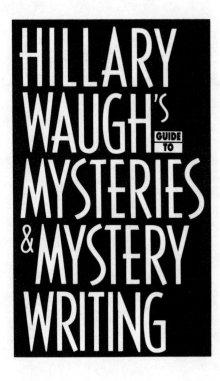

HILLARY WAUGH'S GUIDE TO MYSTERIES & MYSTERY WRITING

HILLARY WAUGH'S GUIDE TO MYSTERIES & MYSTERY WRITING

Writer's
Digest
Books

Cincinnati, Ohio

95 94 93 92 91   5 4 3 2 1

Library of Congress Cataloging in Publication Data

Waugh, Hillary.
  [Guide to mysteries and mystery writing]
  Hillary Waugh's guide to mysteries and mystery writing / Hillary Waugh.
     p.   cm.
  Includes bibliographical references and index.
  ISBN 0-89879-444-7
  1. Detective and mystery stories — History and criticism.
2. Detective and mystery stories — Authorship.   I. Title.
II. Title: Guide to mysteries and mystery writing.
PN3448.D4W38   1991   90-45713
809.3'872-dc20   CIP

Edited by Nan Dibble
Designed by Cathleen Norz

The following page constitutes an extension of this copyright page.

Permissions Acknowledgments

"On Raymond Chandler" (Chapter 8) was written as the introduction to a proposed Bantam Books edition of Raymond Chandler's *The Big Sleep*. Used by permission of Bantam Doubleday Dell Publishing Group, Inc.

"The Police Procedural" (Chapter 10) and "The Mystery Versus the Novel" (Chapter 13) first appeared in *The Mystery Story*, published by University Extension, University of California, San Diego, 1976. Used by permission of *The Popular Press*, Bowling Green State University.

"The Real Detectives" (Chapter 11) originally appeared in *I, Witness: Personal Encounters with Crime by Members of the Mystery Writers of America*, edited by Brian Garfield. Copyright © 1978 by Mystery Writers of America, Inc. Reprinted by permission of Times Books, a division of Random House.

"Plots and People in Mystery Novels" (Chapter 14) first appeared in the December 1969 issue of *The Writer* copyright © 1969. Used by permission of The Writer, Inc.

"The Series Versus the Non-series Detective" (Chapter 15) and "Why I Don't Outline" (Chapter 17) previously appeared in the *Mystery Writer's Handbook* copyright © 1976 by Mystery Writers of America. Used by permission of Writer's Digest Books.

To Shannon,
The Golden Girl who lights up my life.

CONTENTS

INTRODUCTION

The full-time fiction writer faces a fistful of problems, some good, some not so good. To enumerate a few:

1. Writing is the one occupation wherein nobody else ever sees you at work. They will see you in bowling alleys, on the golf course, at parties, at meetings, at various events taking place at any time of day or night. All of which leads non-writers to Conclusion A: *Writers don't work*, and Conclusion B: *Writers are available for whatever purpose you wish to put them to.*

2. Writers don't live in the *real* world. They are somehow exempted from making money, paying bills, being somewhere on time, sweating over the problem of making a living.

3. Writers lead the ideal life. They don't have to get up in the morning, punch time clocks, answer to bosses. Writers don't have to show progress reports.

4. Writers get their words in print, and (due to the impact of the printing press and the "stamped" word) the printed word carries with it the "stamp of truth." If it's in print, it must be true — a fallacy the advertising merchants have been quick to capitalize on.

5. Anyone can be a writer, even the least of us. To wit: Everyone has a story to tell. That much is true. What is not true is that everyone can tell it. Writing is not the easy occupation it appears to be from the outside. Since the outsider doesn't see a writer at the typewriter, since he doesn't comprehend the problems the writer must contend with, writing books, to him, looks like great fun.

6. To the nonwriter, the writer's life seems idyllic. He can go where he pleases, when he pleases, and work at his own pace or take time off if he's not in the mood. In truth, the writer enjoys no such freedom and, in fact, envies the workman who is assured of a lengthy vacation every year. For the writer, there is no such thing as Vacation. A writer can take time off — he can loaf as much as he wants, but, whereas the ordinary mortal can return from a term of absence and find that the project he had left behind has been completed, the writer, upon his return, finds that not one word has been added to the page he left in his typewriter.

There is another problem, unremarked so far as I know, that the fiction writer faces. He cannot read the works of other writers as the reader, the critic, the scholar does. The writer's conditioning makes it impossible. A writer, reading another writer's work, doesn't, to his misfortune, lose himself in the story the other writer is trying to tell. Instead, he's reading the other writer's mind. His attention is upon what the other writer is trying to do, and how well he's doing it. He's not reading and enjoying, he's evaluating.

This is, on the one hand, a curse. On the other, it might be regarded as a blessing. For a writer, there is no mystery about other writers. He knows where they come from.

As a case in point, consider Shakespeare. To critics, savants, and scholars, he's an enigma. He so hides himself behind his genius that they cannot read the man through what he says, and must seek to identify him through what he shows. And what he shows leads them to all sorts of fanciful conclusions, the most notable of which is that Shakespeare didn't write Shakespeare, that the playwright-actor, son of a glove-maker, couldn't do the job. It had to be someone who knew court life they say, who knew falconry (their detective work digs deep); and the list of who wrote Shakespeare's plays is endless, ranging from Bacon to Marlowe. One of the more recent recipients of the honor is Lord Devere, the Earl of Oxford, and there is a group in England so dedicated to this conclusion that its members grow quite misty-eyed in railing against the world for not granting the Lord his due.

To another writer there is no mystery here. Shakespeare was no different from the rest of us, except that he was a genius. Other than that, he's only another member of the fraternity. He did what we all do, and for the same reasons.

Simply put, the plays were written, as purported, by one William Shakespeare, son of a glove-maker; playwright; poet; and actor. When I want an idea for a new mystery, I thumb through collections of true murder stories. When he needed the idea for a new play, he turned to *Plutarch's Lives*.

And he had to turn out plays, one after the other, as, in the early days of live television, people like Paddy Chayefsky and Rod Serling had to grind out dramas for "Playhouse 90."

One can imagine Shakespeare scribbling away, and the director coming in and saying, "Aren't you finished with Act IV yet? The actors are waiting." And Shakespeare, harried, saying, "It's almost done. Give me another hour."

Read *Hamlet* and you can't help feeling that Shakespeare, at the end, must have thought, "You know, if I had a chance to go over this and fix it up, I might have a pretty good play here."

There are those who speak of Shakespeare's knowledge of court life. His knowledge wasn't of court life, it was of human nature. If one of his kings says, "Heavy, heavy lies the crown," they all say it. One need not be a king to feel the weight.

I happened to be watching *Henry IV* on TV with a relative who'd been an actress, and the scene switched from the court and the courtiers to the bawdy Boar's-Head Tavern. "Oh, dear," she sighed. "It's a shame Shakespeare had to write that sort of thing."

To her, Shakespeare was kings and courtiers and quotable lines. I wanted to say to her, "But, don't you see? That's where Shakespeare *lived*. His scenes of courts and kings are sterile. He knows little about court life, not much more than he would have learned from putting on his plays there. But look at the richness of the atmosphere of his tavern scenes. There, he knew what he was talking about."

Critics and scholars, analyzing the works of writers, are akin to entomologists studying a colony of ants, seeking, by observation, to determine what they're up to and why.

A writer is in a different position. He's one of the ants. He *knows* what they're up to and why.

What follows is one writer's view of what the other ants in the anthill are doing.

PART 1

THE HISTORY OF THE MYSTERY

It can be safely said that no one who knew him at the time would have guessed that Edgar Allan Poe, the author of some of the darkest tales of the macabre, the hideous, and the frightening — those emotional products of an obviously disturbed and unfettered mind — could possibly have spawned a field of literature of which clear-headed thinking, ratiocination, the careful analysis of cause and effect, and the creation and solution of puzzles are the hallmarks and essence — the detective story.

In such a field, Edgar Allan Poe would have been voted least likely to succeed. Consider the background of the man.

His Life

Poe was born in Boston on January 19, 1809 to actor parents. Both his mother and father died before he was three and the orphaned boy was taken in by his godfather, John Allan, a wealthy merchant from Richmond, Virginia.

His foster parents eventually took him to Europe and there he was educated for five years in England and Scotland, returning to Richmond in 1820 where he continued his schooling and entered the University of Virginia in 1826. Though he had brilliant scholastic ability, especially in classical and romance languages, he was forced to leave the university after a brief eight months due to quarrels with his father over his gambling debts, his father refusing to support him further.

Poe thereupon moved to Boston where, living in poverty, he published, in 1827, his first volume of poetry, *Tamerlane and Other Poems*.

As might be gathered from Poe's dedication to poetry — hardly the interest of the average male — he was a nonconformist. Poverty, however, pursues poets and even nonconformists must eat. Driven by the need to sustain himself,

BEGIN-
NINGS —
EDGAR
ALLAN
POE

he joined the army, and one must suspect there was a streak of orderliness in him, not just because he chose that means to escape the rigors of penury, but because, in that field, he rose to the rank of sergeant major. Little if anything has been said about this phase of his career, but his success in the army suggests that he might well be one of those people who thrive on, and enjoy, a structured environment, but who flounder and fail to cope if left on their own.

After the death of his foster mother, Poe experienced a temporary reconciliation with his father (probably due to Poe's achievements in the military). This resulted in an honorable discharge from the army and an appointment to West Point in 1830.

His brightening future did not last long. When his father remarried the following year, Poe lost all hope of further financial assistance and, not helping the situation, got himself expelled from West Point for "infraction of minor rules" (drinking and gambling?).

Meanwhile, two more volumes of verse in 1829 and 1831 produced no financial results. He tried to get into the Polish army (more of a crying out for a structured existence?). Failing that, Poe, having no other resources, went to Baltimore and moved in with his aunt, Mrs. Clemm, and her daughter, Virginia. There, he essayed to establish a magazine of contemporary American writing.

Helped by a J.P. Kennedy, he became, in 1835, an editor of the *Southern Literary Messenger* in Richmond. There, he contributed stories, poems, and literary criticism, but his drinking (so often the solace of the gifted when desperate) cost him the job two years later.

Meanwhile, in 1836, he married young Virginia, then only 14. (An earlier romance with a Sarah Royster had been aborted by her father.) Thirteen years his junior, Virginia was much too young. He tended to think of her as a younger sister or daughter. In his letters to her he even addressed her as "Sis," and called her mother "Ma." In the months after the marriage he went through a bad bout of "depression drinking" and was often away from home.

After losing his job with the *Messenger*, he moved "Sis" and "Ma" to New York, where he tried for more editorial work while "Ma" ran a boarding house. As is so often the case with writers, even those with a talent such as his, money was hard to come by, and the lack of it only added to his depression and morbid outlook.

In 1838, Poe published *The Narrative of Arthur Gordon Pym*, his only full-length novel, which, it is reported, W.H. Auden has described as "one of the finest adventure stories ever written . . . an object lesson in the art."

That sobriquet, whether or not warranted, did naught for him at the time and apparently little for him since, for the novel is not included among the works for which he is noted. In 1839, the family moved to Philadelphia, where Poe got a job as editor of Burton's *Gentleman's Magazine* and published his first collection of stories, *Tales of the Grotesque and Arabesque.*

Poe's periodic jousts with the bottle lost him that job, which led to more jousts and, eventually, to complete collapse and delirium. It was at this point, when Poe was recovering and in clearer mind, that, in 1841, George Graham offered him the editorship of *Graham's Magazine*, but on the condition that he "shape up." It was under this dictum that Edgar Allan Poe turned his hand to a new kind of fiction and it was in that magazine, in April 1841, that Poe's "The Murders in the Rue Morgue," the world's first detective story, appeared.

Two other detective stories followed, "The Mystery of Marie Roget" and "The Purloined Letter," but they were not published in *Graham's Magazine*. Poe was gone by then. He had resigned, wanting a magazine of his own — only to find he couldn't raise the funds.

To finish off the unhappy life of a gifted but maladjusted and unappreciated man, Poe moved back to New York in 1844, worked on the *Evening Mirror*, and later edited and owned *The Broadway Journal* — which failed in 1846. (One has to suspect that his business acumen wasn't on a par with his writing talent.) For what it was worth to his morale, his most famous poem, *The Raven*, was published that year to great acclaim.

In 1847, Virginia, Poe's young wife, died in her mid-twenties and Poe turned increasingly to drink.

The following year he was courting the poet Sarah Helen Whitman, but returned to Richmond in 1849 and became engaged to his childhood sweetheart, Sarah Royster, who was now widowed. At this time, he produced his poem, *Annabel Lee* and, at long last, things started to look up. He was engaged, overdue fame was at last alighting, and prosperity lay ahead.

It wasn't to be. On his way north to bring Mrs. Clemm to the wedding, he got into another drinking debauch in Baltimore, which proved fatal, and he died October 7 of that year at the age of forty.

His Art

The nature of a man is imposed upon his art and Poe's nature, judging by his art, is strange indeed. The despair that poverty and frustration bring must account for some of it but Poe's mind, the nurturing medium upon which they worked, had to be unique.

The grotesque horrors that identify most of Poe's short stories — who else could have written "The Black Cat"? — could not have been imagined by anyone else. Only Poe's mind would go in such directions. Try, anyone who will, to turn out such dark terrors. Poe's legacy is that only he could do it and the rest of us should be thankful that our souls have not been so tortured that we could do it too.

Yet, strangely enough, this unusual man, a genius in tales of morbidity and despair, was the first to produce stories in which rationality was the heart and soul, and emotion was supposed to be as nothing. Here, for those whose interest is the "detective story," is where our consideration lies.

The Rational Poe and the First Detective Story

The claim has been made by Joseph Wood Krutch that, "Poe invented the detective story that he might not go mad." That has a nice sound to it, but one has to suspect that it was George Graham's order to "shape up" and Poe's need for his new job as editor of *Graham's Magazine* that got him oriented — briefly at least — in this new direction.

What Poe did — perhaps to prove his metamorphosis to Graham (the story's appearance in *Graham's Magazine* suggests he got no money for it) — was make up a story he entitled "The Murders in the Rue Morgue," and which he published, as mentioned earlier, in the April 1841 issue.

This tale is supposed to represent the *new* Poe, the rational Poe. He tried, and in the view of analysts succeeded, but the darkness that lay upon his soul was not eliminated in his switch from emotionalism to rationalism. Quite the contrary.

Consider his effort. He decides upon the nature of the story. A man with a brilliant mind (representing his own, of course), is going to solve a crime. What kind of a crime? Here his emotionalism returns to the fore: As horrible a crime as his mind can conceive.

To start with, the victims will be women. That's the ultimate in horror — at least it was in his own day and was therefrom until the present era when crimes against women have been so overdone in fiction that the shock value has long since been lost. But until these recent times, crimes against women represented a special evil. Male victims were the literary custom. Males are avaricious, vicious, vengeful, remorseless, arrogant, the embodiment of those qualities readers would like to see eliminated from the earth. Males had created the world in their own image and males were, consequently, responsible for the death and destruction it spawned. Women, on the other hand, were the nurturers, the innocents, the helpless. They had not shaped the world. Men deserved to die, but to have women slain was like having horses burn to death or children mutilated.

As to the way Poe's victims perish, let us add on further horror. One has been throttled and rammed halfway up the chimney. The other has had locks of her hair torn from her scalp, her head "fearfully mutilated" and so severed by a razor that it falls off when attempts are made to lift her.

It might be suggested that, even today, when blood, guts, and gore are frequently introduced into murder scenes for their shock value, such a hideous pair of murders has seldom if ever been equaled.

As for Poe's choice of murderer, it isn't even human. He makes it a beast instead, an apparition more frightening than a mere man. Not even a Mr. Hyde could be so fearful.

While, in actuality, orangutans are peaceful creatures and it is doubtful that any amount of provocation could drive one to perpetrate the acts visited upon the story's poor mother and daughter, in the days in which Poe wrote, little was known about such creatures other than that they bore some resemblance to humans and were incredibly strong. That was all Poe needed.

Nor, when we remark upon the darkness of the author's mind, may we overlook his chevalier, Monsieur C. Auguste Dupin. Dupin is the genius of the piece, the mastermind, the epitome of ratiocination which represents the new Edgar Allan Poe. The height of rationality also is evident in Dupin's nameless chronicler and companion, who leads off the story with a dissertation upon "the mental features discoursed of as the analytical."

Analytical, the pair may be, but Poe darkens and makes weird their characters by creating them as men of the night. Dupin closes the shutters at dawn and the two live by candlelight during the day, only sallying forth into the world with "the advent of the true Darkness." As the chronicler reports, "Had the routine of our life at this place been known to the world, we should have been regarded as madmen."

So even when Poe turns to stories of the intellect instead of the emotions, his own emotions continue to haunt him, at least in this, the first of his tales of M. Dupin.

Other Stories

Thus from his pen came the world's first detective story. Two others involving Dupin were to follow. "The Mystery of Marie Roget," published in *Snowden's Ladies' Companion* (of all places) and serialized in November, December, and February of 1842-43, and "The Purloined Letter," which appeared in *The Gift — 1845*, an elegant, leatherbound display volume — a coffee-table book it would be called today — which was published in the fall of 1844 for the Christmas trade.

A fourth tale, "The Gold Bug," has been claimed as not qualifying as a detective story for a reason we shall dispute shortly. A fifth story, "Thou Art the Man," has been mentioned by Howard Haycraft (author of *Murder for Pleasure*, Appleton-Century, 1941), doubtless the foremost analyst of the detective format, who feels that, except for this same to-be-disputed reason, it "would be a classic detective story."

Some Elements of the Detective Story

Let us take a look at the first of the three Dupin stories. "The Murders in the Rue Morgue" — doubtless familiar to every schoolchild because it was the first, the most famous, and the goriest — starts with an essay by the unnamed chronicler of these tales on the philosophy of analysis (Poe's philosophy of analysis, of course).

Is this the way to start a story? It does not matter. Poe, here, is not only setting the stage for the kind of tale he will tell, he is also showing off the hitherto undiscovered intellectual side of his nature, of which he is suddenly and inordinately — and perhaps rightfully — proud.

The Hero

Poe introduces us to the hero of his tale, M. Auguste Dupin. And who is this C. Auguste Dupin? It's Poe himself, of course. What author does not dress himself in the hero's clothes when he invents a hero? See how he hammers home his thesis of the superiority of the talented amateur mind (his) over that of the professional (i.e, François Vidocq, former head of the Sûreté in Paris — more of him later).

But this is to be expected. What child exists who, in bed at night, does not conjure up tales of glory wherein he or she plays the starring role; that of the bravest and brightest, the fairest and noblest, the savior of the day?

And what does an author do? Only what the little boys and girls do when they're in bed at night, dreaming dreams before they go to sleep. Except that the author writes out his dreams on paper and puts them into stories. And it is the rare author who can keep from making *himself* the hero of his story.

Of course, the author scrubs clean the version of himself he renders to the public as his hero. Nobody is supposed to recognize him. But, of course, the scrubbing is not even skin deep. The author may remove the warts and moles that he thinks make him unappealing, but he will keep, for his hero, all those aspects of his character he cherishes — or fancies he enjoys. And, of course, they may not be the traits and qualities that those around him admire. Nevertheless, the author puts forth, in his hero, those characteristics he most wants to have himself. (Who else is James Bond but Ian Fleming? Who else is The Saint but Leslie Charteris?) We all have our Walter Mitty dreams.

One cannot say, naturally, that the protagonist of every author's story is his idealistic image of himself. There are those tormented authors whose greatness is valued by the presentation of their torments. But those are not the writers of detective stories.

So Poe creates a genius for his hero and establishes his brilliance in two ways. First, Dupin has the awe of his chronicler and this chronicler — though most readers forget it and regard him as somewhat dim-witted — is supposed to be a highly intelligent and thoughtful man in his own right, as witness Poe's starting the story with his lengthy treatise on aspects of the analytical mind. Second, to embed Dupin's genius forever in the reader's consciousness, Poe has Dupin do an elaborate trick of reading his companion's thoughts. The extent to which this mind-reading bit is carried goes well beyond believable limits, but the event successfully serves its purpose, for it is one of the most memorable occurrences in the story and a gimmick which Conan Doyle subsequently appropriated for Sherlock Holmes. And it must certainly be a fictional first.

The Crime and the Clues

Now comes the crime: the gruesome murders of a woman and her daughter. Here, we should note the first example of subtle clue-planting in a detective story. The newspaper reports on the horrible killings tell of the murderer's voice being heard during the commission of the crime, but not in a language those who heard it understood. The hearers, it is mentioned offhandedly, are from a host of different nationalities effectively encompassing all the tongues that would have been known in Paris at the time. It is from this that Dupin deduces the murderer's utterances weren't language at all and the killer wasn't human. And when he reveals this, the reader can nod in the realization that he himself had missed the clue until it was shown to him, and Dupin's acumen has been realistically demonstrated.

At the scene of the crime, Dupin is faced with the detective story's first "locked-room" mystery. The doors have been barred, the windows nailed shut. There is no possible way for the murderer to have left the premises, yet he is gone. Though Dupin promptly solves the problem, Poe does not reveal the solution until later. Instead, he has Dupin, on the way home, scoff at the newspapers' claims that the mystery is "complex because it is outré." He says that, on the contrary, its uniqueness makes it simple and that he has already solved it.

These two circumstances, the outré crime and the locked-room device produced what are claimed by Haycraft to be "the two great concepts upon which all fictional detection worth the name has been based." Dorothy Sayers (in *The Omnibus of Crime,* 1929) expresses it this way: "In this story also are enunciated for the first time these two great aphorisms of detective science: first, that when you have eliminated all the impossibilities, then, whatever remains, *however* improbable, must be the truth; and, secondly, that the more *outré* a case may appear, the easier it is to solve."

The first statement is a truism. It is applied to the locked-room problem and the solution, ultimately revealed by Dupin, as to how the murderer made his escape. Since doors were barred and window-nailed shut, Dupin deduced that, since the doors were impenetrable and the murderer had still made his escape, the window couldn't be nailed shut. He therefore properly deduced that the window only "appeared" to be nailed, and he opened it.

This is great detective locked-room trickery, and so exquisitely justified that Dupin's support of the "improbable" has become a part of the lore, a trough from which all following authors can feed. But that is because Dupin spoke "truth."

On the other hand, Dupin's claim that the more outré the case, the easier it is to solve, is a "non-truth" which subsequent writers have been less willing to support. Though one must grant that the commonest crimes — i.e.: a thief stealing a purse from a stranger — are difficult of solution since the relationship of criminal to victim is based only upon purse possession, it does not necessarily follow that outré crimes must therefore be simple to untangle. The famed Black Dahlia case of 1947, in which the naked, severed body of a young woman, drained of blood and washed clean, was found in a vacant lot in Los Angeles, surely one of the most outré crimes in history, has never, as of this writing, been even close to a solution.

The Solution

To conclude the tale of the Rue Morgue murders, Dupin places an ad in the paper which lures a sailor to their quarters who, it turns out, owned an escaped orangutan and who had conveniently happened to witness the animal's murder of the two women. The explanation of the outré occurrences is thus revealed, and it turns out that no one is really to blame.

Having solved the case, Dupin then elucidates to the chronicler and the reader those aspects of the case which haven't been revealed before.

Thus the essence of the world's first detective story.

The *Essential* Element

Why is "The Murders in the Rue Morgue" called the first detective story and Poe the creator of the detective story? After all, murder is as old as Cain and tales of killing, of tracking down criminals and wreaking revenge, are as old as storytellers. What was the difference here?

The difference is detection. In a detective story, a crime is solved through the accumulation of evidence which points the finger of guilt at the criminal. In a detective story, a detective *detects*; an active effort is made to determine who committed a given crime, and detecting the identity of a criminal could not be done until there were detectives. And detectives did not come into existence until early in the nineteenth century. It started in England with London's Bow Street runners, followed by Scotland Yard; it started in France with the Sûreté in Paris. As the English bibliophile George Bates put it (from Haycraft's *Murder for Pleasure*), "The cause of Chaucer's silence on the subject of airplanes was because he had never seen one. You cannot write about policemen before policemen exist to be written of." Poe was first because there was no one to be first before him.

The First Detective

Well, actually there was a first before him — the source of his inspiration. The real police detective had come into existence in the form of François Eugène Vidocq, former head of the Sûreté, whose autobiography appeared in 1829. Vidocq, a criminal who became a police informer and then, because of his knowledge of crime and Paris criminals, ultimately became the head of the Sûreté and the scourge of criminals, wrote glowingly of his exploits on the side of law and order in his autobiography. The autobiography is regarded as a romanticized account of Vidocq's achievements, however, for it occupies four volumes and would require half a dozen Vidocqs to accomplish the feats therein described.

Nevertheless, it served as source material for Poe and numerous succeeding writers in developing tales of detection. From Vidocq, we may say that Poe gained his inspiration for the fictional exploits of his Monsieur C. Auguste Dupin for there was now, in operation, the field of detection. As Haycraft expresses it, remarking on Vidocq's autobiography, "From about 1830, therefore, it was solely a question of time before the first avowedly fictional detective story would be written." As, in like manner, one could predict, "Given the steam engine, it was only a question of time before trains would cross America and ships would abandon sails," or, "Given the gasoline engine, automobiles and airplanes must follow," or, "Given Columbus, a New World must be born."

Thus, the moment Vidocq's memoirs were published, the fictional detective story was going to be written. Strangely enough, the first such story, though laid in France, was, Haycraft notes, written by an American rather than a Frenchman.

Poe Set the Detective Story Pattern

So the accolade of "first" belongs to Poe. But he is not distinguished because he happened to be the first person to create such a tale. He is lauded for having laid out, "once and for all, the mold and pattern" of the detective story.

Such is the claim, and the claim is universally supported. Poe, in his three Dupin stories, is reputed to have accomplished all that can be accomplished in the detective story. After him there was nothing meaningful to add.

That's a broad statement, and if one wants it to be meaningful, one should include two more Poe tales and, even at that, there is one element of the detective story—the most important element of all—that Poe not only does not include, but was totally unaware of. In fact, it is an element that did not enter the detective story until three-quarters of a century after Poe, and no one seems to have marked its entrance. Suddenly, it is there, and its presence is so vital that it is regarded as always having been there. No one notes its arrival. No one seems to realize it wasn't born with Poe, along with everything else about the detective story.

This is the ingredient known as "Fair Play."

But more of that later. Let us attend now to Poe's other two Dupin stories, then discuss the matter of Poe's contributions to the detective story, what they are, and what they did.

Two More Dupin Stories

In early 1841-42, in the vicinity of New York, a young woman named Mary Cecilia Rogers was found murdered under mysterious circumstances. Due to the mystery surrounding it, her death caused intense and long-enduring excitement. Despite the public interest and police concern, however, the case was never solved.

Now let us imagine the fascination such a case would have for the reformed E.A. Poe who's struck a new chord in literature with his "great detective."

He reads the newspaper articles and applies his own analysis to their reports. He is both dissatisfied and challenged by what he regards as the stupidity of the officials and the reporters of the situation. He's at the height of his own acumen — sober for once? — and gets the idea for a story. From his study of the newspaper reports, he develops his own opinion of what really happened. The police do not know the answer, but he thinks he does.

Being a writer, he does not have to go to bed with his theories, he can publish and present them. Thus there comes from his pen, the second Dupin story, "The Mystery of Marie Roget." What he does is take the Mary Cecilia Rogers murder, transport the case to France, change the victim's name to Marie Roget, and proceed to recount the Rogers murder as reported in the newspapers, not changing any of the facts (for that would destroy his objective), and present in fictional form his solution of the real crime.

And this he does brilliantly, so brilliantly in fact, that, though the crime was not solved, various sources report that it was solved by a deathbed confession which fully confirmed Poe's analysis. It can't be truthfully said that Poe solved the crime, but it must be conceded that his conclusions seem the most likely explanations.

The complaint against "The Mystery of Marie Roget" is aired by Haycraft, who calls "The Murders in the Rue Morgue" the "physical" type of mystery in that we *see* the blood and gore. "The Mystery of Marie Roget," on the other hand, is a "mental" mystery. Nothing is witnessed, only the deductions are reported.

This is true. There is no action. There couldn't be, for Poe was never at the scene. All his analyses were devised and developed through a careful study of newspaper reports. Thus, for those readers who like the excitement and suspense of activity, the story is lacking. However, one might point out that the activity in "The Murders in the Rue Morgue" is extremely limited as well. Dupin does visit the scene of the crime but the only "activity" that takes place is Dupin's prowling around. What he discovers is not learned until the end of the story when Dupin explains all. The goriness of the crime is, as in "The Mystery of Marie Roget," revealed through newspaper reports. At the scene, all Dupin's chronicler says by way of description is, "I saw nothing beyond what had been stated in the *Gazette des Tribunaux*." In each of Poe's three Dupin stories, on-site reporting is virtually nonexistent. Poe's technique is to reveal almost nothing as the story progresses, then tell all at the end. That's not the way it's done today, and not the way it ought to be done. But these were the first detective stories ever written and we can't expect miracles.

More on that, however, later. First let's discuss the tale of "The Purloined Letter."

Briefly, the story is this: The prefect of the Parisian police comes to Dupin with a problem. A certain rascal has stolen a compromising letter from a lady of royal lineage and was using it for blackmail. The letter was known to be in his apartment, but the most thorough searches by police in his absence had failed to uncover it. Could Dupin help?

Dupin tells the prefect to come back in a month, tells his chronicler nothing, and when the prefect comes back, produces the letter. This again is Poe's technique of telling the reader nothing until Dupin explains everything at the end. In this case, Dupin explains that he went to the rascal's apartment on a pretext, knowing from his familiarity with the blackguard's nature that he'd "hide" the letter by leaving it, disguised as an inconsequential note, in plain sight, confident that the police would look everywhere else but at that "inconsequential note."

Dupin, observing the most obvious piece of correspondence in the room, memorized its appearance, returned on another pretext, caused a paid-for commotion to take place in the street below, replaced the letter with a fake while the rascal's attention was diverted and, presto, success.

The brilliance of this piece is Poe's calling attention to man's inclination to overlook the obvious. This is, quite likely, the first time that the tendency for this lapse has been brought to public attention through a story—certainly in a detective story.

Poe's Less-Praised Tales

These are Poe's three Dupin tales. They're good and they're bad from the standpoint of the "detective story." They're good because they introduced into the genre which was being created, most of the permanent essences of that genre. They're bad in that Poe, being the first to write this type of tale, was not aware of certain essences that do *not* go with the detective story.

So now, let us pay attention to what Poe did right in these three stories and what he did wrong. (And let us remember that he was not learning how to do this from anyone else. He was unwittingly creating a whole new field of fiction and little knew that it would outlive him and his concepts. In fact, little did he realize that his place in the history of literature would not stem from his poetry and short stories, but from the genre he created — no, not "created" but was the first to explore.)

And, since he wrote two additional stories which contributed to the field, even though the tendency is to ignore them due to imagined flaws, let us also remark upon "The Gold Bug" and "Thou Art The Man." Only if we consider all five can we encompass all that Edgar Allan Poe contributed to the Detective Story.

"The Gold Bug" is the tale of a man who accompanies a friend and the friend's black servant on a treasure hunt. Due to the black servant's inability to tell left from right (remember this was written in the days of slavery, and certain stereotypical views were held at the time which have nothing to do either with Poe or slaves), the attempt fails but, upon the friend's catching the mistake, a great treasure is uncovered.

After the event — which is Poe's way of relating a story — the friend explains how he came by a treasure map and how, by breaking the code in which the map was written, he achieved success.

The purpose of the story is to show the means by which Poe, the author, goes about breaking down a simple code wherein the letters have been changed. This might seem simple to us now — the defunct N.Y. *Herald Tribune* used to run such coded messages as a daily "problem" for its readers — but the use of code and the breaking of that code was obviously an innovation in Poe's time and we have to give him credit for bringing it to our attention as a means of solving a problem. Coded messages today are far more difficult to decipher, but he, in "The Gold Bug," is probably the first to present readers with code breaking to solve a problem.

Let us now pay attention to Poe's tale, "Thou Art The Man." There are interesting new features here. It seems that the very wealthy Mr. Shuttleworthy's horse, upon which he'd departed in the morning, returned without him. The animal had been wounded by a bullet that had passed right through him. Charley Goodfellow, the missing gentleman's best friend, organizes a search, the results of which implicate Shuttleworthy's dissolute nephew, Mr. Pennifeather, as killing the old man. In fact, Goodfellow's autopsy on the horse's body (it later died) produces a bullet that could only have come from the nephew's gun.

At the end, a confession is gained from Goodfellow by having Shuttleworthy's corpse sit up in his coffin in front of the assemblage and state to Goodfellow, "Thou art the man."

This conclusion has been achieved by the storyteller's affixing a whalebone spring to the corpse so that, when the box containing it was opened, the corpse would sit up. Ventriloquism produced the voice, and the guilty party, Charley Goodfellow, confessed.

This completes Poe's contribution to the mystery. Now let's see what he did and didn't do. Let's examine Poe's "flaws."

Criticism of the Stories

The critics' complaint, mentioned earlier, against "The Gold Bug" being classified as a detective story is that detection isn't utilized. The reader isn't given a chance to break the code himself. He can only watch as Poe breaks the code for him.

That is true. But if we carry that complaint further, we find that Poe never divulges the clues to the reader that will enable him to solve the problem himself. In "The Murders in the Rue Morgue," the reader has no idea what Dupin is up to when he inserts the newspaper ad that will bring the owner of the orangutan to his apartment to reveal to the reader, the chronicler, the police—to all but Dupin himself—what really happened in that apartment in the Rue Morgue.

In "The Purloined Letter," we are not told, until Dupin has produced, turned over the letter to the prefect and received his fee, how it all came about. We, the reader, did not know Dupin had visited the rascal, not once but twice, in seeking out and retrieving the letter. We only learn about it after the fact.

So to complain that "The Gold Bug" is not a detective story because we aren't a witness to events is a "fault" that lies at the doorstep of all Poe's detective stories. This fault was a convention of the era's literature, so Poe can be forgiven for practicing it.

The effectiveness of a whalebone "spring" and ventriloquism to gain a confession in "Thou Art The Man" is as far-fetched as Dupin's mind-reading stint in "The Murders in the Rue Morgue." Nevertheless, these and numerous other Poe innovations have helped make the detective story what it is.

What "Thou Art The Man" can be noted for is that we have here the first illustration of "the least suspected character" being the murderer. It's crude, of course. Good old pal Charley Goodfellow is so obviously the villain that it doesn't need discussing except to say that, the first time it's done, it comes as a surprise and the readers in Poe's day might well have been misled. Poe's gimmick of whalebone and ventriloquism to gain a confession may be regarded as crude, but we should pay attention not to the method, but the concept—which was also a first—of gaining a confession through psychology. (In modern lore, there is the true case of a killer who was "educated" into confession. Evidence against him was insufficient. Spittle found at the crime scene matched his, but, at that time, could have matched innumerable others as well. The suspect, claiming innocence, was indoctrinated into the field of analysis and educated into an understanding of exactly what could be determined from spittle — blood type, and the rest — as a result of which knowledge, he chose to confess.)

Before going further, we must lay rest a claim against "Thou Art The Man." Its failure as a detective story, so the claim goes, is due to its failure to reveal an essential fact. Charley Goodfellow, examining the corpse of Mr. Shuttleworthy's horse, finds a bullet fitting poor nephew Mr. Pennifeather's gun. The flaw in the story is supposed to be that the reader didn't know, until told at the end, that the bullet that fatally wounded the poor horse passed completely through him and therefore couldn't have been recovered from his body.

But Poe — and this is clever clue-planting by a master — mentions on the first page that the wounded horse returned without its master and then, a page later, sneaks in the information that the wounded horse, returning without its master, was "all bloody from a pistol shot, that had gone clean through and through the poor animal's chest without quite killing him. . . ." Thus he certainly did tell his readers that there can be no bullet in him. Poe, here, has confounded his critics.

His critics are confounded another time too. It had been claimed by some that Poe was guilty of a "serious logical flaw" in "The Purloined Letter," the argument being that Dupin, identifying the letter in the blackguard's apartment, could not have seen both the front and back at the same time. This lapse is assumed because Dupin, in explaining matters, contrasts the appearance of the visible part of the letter with the hidden:

> Here the seal was large and black, with the D———
> cipher; there it was small and red, with the ducal arms of
> the family. Here, the address, to the minister, was diminu-
> tive and feminine; there the superscription, to a certain
> royal personage, was markedly bold and decided. . . .

But there has been no lapse of logic on Poe's part. In the sentence just prior to the above, Dupin says, "To be sure, it was, to all appearance, radically different from the one of which the Prefect had read us so minute a description." And, in the early part of the story, the Prefect does just that. To quote: "And here the Prefect, producing a memorandum-book, proceeded to read aloud a minute account of the internal, and especially of the external, appearance of the missing document."

In short, Poe, doing what all good authors do, did not belabor the point. He had twice informed the reader that Dupin already knew what the real letter looked like. Dupin did not have to see the other side in D————'s apartment to know what was there.

Essential Ingredients of the Mystery

We've examined all Poe's tales of detection. Let us now examine the ingredients of the detective story which Poe is regarded as having set down for all time. (They vary in number and nature according to who is doing the analysis.) In essence we can list these:

1. The transcendent and eccentric detective (evidenced by M. Dupin).

2. The admiring and slightly stupid foil. (Dupin's companion and chronicler.)

3. The well-intentioned, blundering officials. (The Prefect friend.)

4. The locked-room convention. ("The Murders in the Rue Morgue.")

5. The pointing finger of unjust suspicion. (The arrest of Adolphe Le Bon in "The Murders in the Rue Morgue.")

6. The solution by surprise. ("Murders" and "Purloined.")

7. Solution by putting one's self in another's position. ("The Purloined Letter.")

8. Concealment by means of the ultra-obvious. ("The Purloined Letter.")

9. The staged ruse to force the culprit's hand. ("The Purloined Letter.")

10. Even the expansive and condescending explanation when the chase is done. ("The Purloined Letter.")

Says Haycraft, "In fact, it is not too much to say—except, possibly, for the influence of latter-day science—that nothing really primary has been added either to the framework of the detective story or to its internals since Poe completed his trilogy," and he continues, "As Philip Van Doren Stern has well said: 'Like printing, the detective story has been improved upon only in a mechanical way since it was first invented; as artistic products, Gutenberg's Bible and Poe's "The Murders in the Rue Morgue" have never been surpassed.' "

Those ten items, however, are not all that Poe contributed. An eleventh is "the hidden clue" (the bullet that passed through the horse in "Thou Art The Man" and the "language" clue in "Murders in the Rue Morgue.") A twelfth would be the "cipher" in "The Gold Bug," but we have to look beyond the "trilogy" of Dupin tales for these last two items. (And there is one feature of the detective novel, vital to its existence, that not only Poe, but all his successors overlooked for more than seventy-five years. That is, as we have said before, the element of Fair Play. More of that anon.)

Examining the Ingredients

Let us turn our attention to the contributions Poe did make, in the form of the ingredients just listed. The critics talk of them as if, somehow, there sprang full-blown, from the mind of this one man, all the requirements of the detective story. From this, one cannot help but conclude that: 1. Poe was a genius who created a genre of literature with one stroke of his pen; 2. Poe was an ultimate craftsman who, by dint of mulling and pondering, selecting and discarding, decided upon just those items that were necessary to produce an art form called "the detective story." A third possibility is that it was an accident. He created the detective story and didn't know he was doing it.

The fourth explanation, and the one that makes the most sense to a fellow writer, is that he sat down to create a certain kind of tale and this is the only way it could be told. There was nothing mysterious nor inspired about it at all. It would have been done the same way by any competent writer who undertook the task.

In defense of this suggestion, and before going into the matter, consider a statement made by Professor George N. Dove, an authority on the mystery story, in the introduction he wrote for an edition of my book, *Last Seen Wearing*. . . . Said Professor Dove, "The plot moves through the six stages of development followed by Poe in 'The Murders in the Rue Morgue' and used by thousands of writers of the formal-problem tale: the Statement of the Problem; the Initial Solution; the Period of Confusion; the Dawning Light; the Resolution; and the Explanation. Often, as in the present case, these last two steps are reversed."

Now this may be true, but I have to say that, in the writing of the story, I was not obediently following precepts laid down by Poe. I did not know nor care about precepts laid down by Poe; I was unaware that he was the father of the detective story; my recollection of "The Murders in the Rue Morgue" was vague. In short, all I was doing was writing a story the way I thought the story ought to be told, which was also the way any writer would think such a story ought to be told.

Let us consider, then, Edgar Allan Poe, an accomplished writer with a keen intellect and a troubled mind. He's got to come up with a saner tale than he's been accustomed to writing. He's familiar with Vidocq's memoirs. He's proud of his brains. Graham wants brains? He'll show him brains, and to spare. He'll out-Vidocq Vidocq.

1. First he needs a hero of the piece and, like any writer, knows his hero has to attract attention. Thus is born Dupin who, as we have noted, reflects the morbidity of Poe's own mind. (Could Poe have produced Leslie Charteris's "The Saint"? Never.)

So Poe creates his protagonist, giving him quirks (that only he could think of) to make him memorable.

2. How then to tell the tale? How much more realistic to have it related — not third person — but through the eyes of a companion? (This would come naturally to Poe, for most of his tales are related in this personal, "I was there" manner.)

We should note that Dupin's companion, who is supposed to be "the admiring and slightly stupid foil," is revealed by Poe as highly intelligent. If he appears "slightly" stupid in the story, it's only to contrast to the brilliance of Dupin, which point serves to heighten the genius of Poe's hero. If this approach has been often copied, it's because there aren't all that many other ways to tell a tale.

3. What else does Poe do? He has the gendarmerie baffled by the problem. (The well-intentioned, blundering officials.) This is a necessity. How else can he get his hero involved?

4. He sets up the "locked-room" convention. Ah, here Poe is original. Unlike most of the other conventions he introduced, a locked room is not a requirement of the detective story. This is a contribution to the detective story that another "first" writer in the genre might well have overlooked. In Poe's case, we can see him conjuring up the idea as a means of demonstrating Dupin's genius. It's all right for Poe to *say* Dupin is a genius — even to illustrate it by throwing in that mind reading act to set the stage. But, as a storyteller knows, it's essential to have Dupin's genius contribute something to the problem in hand. The locked room mystery and Dupin's solution was the means by which Poe solved that problem.

Poe's invention of the locked-room enigma is a real contribution to the field. It's been a pet puzzle gimmick for many subsequent writers, and many have been the ingenious answers mystery writers have developed. A book could be written on that subject alone.

5. As for Poe's being first to point the finger of suspicion at the wrong person, though this was done in "The Murders in the Rue Morgue," it was poorly done for there's no evidence against the man arrested. To find it done properly, we must turn to "Thou Art The Man," where falsified evidence really *does* point the finger at an innocent man.

Poe gets no special accolade here, for such a concept would come naturally to anyone writing a "mystery" and intent upon misleading the reader.

6. The solution by surprise? This would be done by anyone for the same purpose.

7. Solution by putting one's self in another's position (Dupin's method in "The Purloined Letter"). Let's give Poe credit for originality here. At the time this was written, Sigmund Freud was twelve years short of being born. We can't say any other writer would have considered it.

8. Concealment by means of the ultra-obvious. This is one of those magic tricks which, once it's been explained, seems mundane. Nevertheless, it's doubtful that anyone else but Poe would have realized and made capital of the fact.

9. The staged ruse to force the culprit's hand. Give Poe credit for this. It's not a requirement for detective fiction. It's a seldom used ploy but the fact that it's used at all, hands the credit to Poe.

10. "The expansive and condescending explanation when the chase is done." Explanations don't have to be either expansive or condescending, but an explanation is essential. Poe, here, is only doing what has to be done. Stories cannot end with untied strings, so anyone writing this kind of story must, of necessity, answer all unsolved problems. That necessity, in fact, is one of the difficulties that faces the writer of detective fiction. The more complex the plot, the longer the explanation; and who wants to read a dozen or more pages of answers at the end of the book once the mystery of "whodunit" is solved? Poe didn't "invent" the "explanation" part of a detective story; he, like all the rest of us, was stuck with it.

Now we come to what I've chosen to list as number eleven, the Hidden Clue. This is the bit of information presented to the reader in the course of the story, which information, properly assimilated and interpreted, could assist the reader in anticipating the deductions achieved by the detective. In the case of "The Murders in the Rue Morgue," it would be the evidence that the culprit, an orangutan, was not speaking language. Most notable, however, is Poe's classic demonstration of the hidden clue in "Thou Art The Man." He slipped the fact there was no bullet in the horse so deftly past the reader that even the critics were fooled into thinking he never told them.

Fair Play

It's been mentioned previously that the one ingredient essential to the detective story that Poe did not introduce, and which didn't come into existence for another seventy-five years, was the element of Fair Play (meaning the reader must have all the clues the sleuth has). This is not quite right. In his other stories, there was no such thing and, in fact, the need for Fair Play slipped unbeknownst into detective fiction at a much later date.

But here, in "Thou Art The Man," Poe clearly produced the first, though unacknowledged, element of Fair Play into the mystery. The fact that the bullet had passed completely through the horse was the clue to the real killer the moment Charley Goodfellow produced, from the innards of the animal, the suspect's supposed bullet. It is on such hidden clues that Fair Play, the most essential essence of the detective story, the one requirement it must have, exists.

Give credit to Poe. He's the unacknowledged first in this category as well.

We've added the cipher (number twelve), courtesy of "The Gold Bug," as another Poe contribution, but enough of this cataloging. Edgar Allan Poe was a man who wrote detective stories. He was the first, so what he did was automatically, "The First." Any other writer, creating this new field, would have done what he did—because there's no other way to do it—and would be applauded for the "rules" he laid down. Poe earns our respect for those additives to the field which weren't inherent in the nature of the field: the locked room, putting oneself into the mind of the criminal, and putting forth the hidden clue which begets the much later element, crucial to the modern mystery, Fair Play.

The Missing Mystery Ingredients

Now, two complaints about those ingredients of the mystery which Edgar Allan Poe failed to provide, and where his stories failed—by our modern standards.

Motive

In "The Murders in the Rue Morgue," the murders are without motive, and motive is an essential. The case is akin to tracking down a hit-and-run driver who was unaware that he'd hit anybody. Without purpose, there is no guilt and without guilt, there is no case.

Show, Don't Tell

Poe consistently withholds the keys to his stories. He does not *show* you what happens. He *tells* you about it later. Dupin relates how he deduced the ape escaped, not at the scene, but in his recapitulation. In "The Purloined Letter," we do not even know that Dupin visited the black-guard's apartment, let alone retrieved the letter, until after he's been paid for his pains. In "The Gold Bug," all is told by the chronicler after it has happened. The invisible ink appearing after the map was held near the fire, the digging for treasure without the reader knowing what the digging was for — all this reticence must be attributed to the storytelling methods in vogue at the time. These methods, however, are not the present vogue, nor can they ever be the vogue of the detective story, the formula of which is too structured for that sort of approach.

In other words, *approach* is one of the aspects to the detective story that Poe did not generate.

Enough of analysis. The view from here is that Poe did more than write the first detective story. Most of what he brought to it was only what anyone else would have done — there are almost no alternatives. But his agile brain did contribute to the field certain undying elements that can only be called his own.

THE

YEARS

THAT

FOLLOWED

Edgar Allan Poe started it and what is interesting is that he set his detective stories in France and it is the French who next took up the form.

The French Connection

But, of course, there were Vidocq's memoirs — those four volumes of more than four hundred pages each — to trigger their interest. In fact, since Vidocq was French and served also as Poe's inspiration, one might well conclude that Vidocq was the reason Poe's own tales were laid in France.

As for Vidocq, Howard Haycraft notes (*Murder for Pleasure*) that his accounts of his exploits contain most of the essential requirements we've come to accept as identifying the detective story. Since Vidocq's memoirs were published in 1829 (twelve years before "The Murders in the Rue Morgue"), Haycraft suggests that perhaps Vidocq, rather than Poe, was the real "father" of the detective story.

Except, one would hasten to point out, Vidocq was supposedly writing "fact" not fiction. On the other hand, Vidocq's enormous ego, self-aggrandizement, and rogue background, plus the incredible number of cases he's supposed to have been involved with, makes the general assessment of his memoirs more a romantic fancy than fact.

Nevertheless, we will stay with Poe as the creator of the detective story. Never mind where he got his ideas, nor who else was doing what; he produced the first actual fictional detective tales and his imprint, modified by developments over time, marks them to this day.

We should, however, quote Haycraft on the subject. "A whole generation of later writers became indebted to him (Vidocq) as a source. Poe, as we have seen, knew his Vidocq well enough to dispute him; and scores of other authors drew on the *Memoires* to a greater or less degree, including, among many, Hugo, Balzac, Dumas, Dickens, Collins, and Doyle."

Emile Gaboriau

So, also, did the French writer, Emile Gaboriau.

Gaboriau, the son of a notary, born in 1833, served in the army for a term, went to Paris, worked and, for extra sous, wrote on the side.

Ultimately, he was turning out lurid prose on demand, thousands of words a day, and, before he died of exhaustion at thirty-nine in 1873, he had turned out the serial detective novel *L'Affaire Lerouge* for a dying newspaper in 1866, and fourteen more novels, in four of which detection more or less figures. (They can hardly be called "detective stories.") In them, there appears a detective by the name of Lecoq (obviously gleaned from Vidocq).

This is not an advancement of the detective story so much as a carrying-on.

The British are Coming

The next forward step — or next showing of the detective story, we might say, had to wait for Wilkie Collins, who was born in London in 1824 and produced the first British efforts in the field. His younger brother married Charles Dickens' sister and Collins and Dickens were fast friends as well as esteemed writers.

Wilkie Collins

When he was twenty-four, Collins published a memoir of his father. In 1850, he published an historical novel, *Antonia,* with an Italian background based upon his travels. (It did not do well.) His meeting with Dickens occurred a year later and was, notes Haycraft, "an event of the utmost significance to both men." They collaborated on a number of works, and influenced each other. To quote Haycraft, "Though Dickens affected almost every writer of his time, Collins has been declared the only writer who influenced *him.*"

Relevant to detective fiction is Wilkie Collins' *The Moonstone.* It is not detective fiction as we know it today. In fact, we can conclude, from a reading of that book, that Collins was not aware he was writing a detective story. The themes and stresses and opulence of imagery, the thread of plot, go elsewhere. It is a *long* novel — overly long by modern-day standards — and certainly only distantly related to the detective story. Romance and the problems of boy-and-girl are the dominant themes.

There is, however, a detective: Sergeant Cuff, described—and this is interesting—thusly:

> . . . a grizzled elderly man, so miserably lean that he looked as if he had not got an ounce of flesh on his bones in any part of him. . . . His face was as sharp as a hatchet, and the skin of it was as yellow and dry and withered as an autumn leaf. His eyes, of a steely light gray, had a very disconcerting trick, when they encountered your eyes, of looking as if they expected something more from you than you were aware of yourself. His walk was soft; his voice was melancholy; his long lanky fingers were hooked like claws. He might have been a parson, or an undertaker, or any thing else you like, except what he really was.

Pay attention, if you already haven't! Poe had his Dupin. Doyle will later have his Sherlock Holmes. Where did this extraordinary character come from? He seems, almost, to presage Holmes. Who cannot help but be struck by that special attribute of his eyes: "as if they expected something more from you than you were aware of yourself." No other author, before or since, has conceived such a particular, eerie, worrisome attribute to a detective's eyes, or to anything else about a detective hero that is as scary. Collins, here, in *The Moonstone*, created a detective capable of ranking with the best. As an aside, it's been claimed that Collins patterned Sergeant Cuff after the real detective, Inspector Whicher, who was involved in the sensational "Road Murder" case of 1860 and that he used elements of that trial in his own tale. This would be akin to Doyle's patterning Holmes after Dr. Joseph Bell, but the striking point here is Collins' perception of the man, if that be the cause of this notable description. Who else would have seen in Inspector Whicher what Collins has seen and portrayed?

Unfortunately, nothing came of this unique detective. His existence is unremarked. True, *The Saturday Review of Literature* reviewed mysteries under the sobriquet of "Sergeant Cuff," but this is obviously a ploy used as a plaudit to the cognoscenti, and is a nonsense name to the unread (much as the *New York Times*, at a later date, reviewed mysteries under the pseudonym of "Newgate Calendar" which, in fact, was the listing of the scheduled hangings of criminals jailed in Newgate Prison in England).

The reason for Sergeant Cuff's short shrift in the history of detective fiction is because he played but a small part in *The Moonstone*, and so did detection. Collins was unaware of the potential of his austere detective sergeant and of the power of the mystery tale. His focus was on romance and the magic of the Far East. Like Poe with his orangutan and, as we shall see later, Doyle with his evil little native with the blowgun, Collins was incorporating the "mysterious" into his novel—which meant areas of the unknown. Though what was to them The Unknown, and is today, to us, the familiar, does not obviate the purport of their message. Fear of the strange and the weird grips the human soul. How better to tell a scary story than to bring forth all those areas and aspects of the world that lie in mystery? It's like the science fiction tales of today. Today, the mysteries that can grip our imaginations lie out among the stars. A century ago, they lay in "Darkest Africa" and in the mysterious rites and magic of India, with its fakirs, firewalkers, and climbers of unsupported ropes into the sky.

This was the story Wilkie Collins was telling, a tale of mystery and intrigue set against an upfront story of love and romance. Sergeant Cuff played but a small part in *The Moonstone* and so did detection. Nevertheless, *The Moonstone* serves as an incident in the movement (not development) of the detective story as, also, does Charles Dickens' last and unfinished work, *The Mystery of Edwin Drood*.

The Dickens Mystery.

Speaking of Dickens, it seems that he himself, at the end, was sufficiently enamored of the detective story to see what he could do in the realm of mystifying his readers. It's also suggested that he wanted to outdo *The Moonstone*.

If that was his aim, one might suggest that he contrived beyond the wildest dreams of all mystery writers, for he died before finishing the novel and no one, to this day, can determine whom he planned to be his villain.

Thus, we might say, we have here the most mysterious of all mystery novels! Never mind the paltry efforts by others to resolve the problem and finish off Dickens' story. Guess all you want, the answer is something only Dickens could create. And we do not have access to his mind. *The Mystery of Edwin Drood* will forever lie in the realm of mystery.

And more power to it. This is what we read mysteries for—to be mystified.

Except, that there is no solution, and solution is a requirement.

And except that solution was not what the reader of *The Moonstone* and *The Mystery of Edwin Drood* was after. The detective story had not yet come into its own and these books were read for story rather than detection.

3

And Then There Was Holmes

In his book, *Masters of Mystery* (Collins, London, 1931), H. Douglas Thomson introduces his chapter on Sherlock Holmes thusly: "Every one, from Macaulay's schoolboy to the 'every one that matters' of the *Morning Post*, is familiar with the exploits of Sherlock Holmes. Mr. Chesterton regards Sherlock Holmes as the only well-known character of recent fiction. The name is household and has gained the currency of popular conversational usage."

The Holmes stories, he notes, have been published in virtually every language known to man and their circulation runs into the millions. Then he goes on to say something that more nearly approximates the impact of Sherlock Holmes upon the world: "A railway engine, whose decrepitude calls for governmental subsidy, puffs in and out of Baker Street Station flaunting the great name. It is no idle story that a party of French schoolboys on a visit to London demanded to be shown the chambers of their idol before they condescended to be led to the Tower and St. Paul's. . . ."

Ah, yes, those lodgings at 221B Baker Street, an address doubtless more familiar to the world-at-large than Number 10 Downing Street. What visitor to London, if he has any curiosity about him, does not make a trek to Baker Street and acquaint himself with the location of 221B?

To his disappointment, he will find Baker Street a wide, heavily traveled thoroughfare and a large bank or office building occupying the site — at least such was the case in the year 1960 — and the milieu is so different from the image conjured up by the stories that one must doubt that Doyle, in creating the address, had bothered to research the location. Doyle was nothing if not careless — as we shall have further cause to remark upon — in his writing of the Holmes stories.

What is interesting is that Doyle's faults and

foibles in his presentation of this Sleuth of Sleuths are readily not only overlooked, but attended to and justified—no matter how difficult the justification.

Errata: Was Watson's wound in his shoulder, or his leg? (Doyle seems to have forgotten.)

Answer (by the faithful): Obviously, the same bullet must have gone through the one and penetrated the other.

This answer, in itself, bespeaks the impact of Sherlock Holmes upon the readers of his tales.

So great, in fact, is the impact, that any number of readers believe that Sherlock Holmes actually lived, and this includes people in high places. Howard Haycraft, in his *Murder for Pleasure* (Appleton-Century, 1941), reports that during the First World War, Conan Doyle, upon being introduced to a French general, was asked what rank Sherlock Holmes held in the English army. Nor is this to overlook the hundreds of letters that still come addressed to Sherlock Holmes at his unforgettable address.

The Mystique of Sherlock Holmes

So what is it that Sherlock Holmes has that makes him the most memorable character in the history of fiction? Wherein lies the secret?

Thomson quotes a reviewer in the *Times* (of London) as saying, "Where would Sherlock Holmes be in our memories without his drugs, his dressing gown, and his violin? Where would our detectives be without their endearing quixotry, their disarming cynicism, and their thousand and one affectations?"

Haycraft regards William Bolitho as coming "close to the heart of the secret when he wrote of Holmes: 'He is more than a book. He is the spirit of a town and a time.' "

Then there is Vincent Starrett's paean (from Haycraft's *Murder for Pleasure*), which must affect us all:

> Granted the opportunity, gentlemen—one might cry, in paraphrase of Dr. Bell—of recovering a single day out of the irrecoverable past, how would you choose to spend that sorcerous gift? With Master Shakespeare in his tiring room? With Villon and his companions of the cockleshell? Riding with Rupert or barging it with Cleopatra up the Nile? Or would you choose to squander it on a chase with Sherlock Holmes after a visit to the rooms in Baker Street? There can be only one possible answer, gentlemen, to the question.

Who can quarrel with Starrett's proposition?

But why do we agree?

What mystical force draws us to this mythical man as to no other? What has happened? What has Doyle done? Is it really dressing gowns and violins? It can hardly be cocaine, the effects of which Doyle shows less knowledge of than one should expect from a medical man (and Doyle later pretty well drops it from Holmes' realm of eccentricities).

And what makes us forgive Holmes' shortcomings, belove his absurdities? Haycraft explains it this way: "The quality is at once simple and difficult to define — and one that many abler technical achievements sorely want. Lacking a single *mot juste* we may speak tentatively of 'flavor.' Or, to choose a hardier word, 'gusto.' One hesitates to use the overworked phrase 'born storyteller'; yet Doyle's almost naive zest was certainly a factor."

He goes further and suggests "It is the 'romantic reality' of their comfortable, nostalgic British heartiness. It is the small boy in all of us, sitting before an open fire, with the winter wind howling around the windows, a-wriggle with sheer pleasure."

True. All this is true. Around the Holmes stories we conjure up all sorts of delicious sentiments. Nowhere else could one be so happily alive except with Holmes in a London fog (actually a poisonous concentration of fumes from millions of Londoners' coal fires, which stagnant weather conditions allowed to settle over the city and smother the populace at the cost of hundreds of lives).

Nowhere else would one want to live except with a man who shoots bullets into the wall (a later quixotic Holmes gesture, about which the compliant Mrs. Hudson apparently said nothing), mainlined drugs (early on), and led a life aloof, not only from mankind, but apparently from his roommate as well. Well, Holmes is not inconsiderate of Watson. The bullet holes in the wall, cigars in the coal scuttle, tobacco in the Persian slipper, unanswered correspondence transfixed to the mantel by a jack knife (see *The Musgrave Ritual*) mainly occurred in Watson's absence, for Holmes' bad habits, by his own confession in *A Study in Scarlet*, consist of, "You don't mind the smell of strong tobacco, I hope?" Also, "I generally have chemicals about and occasionally do experiments. Would that annoy you?" Lastly, "I get in the dumps at times and don't open my mouth for days on end." As a coda, he asks if his playing the violin would be objectionable. It's upon this limit of annoyances that Watson takes Holmes on as a roommate.

As for Watson's faults, the good doctor says, "I keep a bull pup" (of which no more is heard). "I get up at all sorts of ungodly hours, and

I am extremely lazy." (No more is heard about that either.)

There is a difference between the (by now famous) Sherlock Holmes that Watson is sharing rooms with in *The Musgrave Ritual* and the eager, (newly created) young chemist of *A Study in Scarlet*. The later Holmes might be more memorable — excruciatingly so — but the early Holmes would make a more companionable and endurable roommate for the supposedly irretrievably ill (may we add, even a healthy) Watson.

So is it really the eccentricities that make the man? And if so, how many does one need? Would not the deerstalker's cap, magnifying lens, and meerschaum pipe be enough? The Persian slipper for keeping tobacco and the coal scuttle for storing cigars are brought to the public's attention only well after Sherlock Holmes had achieved renown. He didn't require those idiosyncrasies to make him famous.

The Baker Street Irregulars

What, we may continue to ask, is there about the Holmes-Watson tales that prompted Christopher Morley, in 1934, to create "The Baker Street Irregulars," a group of dyed-in-the-wool Holmes-and-Watson lovers, which Morley headed until he died? And which flourishes today under the aegis of one Tom Stix, its fourth president, whose predecessor is the only president not to have died in office? There are, in this organization, some 270 members, of whom 60 are investitured — one for each of the Holmes stories (fifty-six short tales and four novels). It's a labor of love. There are no dues, and membership depends upon interest; investiture on dedication. The reason for its being is perhaps best explained by Morley in the Introduction to *The Complete Sherlock Holmes* (Garden City, 1938) when he says: "It is a kind of piety for even the least and humblest of Holmes lovers to pay what tribute he may to this great encyclopedia of romance that has given the world so much innocent pleasure. Already the grandchildren of Holmes' earliest followers are beginning upon him with equal delight."

And he speaks for many when he says: "One of the blissful ways of passing an evening, when you encounter another dyed-in-the-wool addict, is to embark upon the happy discussion of minor details of Holmesiana. 'Whose gold watch was it that had been so mishandled?' one may ask; and the other counters with 'What was the book that Joseph Stangerson carried in his pocket?' "

And one might equally well ask, "What is there about Sherlock Holmes and Dr. Watson that elicits such devotion?" Surely, in the annals of fiction there has been nothing like it.

Morley says: "Even in the less successful stories we remain untroubled by any naiveté of plot; it is the character of the immortal pair that we relish. It is not mere chance that they are well-loved. Doyle himself must have been a singularly lovable man."

Is it character then, the character of the pair as Morley suggests? Apart from his idiosyncrasies, is it the eagerness of Holmes on the scent, his willingness to draw his own blood to test a thesis, his ego, his singleness of purpose, his scorn of emotion?

Or is it a combination of factors that explains Holmes' grip on the public imagination: the romance of the tales, the eccentricities of Holmes, the propitious meshing of his character with Watson's, the atmosphere of a London we never knew?

Or is there more? Do the real reasons lie elsewhere?

Influences from Doyle's Life

To analyze the matter, let us start at the beginning. Let us trace the creation and development of this most remarkable character in the annals of fiction. Let us see how and why Sir Arthur Conan Doyle brought Holmes into being and what happened to the author and the character thereafter.

Arthur Conan Doyle was born in Edinburgh on May 22, 1859, in modest circumstances, was educated at Jesuit schools, and studied to become a doctor at the Royal Infirmary in Edinburgh. There, as virtually everyone now knows, he came under the influence of one Dr. Joseph Bell. Bell had acute powers of observation and deduction, a fact now known worldwide, which were quite the marvel of his students and which made an appropriate impression on young Doyle. A sample of Dr. Bell's technique is provided by Doyle's own account of Bell (from Thomson's *Masters of Mystery*):

> In one of his best cases he said to a civilian patient:
> "Well, my man, you've served in the army."
> "Aye, sir."
> "Not long discharged?"
> "No, sir."
> "A Highland regiment?"
> "Aye, sir."
> "A non-com officer?"
> "Aye, sir."
> "Stationed at Barbados?"
> "Aye, sir."

"You see, gentlemen," he would explain, "the man was a respectful man, but he did not remove his hat. They do not in the army, but he would have learned civilian ways had he been long discharged. He has an air of authority and he is obviously Scottish. As to Barbados, his complaint is elephantiasis, which is West Indian and not British."

Doyle, with scant funds, worked his way through medical school and, in 1882, set up his practice in Southsea, a suburb of Portsmouth. Though he chose Southsea with high expectations, his practice did not materialize and, having married in 1885, by 1886 he found himself debt-ridden, with a sick wife. In these straits, and with time hanging heavy, he turned, for income, to writing short stories for some of the cheaper magazines. Though he had some success, he soon saw that if he really hoped to make any substantial money from writing, he should turn out a full-length novel. He tried his hand at one and circulated it till its pages were tattered, to no avail.

The Birth of Holmes

Now we come to the heart of the tale. He needed to try again. He had to write a second novel. So, in casting about for what to write about, he recalled his old mentor, Dr. Bell, and Bell's exceptional ability at observation and deduction.

From here we shall quickly leap ahead to the outcome of this idea of Doyle's, then return for a look at it in detail.

The result was a novel ("novelette" would be a more appropriate label) entitled *A Study in Scarlet*, about a detective who looked like Joseph Bell and used Bell's technique of observation and deduction and whom Doyle started off calling Mr. Sherrington Hope but — Oh great good fortune — changed to Sherlock Holmes.

A Study in Scarlet made the rounds as had its predecessor and seemed destined to the same luckless fate until Doyle got an offer of £25 outright from Ward, Lock and Company. Sufficiently discouraged and disgusted, he took it and *A Study in Scarlet* made its first public appearance in *Beeton's Christmas Annual*, in December 1887.

Though December 1887 is now a memorable date in publishing history, at the time it passed unnoticed. *A Study in Scarlet* did not set the world on fire, nor should it have, for it is not a very good story. In fact, that single tale would doubtless have marked the one and only appearance of Sherlock Holmes had not, more than a year later, Doyle been summoned to meet an editor of the American magazine, *Lippincott's*, who had liked the story and made a substantial offer for another. Sherlock Holmes' life had been spared.

From there on, Holmes' existence has historical significance so let us go back to the days of creation and study the way that existence came into being. Let us put ourselves in Doyle's shoes, see what he did and how he did it, for the approach to how Doyle introduces Holmes into history is worth a great deal of attention.

In view of Doyle's dealing with Holmes in his second appearance, it's hard to deduce whether Doyle, in the first novel, was preparing his detective for a series — if all went well — or was using him merely as the one-time protagonist in a new novel.

In either case, the novel doesn't go well, and the reason is because Doyle introduces his detective in a strange tale dealing with areas (Mormonism and America) of which Doyle knows nothing more than what he's read, trusting that the readership knows even less. Customarily, this is a fatal mistake. In his case it was, by great good fortune, only "*almost* fatal."

Holmes' First Appearance

But WHAT an introduction! Critics, scholars, and all fans of Sherlock Holmes debate and wonder at the grip the man has on the world. He's analyzed and criticized, adulated, parodied, imitated. But has anyone really studied the beginning of that otherwise dreadful novel, *A Study in Scarlet*, and paid attention to what is said there? Let us do that. Let us first meet, then go along with, Dr. Watson as he forms the most fortunate partnership in the annals of fiction by sharing rooms with Mr. Sherlock Holmes.

The Reader Meets Dr. Watson

Doyle introduces his storyteller, as follows: Chapter head: "Being a Reprint from the Reminiscences of John H. Watson, M.D., Late of the Army Medical Department," and introduces his detective under "Chapter I, Mr. Sherlock Holmes."

Watson describes himself, after a brief résumé of his army experiences, as a man whose health has been "irretrievably ruined" (a fact thereafter soon forgotten), living on a government subsidy of eleven shillings and sixpence a day. With no kith nor kin in England, he gravitates to London, "that great cesspool into which all the loungers and idlers of the Empire are irresistibly drained."

There, in the Criterion Bar, he encounters an acquaintance named

Stamford who describes Watson thusly: "You are as thin as a rail and brown as a nut." This description, judging from the general view of Watson as plump, hale, and hearty (the image of Doyle himself) is, for some strange reason, totally ignored.

Watson, like Dupin's chronicler, is also regarded as not overly bright, but again we must regard this as merely a contrast devised by the author to set off the brilliance of Holmes. Watson, in fact, despite this early report on his health, is conveniently capable of resuming his medical career and shows himself as courageous and quite capable of handling a revolver when Holmes wants him armed. We must therefore regard his health as not irretrievably ruined, but we are also left to wonder how he gained all the weight everyone thinks he carried, for no further description, beyond Stamford's "thin as a rail, brown as a nut" is ever given of the man. And what, outside of his amazement at Holmes' deductions (which must amaze us all) labels him a bumbling buffoon?

Watson Seeks a Roommate

But never mind Watson. Holmes is the man we all wish we knew, and a good part of the reason is the way Doyle introduces us to him.

Holmes, Watson's possible roommate, is first described by Stamford in provocative terms, bound to arouse our interest. Stamford says he knows a man who's looking for someone to go halves on a room with him. Watson leaps at the opportunity. Stamford's reply is, "You don't know Sherlock Holmes yet. Perhaps you would not care for him as a constant companion."

"Why, what is there against him?"

Stamford answers, "Oh, I didn't say there was anything against him. He is a little queer in his ideas—an enthusiast in some branches of science. As far as I know he is a decent fellow enough."

"A medical student, I suppose," says Watson.

"No—I have no idea what he intends to go in for. I believe he is well up in anatomy, and he is a first-class chemist; but as far as I know, he has never taken out any systematic medical classes. His studies are very desultory and eccentric, but he has amassed a lot of out-of-the-way knowledge which would astonish his professors."

Ah, what an introduction! Much of Watson's (Doyle's) first revelations about Holmes are forgotten by Doyle, who is only starting off a lengthy and not very good novel, and who obviously didn't reread and refresh his memory on details when circumstances persuaded him to continue the saga of Holmes (he later refers to Watson as "James" rather than "John" and forgets that Watson's wound by a Jezail bullet was in the shoulder "which shattered the bone and grazed the subclavian artery" rather than in his leg). Nevertheless, pay attention to the way Doyle builds up interest in the man.

Stamford takes Watson to the hospital and the chemical laboratory where Holmes is to be found. En route, he gives Watson additional warning about the man, the further to pique our interest. "You mustn't blame me if you don't get on with him," Stamford insists, washing his hands of the matter. Pressed as to what's wrong with the man, Stamford says it's not his temper or disposition, only, "Holmes is a little too scientific for my tastes — it approaches to cold-bloodedness." Then he adds mystery: He's seen Holmes beating the subjects in the dissecting rooms with a stick "to verify how far bruises may be produced after death."

Then comes the actual meeting. We quote:

> "Dr. Watson, Mr. Sherlock Holmes," said Stamford, introducing us.
>
> "How are you?" he said cordially, gripping my hand with a strength for which I should hardly have given him credit. "You have been to Afghanistan, I perceive."
>
> "How on earth did you know that?" I asked in astonishment.

There we have it: The first inkling of what Sherlock Holmes is all about.

But does Doyle tell us? Not yet. He's building up mystery about this man. This is a natural storyteller at work. Says Holmes, excited about a chemical discovery he's just made, "Never mind. The question now is about hemoglobin," and he claims his discovery gives an infallible test for bloodstains, which he goes on to demonstrate.

Who can read all this and not want to know more about this very odd individual? For one thing, how the devil did he know Watson had been in Afghanistan? We are left hanging.

Nor is the reader quite allowed to forget that "throwaway" remark. Rooming arrangements are made, Stamford and Watson leave, and Watson says, stopping and turning on Stamford suddenly, "By the way, how the deuce did he know that I had come from Afghanistan?"

And Stamford answers with an enigmatic smile, "That's just his little peculiarity. A good many people have wanted to know how he finds things out."

And, of course, so does the reader.

A Mystery on Baker Street

Holmes and Watson move into rooms at 221B Baker Street and the mystery grows. Watson has time to reflect upon his strange suite-mate for Doyle has not yet forgotten that Watson is ill. ("My health forbade me from venturing out unless the weather was exceptionally genial." — This restriction won't last beyond its present need.) Holmes, unaware and unconcerned about the Copernican theory, declares that he would acquire no knowledge that did not bear upon his subject. Since he does not say what his subject is and Watson is afraid to ask, Watson tries to deduce the answer by categorizing the areas of Holmes' knowledge.

By now, understand, we are a good eight pages into the story and nothing has happened. The whole time has been spent trying to solve the mystery of what Watson's roommate is all about.

As for Watson's list of Holmes' areas of knowledge, the results are so baffling that he throws it in the fire.

Then there are the visitors who call upon Holmes, a motley crew from all walks of life. More mystery.

Whereupon, on the fourth of March, there comes the moment when Watson reads a magazine article entitled, "The Book of Life," that "attempted to show how much an observant man might learn by an accurate and systematic examination of all that came his way." Watson regards it as a remarkable mixture of shrewdness and absurdity. (As a matter of fact, that should be an appropriate description of the Sherlock Holmes tales and Holmes' deductions — a mixture of shrewdness and absurdity.)

"What ineffable twaddle," exclaims Watson, only to learn that Holmes had written the article and can back up everything it says. In fact, he announces, he depends upon observation and deduction to earn his "bread and cheese."

"And how?" Watson asks involuntarily.

Then comes the revelation: "Well, I have a trade of my own," Holmes answers. "I suppose I am the only one in the world. I'm a consulting detective, if you can understand what that is."

It's ten pages into the story and we've only just found out who Sherlock Holmes is. There's been no action yet. The whole time has been spent introducing us to the most memorable character in the whole of fiction, and the way in which Doyle has handled the introduction is, unquestionably, a significant factor in creating the legend of Sherlock Holmes. Becky Sharp's arrival (in *Vanity Fair*) is anticipated well in advance of her coming, which lends interest and enchantment to this person we are about to meet. Doyle does much the same thing, except that Holmes is on hand, and what is good about that is that the mystery about the man deepens, even as we learn more and more about him.

The reader, interestingly, is not bored waiting for some action to take place. The reader becomes fascinated by the enigma of Watson's suite-mate. This, the ten opening pages of A *Study in Scarlet*, perhaps ranks first in the introduction of a character in fiction. Could any character start out by being more indelibly impressed upon the mind of the reader?

Escaping Dupin's Shadow

Of course, while first impressions are lasting, Holmes would not remain memorable if he didn't do something to live up to the buildup. And this he soon does.

First, however, Doyle must rid himself of the image of Poe's Auguste Dupin which, as well as Dr. Joseph Bell, is hovering over the scene. For instance, says Watson, upon learning what a "consulting detective" is, "But do you mean to say that without leaving your room you can unravel some knot which other men can make nothing of, although they have seen every detail for themselves?"

"Quite so," says Holmes (shades of Dupin unraveling the mystery of Marie Roget). Then he adds (fortunately for the world), "Now and again a case turns up which is a little more complex. Then I have to bustle about and see things with my own eyes." And thus is laid the groundwork for most of the cases Watson records for us, cases wherein the two of them venture forth from 221B Baker Street, into hansom cabs, London fog, and adventure.

Doyle, in real life, may have conceded the debt he owed to Dupin, but not Sherlock Holmes. When Holmes explains how he knew Watson had come from Afghanistan, Watson says, "You remind me of Edgar Allan Poe's Dupin . . ." and Holmes puts Dupin down with, "Now, in my opinion, Dupin was a very inferior fellow. That trick of his of breaking in on his friends' thoughts with an apropos remark after a quarter of an hour's silence is really very showy and superficial. He had some analytical genius, no doubt; but he was by no means such a phenomenon as Poe appeared to imagine."

Here, Doyle is puffing up his own creation and, perhaps inadvertently, giving Holmes the ego for which he is noted—it might even be that, in fulfilling the need to show Holmes' superiority, and the necessity of putting the words in Holmes' mouth, he got the idea to make "ego" a characteristic of his newly invented detective.

As for Gaboriau's Lecoq, Holmes puts him down as a "miserable bungler." Holmes could have solved in twenty-four hours what it took Lecoq six months to accomplish. (Well, we can see why Doyle gave

Holmes an ego. It's the only way he could present Holmes as superior to all prior fictional detectives.)

In establishing that, though Doyle has Holmes pooh-pooh Dupin's "mind-reading" ability as showy and superficial, Doyle doesn't forget the trick. And he knows anybody who's read Poe (which would include most of those who would read Doyle—at least that would be his view at the moment of Holmes' creation, little dreaming that the number of his readers would shrink Dupin to obscurity) won't forget it either. He has to have, and does have, Holmes pull the same trick on Watson.

But that's later, when the reader has presumably forgotten that Dupin did it first. Right now, Doyle must give the reader and Watson an illustration of the Holmes deductive technique. Watson, thinking Holmes conceited, notes a man on the street outside. Holmes, with a glance, says, "You mean the retired sergeant of the Marines?" which deduction is promptly confirmed when the man comes to their door. And here, for the first time, we see Sherlock Holmes in action. Doyle has given us a dozen pages of buildup. Now the legend begins.

Flaws in the First Holmes Novel

Unfortunately, as has been noted, *A Study in Scarlet* is not a good novel. Doyle, after introducing us to his detective, presents the reader with a bizarre murder and has Holmes promptly solve it, snapping handcuffs on the wrists of a cabman come to fetch a portmanteau, and announcing to the amazement of Watson, Gregson, Lestrade, and the reader, that this is Jefferson Hope, the murderer. At this point, there have been twelve pages introducing Holmes and thirty pages of story. Now follows twenty-nine pages of confession in the form of a flashback and eleven pages of explanation by Holmes as to how he solved the mystery.

That is not how detective stories are told today, but we mustn't blame Doyle for that. Poe told his stories the same way. What we can do is note and comment on some disparate points of interest.

The Ash Deduction

For instance, Holmes, at the scene of the crime, says that the murderer smoked a Trichinopoly cigar and explains, "I flatter myself that I can distinguish at a glance the ash of any known brand either of cigar or of tobacco." (In *The Sign of Four*, he'll go even further and say he's done a monograph identifying 140 forms of cigar, cigarette, and pipe tobacco, "with coloured plates illustrating the difference in the ash.") That's all well and good, but modern authorities claim that tobacco ashes are tobacco ashes and there's no way to distinguish brands from ashes—a revelation which is hardly surprising. However, let us not be picky. Holmes' claim is a nice touch and, doubtless, at the time no one had yet thought of investigating the matter. (Maybe Sherlock's statement got them to do it.)

Doyle's Use of Dialogue

At one point in the tale, Gregson explains his solution of the case. This does not sound like a policeman talking, it sounds like Doyle. In short, there's no characterization in his dialogue. But that, we will find, is true throughout all the Holmes stories. Whenever someone comes to the great detective with a tale to tell, that tale is told as Conan Doyle would tell it, not as the client in question would. In a literary sense, this is a flaw, but from a storytelling sense, it's a plus, for it moves the story and maintains interest. Dickens might not have approved, but Sherlockians will. After all, these aren't really stories that are being offered to the reader, but puzzles; and what matters is having all the pieces of the puzzle presented clearly.

Final Revelation of Clues

And there's a touch of Dupin in Holmes' revelations at the end. Says Holmes, "I have already explained to you that what is out of the common is usually a guide rather than a hindrance." That's Dupin saying that the more outré the case, the easier it is to solve, a statement we've challenged. And he does say something else: "In solving a problem of this sort, the grand thing is to be able to reason backward." Is that new, or is it only another way of saying, "Put yourself in the criminal's mind and think as he would think"? (Which Dupin did.)

Medical Mistakes

Unfortunately, there is one matter for which we should take Conan Doyle severely to task. Being a doctor, Doyle should have known better when he claims the expression on the dead man's face indicated the victim foresaw his fate. This refers to Holmes deducing, upon smelling poison on the dead man's lips, that the poison had been forced upon him. Holmes concludes, "I argued that it had been forced upon him from the hatred and fear expressed upon his face."

We can expect such medical mistakes from writers who aren't doctors, but anyone who has been around a morgue or a medical school and has seen corpses, should be familiar with that "unstrung puppet" look they have which separates the dead from the merely sleeping. The faces of dead people have no expression. It doesn't matter how they died. Once they're dead, they're dead. (As Dr. Elliot Gross, former Chief Medical Examiner of the City of New York, puts it: "If the expression on a dead man's face revealed the nature of his death, forensic pathologists would be the greatest detectives in the world.")

And it turns out that the key clue that enabled Holmes to solve the case was just that: the expression on the victim's face. The real mystery here is: Didn't Doyle know any better, or did he think the reader wouldn't know any better?

Or was he, perhaps, unable to devise another way to solve his mystery?

Clever Deductions

But let us not carp. The novel may not be very good, but the Great Man has been born. The recommendation here, regarding *A Study in Scarlet* is: Skip the flashback, never mind how it all came about — only read about Holmes.

But isn't that the reason for reading the Holmes tales in the first place? It's he and Watson who fascinate us — actually, it's Holmes who fascinates us — and the tales are only vehicles for the purpose of letting us see the Great Man in action.

There is a good deal of deduction at the end of *A Study in Scarlet*, by the way, some of it excellent — the conclusion that the cab driver was the murderer being best. Some are not so good: the expression on the dead man's face for one, and that gimmicky conclusion of the murderer having a florid face and bursting a blood vessel.

But we must remember that Doyle had set no easy task for himself. Once he decided that Holmes' deductions (à la Dr. Bell) would be the mark of the man, he had to figure out ways to have Holmes deduce things.

Holmes' Real Appeal

And now let us propose the *real* reason for the magical grip Sherlock Holmes has on the mind of the public. It isn't Doyle's romanticized London, nor Holmes's personality that keep us going back again and again to the canon. Nor is it the rooms at 221B Baker Street, nor the detective's idiosyncrasies. Nor is it Doyle's storytelling ability, great as it is. They're a part of it, that's true, but only after the Fact.

The Fact that makes Holmes so memorable, and the envy of us all, is his ability to observe and deduce. To express it à la Starrett (from

Haycraft's *Murder for Pleasure*): "Gentlemen, I propose to you; *there* you have it. THAT is the Essence!"

Holmes appeals to the puzzle-solving urge in mankind. We pick up each new Holmes story eager to see what "Amazing, Holmes!"— "Elementary, my dear Watson" deductions Holmes will charm us with next. And we go back and reread in the hope that we've forgotten some and can gain the pleasure of rediscovery. Or we wish to relish once again Holmes' astounding pronouncements and, like Watson, find ourselves asking, "How the deuce did he know that I had come from Afghanistan?"

Agree or disagree as you choose, Doyle, in this first tale, gives us a fulsome sampling of Holmes' observations and deductions, with the result that the editor at *Lippincott* who hired him to write another story realized what it was that Holmes had and capitalized on it.

But one can imagine the strain that this was on Doyle. Holmes' prime characteristic was to observe and deduce. This meant Doyle had to keep coming up with clever deductions—well, at times, *any* kind of deduction. The result of this demand was, naturally: some good, many far-fetched. There are times when Doyle really had to reach (i.e., the scratches on Watson's shoes indicating a careless maid in "A Scandal in Bohemia")—which is why Holmes lends himself so well to parody.

But it is this deductive ability, quite apart from Holmes' other eccentricities (Doyle brings in too many: Bullet holes in the wall and the drug use we can do without) that makes us eagerly pick up an unread tale, and makes us regret it when there are no more.

The Second Holmes Novel

With the *Lippincott* commission, Doyle sat down to write another Sherlock Holmes novel, which he entitled *The Sign of Four* and which was published in February 1890 on both sides of the Atlantic. Howard Haycraft says that, "due to the substantial advance, Doyle worked with greater care."

If so, the evidences are hard to come by. One would gather that Doyle did not reread Holmes' first adventure to reacquaint himself with the detective and his chronicler, for this is where he puts the Jezail bullet wound in Watson's leg instead of his shoulder. Doyle seems quite sloppy in a good deal of his work—which causes great difficulty to members of "The Baker Street Irregulars" whose intent, among other things, is to justify every utterance of the "canon."

That, however, is for the "Irregulars" to cogitate over. Our concern is Doyle's approach to a second novel about Sherlock Holmes whom, we have to guess, Doyle had only regarded as a one-time protagonist. If he relied on a faulty memory and mixed up the location of Watson's bullet wounds, the one thing he did not forget was that the secret of Holmes' impact upon the story was his deductive ability. Here, we will pardon Doyle for quoting from Poe when he has Holmes say, "Eliminate all other factors, and the one which remains must be the truth," and pay attention to, perhaps, the most dramatic — certainly most memorable — bit of deduction Holmes ever produced.

A Most Memorable Deduction

Again, remembering Doyle's storytelling ability (the way he introduced Holmes in *A Study in Scarlet*), note that, after a quick connective link to show that *The Sign of Four* is the sequel to *A Study in Scarlet*, Doyle has Watson give Holmes his gold watch to see what Holmes can deduce from it.

Holmes examines the timepiece, hefting it, opening its back, examining it with lens as well as eye, and hands it back with a crestfallen face. "There are hardly any data," he complains. "The watch has been recently cleaned, which robs me of my most suggestive facts."

Watson and the reader smile. Holmes has been put down.

"Though unsatisfactory," he remarks, "my research has not been entirely barren."

Now what?

Holmes notes from initials and date that the watch had been handed down to Watson from his father through an older brother. So much could anyone deduce, as Sherlock points out, and Watson and the reader will agree.

Now Doyle *has* you. Everything the watch can say has been said. *We're* as smart as Holmes.

Except Doyle now pulls the rug out from under the reader. "He (the brother)" says Holmes, "was a man of untidy habits — very untidy and careless. He was left with good prospects, but he threw away his chances, lived for some time in poverty with occasional short intervals of prosperity, and finally, taking to drink, he died. That is all I can gather."

The reader is stunned. Holmes may explain how he reached these conclusions and the reader may agree that they are justified, but who is going to *forget* the man who called these things to our attention?

Romance — and Watson's Future Wife

Then comes the story part of *The Sign of Four*, and with it romance. There is a damsel in distress, Mary Morstan by name, and there is a knight in shining armor (even if his health isn't supposed to be good, and even if we know nothing about him as a ladies' man), Dr. Watson himself. (Holmes, as painted, won't serve as a Lochinvar. He isn't interested in emotion, and—a point that isn't relevant now but will be later—series detectives don't make good husbands or wives.)

So Watson becomes a Romeo in Doyle's second saga, and Mary Morstan a Juliet. Neither fits the role, but this we must blame on Doyle, not on John and Mary. Doyle is good at adventure tales, not billing and cooing.

That, however, is not the point. What Doyle sees here, and what he's doing, is writing a sequel to *A Study in Scarlet* and wrapping it up. That first novel went nowhere. This second, manna from heaven in the guise of *Lippincott's* offer, is as far as he expects the tales of Sherlock Holmes to go.

Ergo, he introduces a love story to add a little interest and figures, at the end, that Watson marries Morstan and lives happily ever after, Holmes goes about his business *sans* roommate and chronicler, end of saga. (May we not regard this as Doyle's first attempt to get rid of Sherlock Holmes? The difference between this and future attempts, however, would be because he thought the character was going nowhere, not because there was no way to stop him.)

Borrowed Story Elements

As to the story, it is noted that Doyle borrowed some of the atmosphere of *The Moonstone*. He also did some direct borrowing from Poe. In the murder of Mr. Sholto, he presents the same "Rue Morgue" question, "How did the murderer escape from the locked room?" The explanation is simpler than in Poe's story, but, as if he originated it, Doyle has Holmes state: "How often have I said to you that when you have eliminated the impossible, whatever remains, *however improbable*, must be the truth?"

And, at the end, on a totally different subject, one cannot help noting Watson's (Doyle's) description of Tonga, the native with the poisoned darts: "venomous as a young snake . . . little black man—the smallest I have ever seen—with a great, misshapen head . . . Never have I seen features so deeply marked with all beastiality and cruelty. . . ."

Doyle's vision of the populace of undeveloped countries is reminiscent of Poe's equally awry picture of orangutans, and suggests that this was the nineteenth century concept of "The white man's burden."

The Adventures of Sherlock Holmes

How immediately successful *The Sign of Four* was is open to some debate. In any case, it couldn't have been spectacular for, early in 1891, Doyle opened a practice in London as an eye specialist with an office at 2 Devonshire Place, near Harley Street. As before, patients failed to come, and Doyle had to keep on writing to keep the wolf from the door. What he wanted to write, and worked hard at, were historical novels. Haycraft says he "had a strong sense of the pageantry of history" and wanted to do for England what Scott had done for Scotland. Thus, was published, in 1891, *White Company*, a tale set in fourteenth century England and France. This was not sufficient so Doyle took on the assignment of turning out a dozen Holmes short stories for the young *Strand Magazine*, the first appearing in July 1891, and with these came fame and fortune. Collected between covers, they were called, *The Adventures of Sherlock Holmes*.

The series starts with "A Scandal in Bohemia" and, if we read Doyle's mind correctly, he sought to establish two things: That Holmes' abilities were sought by people in high places (even royalty) — always a good ploy — and that Holmes was fallible (and therefore human) — an equally desirable ploy.

We should note the date of this case: March 20, 1888. This is after Watson's marriage and he has "seen little of Holmes lately." His marriage had "drifted us away from each other." This is obviously their third adventure together, and while Doyle can have Watson chance to drop in on Holmes this time, he can't have this happen for all the other fifty-five short adventures they share. He has it happen again in the next story, "The Red-Headed League," (surely one of Doyle's best) but soon he's going to have to face the fact that the wife is in the way. Spouses of series detectives (and their narrators) are a bad idea and usually come to no good end, either dying or disappearing.

In any event, in "A Scandal in Bohemia," Holmes makes a statement that is uniquely his own and sets him apart from his predecessors and could only be copied by his followers. Says Sherlock, and this defines the man: "You see, but you do not observe."

In the story, dealing with the attempt to retrieve a compromising photograph damaging to a royal personage, Doyle borrows heavily from Poe's "The Purloined Letter." Here it's a photograph rather than a letter, but the threat — blackmail — is the same. Doyle also uses the same ploy of creating a fake disturbance to trick the victim and regain the valuable property. In Holmes' case, it doesn't work. However, all is well at the end. Irene Adler's convenient marriage assures that the damaging evidence will never be used (more believable of a woman than a man).

This contrivance (Irene's marriage) to produce a satisfactory conclusion is reminiscent of Jefferson Hope's convenient death in *A Study in Scarlet* and Jonathan Small's innocence in *A Sign of Four*.

Let us not, however, assume that Doyle was tender-hearted. He knew his audience and was doing what Dickens did—producing happy endings (in Dickens' case sometimes unbelievably).

An Innovative Gimmick

Next in *The Adventures* is "The Red-Headed League," but it appears to be misplaced. Watson visits Holmes, who mentions the "Mary Sutherland" case of a few days before and Mary Sutherland appears in "A Case of Identity," which follows. It's a matter of small moment, but it should be noted.

"The Red-Headed League" invokes a really great gimmick, so far as I know, a first. No wonder this story was so popular. A mysterious situation is set up that defies explanation. Then the explanation is introduced and it goes in a totally different direction. That's the essence of humor, the switch that catches us completely off guard. And if humor delights us, why not use the same kind of switch in storytelling of a nonhumorous vein? We are sure to be delighted.

The Problem of the Wife

In skimming over the rest of the adventures, let us consider the problem of the wife. In the above cases, Watson, married and living with his wife, has been dropping in on Holmes at convenient times. Now, in "The Boscombe Valley Mystery," comes an out-of-town case which Holmes wants Watson to go off with him on. Mrs. Watson urges him to do so, which is extremely generous of her, but how long can this go on? If Holmes and Watson are to solve innumerable cases together, they should be back sharing rooms at 221B.

The next tale, "The Five Orange Pips," opens: "When I glance over my notes and records of the Sherlock Holmes cases between the years '82 and '90, I am faced by so many which present strange and interesting features that it is no easy matter to know which to choose and which to leave."

It's September 1887, and Watson is back at Baker Street, sharing rooms with Holmes. Is Mrs. Watson gone? No, she isn't. He's back with Holmes, it turns out, only because his wife "was on a visit to her mother's, and for a few days I was a dweller once more in my old quarters at Baker Street." (What mother? Mary Morstan's mother was dead.)

(Let's face it, spouses have absolutely NO business in series detective stories!)

Doyle avoids the existence of a wife in "The Adventure of the Speckled Band" by casting the time as "in the early days of my association with

Holmes, when we were sharing rooms as bachelors in Baker Street," setting the date as April 1883.

For fun, and for the record, which Doyle has to keep monkeying with because of the inconvenient wife, we have as follows: Watson became a doctor in 1878 (*A Study in Scarlet*). He's already married in 1887 ("The Five Orange Pips"), and in "The Adventure of the Engineer's Thumb," set in the summer of 1889, Watson says it's "not long after my marriage."

In short, what Doyle had to do was get around the mistake he made of marrying Watson off after his second case with Holmes. He started off trying to have the next cases take place after the marriage. That, however, was tedious, so he ultimately inserted countless cases, and referred to countless more, as having taken place after meeting Holmes and before getting married. Thus, in the last three of the *Adventures*, one is before his marriage, and the last two have Watson living with Holmes with no mention of a wife.

In short, Doyle was doing what any other writer would do faced with the same problem. He fudged, manipulated dates, inserted cases, dismissed the wife, and sometimes pretended she didn't exist. The reader was more than glad to go along. He didn't want her around anyway.

Christopher Morley (*The Complete Sherlock Holmes*) puts it best: "We had been tolerant of Mrs. Watson because she was nee Mary Morstan in *The Sign of Four*, but obviously she was a little in the way. Her patience was certainly exemplary in allowing the doctor to rush off on various expeditions: but it could not last."

Morley then concludes with a little mystery of his own: "One of the unsolved questions, by the way, is the second Mrs. Watson. Evidently the good doctor, who was always persevering, had tried again; for Holmes in January 1903 (see "The Adventure of the Blanched Soldier") refers to an existing Mrs. Watson. But who or why this second lady we have no data."

So let us deal with the wife — wives? — establish what we can (according to Doyle), and see what we can establish as Doyle's solution of the problem.

From the *Memoirs of Sherlock Holmes*, which follows *Adventures*, we can conclude that Watson married in the late spring of 1887 (in "The Reigate Puzzle," April 18, 1887, he had no wife, but in June, when the affair of "The Stock-Brokers Clerk" came about, he was newly wedded). Prior to that time, we are left to conclude that Watson had shared rooms with Holmes and recorded Holmes' cases for at least five years. (But Watson, later, will report that he was with Holmes for seventeen of his twenty-three years of practice.) Arthur Conan Doyle did have his problems with Holmes, Watson, and the calendar. But one must acknowledge that, despite the difficulties of the unwanted wife (whom Doyle inexplicably reintroduces in a case taking place in 1903 — evoking Christopher Morley's reference to a second Mrs. Watson) Doyle was not attentive to calendars. He makes the mistake, for example, of setting "The Adventure of the Solitary Cyclist" on Saturday, April 23, 1895, when April 23 fell on Tuesday that year. One must grant Doyle high marks as a storyteller, but we must fail him on reliability, even when he isn't having to squeeze Holmes' cases into the time frame he inadvertently imposed upon himself.

The Demise of Holmes

The problem for Doyle wasn't really with dates and wives, the problem was Holmes himself.

The success of the *Strand Magazine* series, appearing in the U.S. through McClure's Syndicate, was such that Doyle was commissioned to do another dozen for *Harper's Weekly*. For these he was paid £50 each, twice what he got for the complete rights to *A Study in Scarlet*. (Eleven of the twelve were collected in *Memoirs of Sherlock Holmes*, the twelfth appearing in *His Last Bow*.) Their popularity was so great that, in 1894, Doyle was invited on an immensely successful lecture tour of the United States. It would appear that all was right with the world.

It wasn't. Despite the success, Doyle was tired of Holmes and deadlines. He felt trapped by his creation. He wanted to be known for his "serious" work, the historical novels. Instead, everywhere he went, he was associated with Holmes and was constantly expected to solve every sort of real puzzle and problem, great and small. (In actuality, he was very good at it. He played a successful role in two *cause celebres*, the Slater and Edalji affairs, and it is claimed that his "brilliant" analysis of the evidence helped prevent a serious miscarriage of justice.)

He was plagued by the problems which serial detective story writers have to face: 1. The necessity of trying to maintain quality; 2. The fatigue of endlessly repeating oneself; and 3. The need to grow. And, in Doyle's case, we can add a fourth: those numerous, fascinating deductions Holmes was expected to surprise us with, not only to solve a case, but to entertain the reader before the case was ever undertaken.

In Doyle's case, he faced the ultimate. Most creators of detective series find that their readers tire of their protagonist at nearly the same rate that they do. Thus, when they decide to explore another realm, the outcry from the faithful is but slight and can be ignored. Not so with

Doyle. He had created a monster which dominated him to the same degree that Dr. Frankenstein's creation dominated *him*. (To wit: Most people think "Frankenstein" is the name of the monster, not the doctor who created him.)

The Arch Villain

Doyle decides the solution is to get rid of Holmes. And into the canon, in "The Final Problem," the twenty-fourth short story, he introduces an arch villain named Professor Moriarty. The only significant thing to be said of the professor is that he doesn't "belong" in the Holmes stories. He doesn't fit. In fact, until this story, he's never been heard of.

But how else can Doyle end the series? He can't have Holmes fall to an inferior adversary, but Holmes has no equals. Doyle has to create one. Thus there comes into being a brilliant mind (we make him a professor to prove it), as dedicated to evil as Holmes is to good. This is the forerunner of Fu Manchu, of Goldfinger and untold others — the threat to humanity and all that is worthwhile in life. (The real embodiment would be Adolph Hitler, but no fiction writer could have imagined a Hitler — all of which says something about the limits of the creativity of writers. We can't imagine what we haven't experienced.)

Doyle creates — tries to create — an evil equal to Holmes in order to get rid of Holmes. But, of course, Holmes cannot lose! Thus, they must go down together. (Both are presumed to have fallen to their death, locked in each other's arms, in a plunge over Reichenbach Falls.) Here we have the satisfactory (to Doyle's way of thinking) end of Holmes. (Well, it can't be perfectly satisfactory, for Doyle can't really believe Holmes can be equaled — never mind the Mycroft bit.) But it's the best he can do. How else can he get rid of Sherlock Holmes in any kind of manner his readership will accept? (You can hardly have him accidentally trampled to death by a coachman's horse.)

But Doyle is smart enough not to produce a body. This for two reasons: 1. The enormous readership his Holmes tales have evoked would have been revolted at the sight of Holmes' corpse (this would have been too much — particularly in his day); and 2. Which is really # 1 — he must leave himself an out. (No author who has any idea of what he's doing boxes himself into a corner. That's the predicament he puts his hero into — that's good storytelling. But he doesn't do it to himself — though one must admit that Doyle came as close to it as he could. His resurrection of Holmes was hard to manage.)

The Resurrection of Holmes

The outcry at the demise of Holmes was instant and voluminous. One woman wrote, "You beast!" It is even said that Queen Victoria expressed the desire to see more stories and Doyle felt obliged. In any event, he resisted the pressure until 1901 when, faced with money worries and with his imagination stimulated by the story of a gruesome death and a ghostly dog on Dartmoor, he wrote the best and most famous of the Holmes novels, *The Hound of the Baskervilles*, which appeared in 1902.

He had Watson explain the novel as being an early adventure but, in 1903, he was finally persuaded, by an offer from *Lippincott* at $5,000 a story, and a *Strand* offer of £100 per 1,000 words, to turn out more tales.

The result was a new collection entitled (in book form), *The Return of Sherlock Holmes*, in the first of which tales, "The Adventure of the Empty House," Holmes reappears. (Though its publication was 1903, Watson dates the case as 1894.)

Doyle makes the resurrection as dramatic as possible by having Holmes remove a disguise, but, in all honesty, it is nothing like the drama that attended his introduction in *A Study in Scarlet*. In fact, the new set of tales is regarded as not on a par with the earlier ones. Doyle used to tell of a Cornish boatman who reflected the public mind by saying to him, "I think, sir, when Holmes fell over that cliff he may not have killed himself, but he was never quite the same man afterwards."

Be that as it may, when the first story appeared in the *Strand* for October 1903, queues lined up at the London stationers' on publication date.

Including the Villain

Back to Moriarty. Doyle, in the new series, now is faced with the difficulty of presenting this demon, whom Holmes only first mentions in "The Final Problem," as someone Holmes has had to grapple with throughout his career. He does what he can, mentioning him in further cases which supposedly took place earlier. It doesn't really work, as of course it can't, but Sherlockians willingly accept Moriarty as the arch criminal who was Holmes' constant threat. In fact, there are some who suggest that Moriarty himself survived the struggle at Reichenbach Falls and surfaced again as Adolph Hitler (an antiquated, doddering Hitler if so).

A Final Word on Holmes

With evident reluctance, Doyle produced three more Holmes books: *The Valley of Fear* (1915); *His Last Bow* (1917); and *The Case-Book of Sherlock Holmes* (1917).

Of *The Valley of Fear*, Haycraft says, "It is to be feared posterity will pronounce (it) sadly inferior to anything in the saga." The other two were the "familiar groupings of short stories that had previously appeared in a number of English and American journals over a period of years."

As *Adventures* were better than *Memoirs*, so *Memoirs* were better than *Return*, and *Return* better than what followed.

But does that really matter? What we have are fifty-six short stories and four novels and we only wish there were more, not less.

Oh, there are the careless mistakes Doyle made, there are the awkward attempts to deal with the unnecessary wife, and the belatedly arrived Professor Moriarty, but that's not what Sherlock Holmes is all about. The opening of "The Adventure of the Abbey Grange" says it best:

> It was on a bitterly cold night and frosty morning, toward the end of the winter of '97, that I was awakened by a tugging at my shoulder. It was Holmes. The candle in his hand shone upon his eager, stooping face, and told me at a glance that something was amiss.
>
> "Come, Watson, come!" he cried. "The game is afoot. Not a word! Into your clothes and come."

Who could resist such a summons?

4

FROM
DOYLE
TO
CHRISTIE

The shadow cast by Sherlock Holmes has been long indeed, affecting the progress of the detective story from his time forward. Never mind that Auguste Dupin did it first, nor that Poe's tales established the rites of what we call the "mystery story," the overwhelming presence of Sherlock Holmes obliterated all that. Only the scholars would note that Holmes had a predecessor, that he didn't start it all.

But then, as we have pointed out, Poe didn't lay down the rules of the detective story, he only utilized the rules in creating his own. The rules are implicit in the nature of the art. Anyone who wishes to write a detective story — or a novel of any kind (see chapter thirteen, The Mystery versus the Novel) — must obey the strictures. They are the *form* of storytelling, from the *Bible* through the *Iliad* and the *Odyssey*, through the plays of Shakespeare, and down to today's best-seller.

All subsequent writers of detective fiction pay a debt to Sherlock Holmes. They all seek to establish a detective hero who will be, in whatever way — and this varies with the changing times — memorable, likable, enduring, capable of catching the reader's attention; all for the purpose of making the reader want to encounter this unique personage in further adventures.

In the years which followed Holmes's appearance on the stage, the mystery form gripped the imagination of subsequent writers and readers, and the years from 1900 to 1920, witnessed the introduction of a great number of protagonist detectives who were unique in their being and who devoted their time to solving mysteries.

It is not the purpose here to list all the authors of detective fiction and the titles of their works. For such a compendium, one should turn to Allen Hubin's *The Bibliography of Crime Fiction 1749-1975*, which is as complete as his dedication to the subject can make it. (And even Hubin, in his research, will admit to new discoveries.)

Nor can we, here, even list all the mystery writers of importance, those of great and good reputation whose readership thrives on their continued production. All we seek to do is note those moments in the history of the detective story when significant changes in the nature of the medium took place, and take cognizance of those particular authors who produced the change.

On the side, we shall mention certain other authors who, while they didn't motivate change, contributed to the field and were, for one reason or another, interesting for what they did or for what they wrote. In short, it would take pages to record the names of those who deserve to be noted for their excellence, for their reputations, and for the renown of their detective heroes. We can only mention a few and not necessarily for their excellence, nor for the renown of their detective heroes, although the names we do mention should be, in some degree, familiar to the reader.

Mary Roberts Rinehart

Now, having said all that, the first person we shall mention, one whose name rings many bells, is a writer who did none of the above. She did not follow in the footsteps of Sherlock Holmes, she did not create a memorable detective, nor try to. She just wrote mystery stories to her own liking — and to the liking of an enormous readership, so she certainly deserves a mention here. We mean, of course, Mary Roberts Rinehart.

Born in 1876, married at nineteen to Dr. Stanley Rinehart; the mother of three sons, Mrs. Rinehart, to contribute to the family support after the stock market slump of 1903 left the family distressed, started writing stories. Her first mystery novel, *The Man in Lower Ten*, was serialized in 1907. Her first hardcover novel, one which lasts today, *The Circular Staircase* (1908), was an immediate success and led to a career in the field which credited her with being the highest paid author in America. In fact, she even founded her own publishing company to handle her works.

The "Had I But Known" School

She is regarded today as a "woman's author," and a devotee, if not a creator, of what is called and condemned as the "Had I but known" school of detective writing.

The condemnation of the "Had I but known" school is not because, due to the fallibility of the human animal, we fail to foresee the results of our own actions. It's because, in feminine novels, such as Mrs. Rinehart wrote, this inability is stated by the valiant heroine of the tale who suggests that, had she realized what future horrors would result from her present innocent or bewildered behavior, she would never have done what she will now proceed to do.

What is interesting about the disrepute of this form of writing is that it preceded the recent sexual revolution. Even before feminists attacked this portrayal of the female as a helpless idiot, editors and readers had already rejected such ineptitude on the part of storybook heroines.

Nevertheless, pay Mary Roberts Rinehart her regards. Never mind her flaws. Pay attention to her storytelling ability. She holds our attention, not because she creates great detective fiction, but because she tells Great Stories. And she's one of the few.

Detectives between 1900-1920

Detective as Culprit

As for the genuine detective stories in the first two decades of this century, let us mention French author Gaston Leroux's *Le Mystere de la Chambre Jaune* (*The Mystery of the Yellow Room*), which is called the most brilliant of all "locked room" novels. What, in addition, was a most original concept at the time, was Leroux's making the detective the culprit. If it is not so original today, it is still a good gimmick in the art of trying to produce the "least likely" suspect as the villain of the piece.

Dr. Thorndyke

Also to be noted is R. Austin Freeman's creation, medical-legal expert, Dr. Thorndyke, who made his first appearance in 1907. Dorothy Sayers will have some words to say about Dr. Thorndyke in the following chapter, but Howard Haycraft's assessment is worth repeating now: "From the earliest days of the police novel," says Haycraft, "there has been a vast deal of high-flown talk about the 'scientific' detective. The plain truth is that few of the sleuths of fiction wearing this designation would know which way to turn if they found themselves in a real-life laboratory." He goes on to say that the "shining exception" is Dr. John Thorndyke, and explains, "No other literary criminologist, as far as this writer knows, has been paid the tribute of having his fictional methods put into use by the real police."

Why Detectives Are Never Police

Note, particularly, what Haycraft says about the customary fictional sleuth's inability to find his way around a laboratory. This critical flaw in the makeup of the fictional detective, which will not be corrected until the advent of the Police Procedural fifty years down the line, is due to the lack of interest of fiction writers throughout this period in researching how the real police go about their business. As a result, most fictional detectives here and in the Classical Age that follows, are represented as amateurs. This serves the handy purpose not only of making police research unnecessary, but also explains why the brilliant genius is not a member of the forces of law and order. The super-intellect of their super-sleuths is too great for such a "mundane" occupation. And, of course, the super-detective must be unhampered in his investigation by such things as rules, regulations, and the mountain of paperwork that is the baggage borne by the police professional.

What this reflects, incidentally, is the commonly held view of the "intellectual" (if we can classify writers as being in that category) as to the mental qualifications of policemen. The highbrows of society (meaning writers who, because they are articulate, are the tastemakers and the naysayers) tend to regard the police as lowbrows and never, by the remotest possibility, can they envision the smartest detective character their minds could create as dealing with the police on anything like an equal level.

Even those writers who gave their detectives official police titles, such as *Lieutenant* French and *Inspector* Maigret, were not writing about policemen. Their heroes were supposedly high enough up in rank so that their connection with the Department never showed.

For it is quite one thing to say that "so-and-so" was a member of the police department, it's quite another to make him that—meaning, for the author to demonstrate that his hero is, indeed, attached to a given police force, bound by its dictums, shackled by the rules of evidence, the laws of the land, the strictures which impose their restrictions upon everything a real policeman *can* do. (This is the difference between these so-called "police" novels, and the "police procedural.")

The Old Man in the Corner

Detectives to note in the period between 1900 and 1920 include Baroness Orczy's "Old Man in the Corner" (1909). Here is a detective—the Old Man—who represents Sherlock Holmes's ideal situation, that of sitting at home and unraveling cases brought in to him from outside, without stirring from his seat.

This detective's distinctive characteristic is that he sits in a corner tying and untying complicated knots in a piece of string while he, without moving, solves the cases brought to him.

As we have noted—Thank God the cases Watson recorded were

the ones where Holmes had to get up and move around a bit. Tales wherein the detective is sedentary and omniscient, never having to move from his chair, must inevitably not only be static, but tedious. It's no fun if everything is reported to the detective and nothing is seen (which is the valid criticism of "The Mystery of Marie Roget," which, otherwise, is fascinating from the view of how Poe's mind worked). In storytelling, the overpowering maxim is "Show, don't Tell."

Father Brown

The Baroness's tales are short stories and so are the tales of G.K. Chesterton's famous detective, Father Brown (1911). Father Brown's unique quality was that he was a priest rather than a detective. Father Brown, unlike the Old Man in the Corner, got out and about a bit, but the Father Brown stories aren't noted so much for detection as for a professed understanding of human nature. Father Brown solves cases because of his background as a priest and the insights that resulted.

Philip Trent

Most of the detective tales in this period were short stories, but there was one product of the era, E.C. Bentley's *Trent's Last Case* (1913), which was a novel.

Edmund Clerihew Bentley, born in 1875, was a lifelong friend of Chesterton's and his career was as a newspaperman. *Trent's Last Case*, his first venture into detective fiction, was perhaps motivated by Chesterton's efforts, although Bentley says it was motivated by the belief that "It should be possible, I thought, to write a detective story in which the detective was recognizable as a human being" (from *Murder for Pleasure*). His detective, Philip Trent, artist and journalist (the author himself, as is usually the case), was used to make this point, and the novel is regarded as the forerunner of the Classical Period that followed. Trent's "Last Case" wasn't really his "one and only" as Bentley had suggested, for he did produce an encore, *Trent's Own Case*, done in collaboration with H. Warner Allen, circa 1936.

Dorothy Sayers admits a debt to Philip Trent, which, in effect, indicates that the rise of the Classical Age of detective fiction started before her, and before the 1920s.

Be that as it may, the time between Conan Doyle and Agatha Christie should be regarded as a "waiting period." Never mind who wrote what about what in that era, the shift that was going on in detective fiction was the transition from the reader as ineffectual witness to the storied events, to the reader as competent competitor against the detective hero.

Just how and when and where it came about is difficult to pinpoint (because it was a growing thing during this period), but with the advent of the Classical Age of the mystery, which started with Christie in 1920, the era of Fair Play in detective fiction was now established.

5

THE QUEEN

The title "Queen of the Mystery" goes, of course, to Dame Agatha Christie. She earns that title not only for her ingenuity, in which category she stands alone, but for output (some eighty-three detective novels, a dozen plays, innumerable short stories); for reputation (she created not one, but two internationally known detectives); fame (sale of her books are estimated in excess of 400 million copies); and wealth. As one article writer said of her, "Agatha Christie isn't just rich, she's Big Rich." Or, as Jeffrey Feinman put it in his 1975 biography, *Agatha Christie*, "In poor years, Agatha Christie's income never drops below $5,000 weekly. Currently she tops $10,000 a week . . ."

How did she get that way? Who was this woman? Where did she come from? What, exactly, did she do? What were her talents and her flaws?

Her Life

To begin at the beginning, Clarissa Mary Agatha Miller was born September 15, 1890 in Torquay, Devonshire, a village on the English Channel, following an elder sister, Madge, and a brother Monty. The family was well-to-do, her upbringing proper and comfortable. There were four servants, a cook, parlormaid, housemaid, and nurse. Her father, Frederick Miller, was a wealthy American stockbroker who spent his days, not at work, but at the club.

With his death, when Agatha was eleven, financial problems ensued, but they weren't calamitous. Madge married well, Agatha went to finishing schools in Paris, and continued to enjoy the upper-class life of the times.

Then she met, at a house-dance, the dashing Captain Archibald Christie who quite swept her off her feet. Their engagement, which was according to Gwen Robyns, "a tempestuous affair," lasted nearly two years before Agatha Miller and Archibald Christie were married by special license on Christmas Eve 1914, "at the parish church of Emmanuel, Clifton, a fashionable suburb of Bristol." Gwen Robyns, in her book, *The Mystery of Agatha Christie* (Penguin 1928), says, "There is no doubt from her autobiography that Agatha Miller would have preferred to wait." To Robyns' question, "Why the haste?" one may only note that a war was on and marriages mustn't be delayed when a soldier goes off to battle.

Poison — the Instrument of Choice

With Archie in France, Agatha moved back to Torquay and took up nursing, being assigned to the surgical ward of the Torquay hospital where she stayed two years. There, to quote Robyns, between "rapturous re-unions with Archie when he came home on leave," Agatha advanced to the dispensary which she found, "Very rewarding, very enjoyable; you had a lot of responsibility," and it was there that she gained an accurate knowledge of poisons, which she put to effective use in her novels. Agatha not only used poisons in her stories, she *knew* them. As she later said, "I know nothing about pistols and revolvers, which is why I usually kill off my characters with a blunt instrument — or better still with poisons. Besides, poisons are neat and clean and really exciting. . . . I do not think I could look a really ghastly mangled body in the face." Added Agatha, "It is the means I'm interested in. I do not usually describe the end, which is often a corpse."

This, one might suggest, is "female thinking" — neatness, no mess: do the job and get on with the case. However, we should note that it wasn't only female writers who resorted to poisons, neatness, and no mess in those days. This was before Hammett and the advent of blood and gore. This was when the purpose of the novel was the solution of the crime, not the horrors of it. Thus poison was an easy out. But, we should also note, when other methods were used — guns, blunt instruments, or whatever else the writers of the period could devise (arrows in an Ellery Queen mystery of the period), gore was either not in attendance, or the description was omitted. (Gunshot wounds were usually limited to a small round hole in the middle of the forehead. Horror was not apropos of the plot.)

The point to be made here is not that, as the saying goes, "Poison is a woman's weapon." Poison was a *common* weapon. And Agatha seized upon her knowledge of poisons as providing the ideal way to get rid of victims: 1. No mess; and 2. Great mystery as the detectives pondered how the victim died.

This, for a while, begat all sorts of bizarre poisons — we can see mystery writers of the period combing the medical journals for the rarest, hardest to detect anathemas to the human body (perhaps making up their own), all the better with which to bewitch not only the police, but the hero-detective and the reader.

Agatha was well placed to utilize this ploy but, ultimately, rare poisons got done to death and readers could complain that it wasn't "Fair Play." How were they supposed to approach and have a chance to solve the mystery without a thorough indoctrination into the field of poisons?

Dorothy L. Sayers expresses it this way in her Introduction to the anthology, known in England as *Great Short Stories of Detection, Mystery, and Horror* (Gollancz 1928) and in America as the first *Omnibus of Crime* (Payson & Clarke, 1929):

> The reader must be given every clue — but he must not be told, surely, all the detective's deductions, lest he should see the solution too far ahead. . . . Various devices are used to get over the difficulty. Frequently the detective, while apparently displaying-playing his clues openly, will keep up his sleeve some bit of special knowledge which the reader does not possess. Thus, Thorndyke can cheerfully show you all his finds. You will be none the wiser, unless you happen to have an intimate acquaintance with the fauna of local ponds; the effect of belladonna on rabbits; the physical and chemical properties of blood; optics; tropical diseases; metallurgy; hieroglyphics, and a few other trifles.

These "trifles," as she calls them, are not "Fair Play," a subject to be dealt with later.

The First Novel

But let us return to Agatha. In 1916, she was given a leave from the hospital. At this point, all she's read in the field of the mystery is Sherlock Holmes and *The Secret of the Yellow Room*, which might be considered the stock-in-trade of the nondevotee. And it is now that, so the story goes, her sister Madge gives her a dare. The talk is mysteries and Madge says: "I bet you can't write a mystery in which I can't guess the ending."

"Wait and see," answers Agatha. "I have an idea going round in my head about medicine."

Her mother suggests she write it at Dartmoor and Agatha proceeds there and produces her first novel, *The Mysterious Affair at Styles* in three weeks.

Hercule Poirot

Out of this came Hercule Poirot, doubtless the most familiar name in detective fiction next to Sherlock Holmes. She makes him Belgian and, though a direct connection cannot be established, the fact that Torquay had opened its doors to Belgian refugees suggests that, at least subliminally (Agatha claims the idea "just came to her"), this is where she got the inspiration.

Now let us come to the other impacts that helped Agatha Christie create her Hercule Poirot: She's read the Sherlock Holmes tales. Anyone who has this as background, is, in a maiden attempt, going to go with the tried-and-true. Holmes grips the readership, not by Doyle's plots, but by *himself*—by Holmes' appearance on stage.

The thing to do, therefore, from a tyro's point of view is, create a "memorable detective." Now, let's face it, no one is going to come forth with a detective so memorable that he will eclipse Sherlock Holmes. So an Agatha Christie, or anyone else (and we will find they were many), has to create a detective "almost as memorable" as Holmes. The name of the game is, "You can't out-Sherlock Sherlock. Therefore, create a character as nearly Sherlockian as you can."

Thus Agatha, if we read her correctly, produces a Belgian detective in England. The problem here is that he's commonly thought of as French. Be that as it may, we describe him: Short, egg-headed, mustachioed. (How unlike Sherlock can we get?)

Unfortunately, physical description isn't all that memorable. We have to give him characteristics, things that will separate him from the mass. One of the things we can do is program classroom French phrases into his speech. (That hasn't been done before and it makes Poirot distinctive.) We can have him talk about "little gray cells"—again unique.

Bit by bit, we create a detective who, like Sherlock Holmes, will be *distinctive* and, therefore—hopefully—(the failures are legion) *memorable*.

Poirot's "Watson"

This, we can imagine, was Agatha Christie's thinking when she sat down to produce her first mystery novel. Again borrowing from Doyle, she also introduces a "Watson," Captain Hastings, the person who would recount the exploits of her M. Poirot.

Robyns remarks: "The fact that she (Christie) gave M. Poirot an assistant named Captain Hastings, an army officer who had recently been invalided home from the front, is reminiscent of Sherlock Holmes and Watson. Hastings was as slow-witted and obvious as Poirot was mercurial-thinking and obscure."

(One cannot help wondering just how "stupid" Watson and Hastings really are, vis-à-vis not just us readers, but in contrast to everyone else except Holmes and Poirot. This supposed "stupidity" and the amount of it might well await a thesis on the subject.)

The "Cute Young Couple" Detectives.

This first mystery novel of Agatha Christie's, a landmark in the field, did not meet with the immediate success we might anticipate. It went the rounds of half a dozen publishers for four years before finally being accepted by John Lane of Bodley Head.

Meantime — and note this — Agatha Christie was not sitting idle. Sharp and shrewd, she had nearly finished a second novel, *The Secret Adversary*, featuring Tommy and Tuppence Beresford, the first of the cute young couple school of detective fiction, which came out in 1922.

As for her private life, Agatha and Archie had a daughter, Rosalind, in 1919, her only child. In 1922, she and Archie took a trip around the world as he promoted the British Empire Exposition of that year, and by the mid-twenties, with three more books to her name, they were pretty well-off financially, assisted, no doubt, by Agatha's output. But the marriage was crumbling.

Fooling the Reader

Now we come to 1926, the year in which Agatha published the most talked about novel in detective history, *The Murder of Roger Ackroyd*, made famous, as nearly everyone knows, by the fact that the first-person storyteller turns out to be the murderer.

When it comes to fooling the reader as to the identity of the murderer, the concept of having the storyteller the guilty party hadn't ever been considered before. This went beyond all previous efforts and is the most obvious illustration of her great ability to come up with the "least suspected" character as villain. But this was her forté. This particular ability is what sets her ahead of all other mystery writers in this regard. In her books, no matter whom you think you've picked out, it's almost certain she's going to fool you. A reader familiar with the works and therefore the mind-set of a particular author, can, in time, get pretty adept at figuring out who the author is going to throw at you as the guilty party. This isn't done, mind you, through careful attention to the clues, the neat sidestepping of red herrings, or the ability to remember what casual remark in the beginning is going to be the key clue at the end. It is, instead, an acquaintance with how the author thinks. Never mind the clues. Never mind the red herrings nor the direction the story seems to take. It's all a question of reading the author's mind, of being aware of traits that he doesn't know he's got.

For instance, in an Ellery Queen book, it's easy to pick out the murderer. It's going to be the *one* person who simply couldn't have done it. The reasons why he couldn't have done it may vary: It could be the absolutely ironclad alibi (*The Chinese Orange Mystery*); or that he's thought to be the victim and is dead (*The Egyptian Cross Mystery*); or because he's the victim's most devoted friend. (That's the one with the arrows.)

Sometimes an author, without being aware of it, will introduce the murderer first in the story, and the perceptive reader, ahead of the author on this, will know the identity of the murderer before the first few pages have passed.

It takes a clever author to be mindful of his own idiosyncrasies and vary his tactics in order to keep the perceptive reader fooled. And at this, nobody was better than Agatha Christie. (One should note a trick of hers which she has used more than once, however — the murderer, though present throughout, is not listed as one of the suspects. This is, in fact, the ploy she used in *Ackroyd*, the storyteller apparently being Poirot's righthand man while the fingers of suspicion point to everyone else.)

So there was a great howl of protest when Agatha fooled everyone with her *The Murder of Roger Ackroyd*, and great were the cries that she had "cheated," that she hadn't played fair. But, in reality, the clues were properly planted — or, shall we say, as "properly" as Agatha was prone to plant them, which isn't as proper as she would have you believe.

So the howls of protest could best be described as sour grapes because she'd pulled a fast one. Dorothy Sayers was one who supported Christie's tactic, reminding the reader that, in a mystery novel, absolutely *nobody* was above suspicion, saying, "Fair!" and "Fooled You!"

One of the complainers of Agatha Christie's methods and technique was her contemporary peer, Willard Huntington Wright who, under the pseudonym S.S. Van Dine created the enormously popular, if now all but forgotten sleuth, Philo Vance. Said Wright in the Introduction to *The Great Detective Stories* (Scribners, 1927):

> Hercule Poirot, Agatha Christie's pompous little Belgian sleuth, falls in the category of detectival logicians, and though his methods are also intuitional to the point of clair-voyance, he constantly insists that his surprisingly accurate and often miraculous deductions are the inevitable results of the intensive operation of "the little gray cell." Poirot is more fantastic and far less credible than his brother crimi-

nologists of the syllogistic fraternity. The stories in which he figures are often so artificial, and their problems so far fetched, that all sense of reality is lost, and consequently the interest in the solution is vitiated. This is particularly true of the short stories gathered into the volume *Poirot Investigates*. Poirot is to be seen at his best in *The Mysterious Affair at Styles* and *The Murder on the Links*. The trick played on the reader in *The Murder of Roger Ackroyd* is hardly a legitimate device of the detective-story writer; and while Poirot's work in this book is at times capable, the effect is nullified by the denouement.

Dorothy Sayers answered S.S. Van Dine in the *Omnibus of Crime*, saying:

An exceptional handling of the Watson theme is found in Agatha Christie's *Murder of Roger Ackroyd*, which is a *tour de force*. Some critics, as, for instance, Mr. W.H. Wright in his introduction to *The Great Detective Stories* (Scribners, 1927), consider the solution illegitimate. I fancy, however, that this opinion merely represents a natural resentment at having been ingeniously bamboozled. All the necessary data are given. The reader ought to be able to guess the criminal, if he is sharp enough, and nobody can ask for more than this. It is, after all, the reader's job to keep his wits about him, and, like the perfect detective, to suspect *everybody*.

Of a different book, *Murder on the Orient Express*, Raymond Chandler takes Christie to task thusly:

. . . there is a scheme of Agatha Christie's featuring M. Hercule Poirot, that ingenious Belgian who talks in a literal translation of schoolboy French, wherein, by duly messing around with his "little gray cells," M. Poirot decides that nobody on a certain through sleeper could have done the murder alone, therefore everybody did it together, breaking the process down into a series of simple operations, like assembling an egg-beater. This is the type that is guaranteed to knock the keenest mind for a loop. Only a halfwit could guess it. ("The Simple Art of Murder," *The Atlantic Monthly*, Dec. 1944)

Raymond Chandler, as witness the above, had little patience with the novels of the Classical Age, as we shall see in greater detail later.

As for Agatha, and her so-called "reprehensible" sin of introducing a first-person murderer, it should be noted that many other authors in subsequent books have since followed in her footsteps and had their own first-person storyteller turn out to be the villain. So much for the lack of Fair Play concept. (And, also, so much less the surprise.)

Fair Play

While we're on the subject of Fair Play, let us discuss it for a bit and apply the rules to Agatha and see just how "fair" she is.

Fair Play did not become a feature of detective stories until the advent of the Classical Period and it would appear to have arisen full-blown and without introduction. It marked the removal of the reader from the position of looking over the great detective's shoulder, marveling at what he was doing, and needing it explained to him at the end. Fair Play became a requirement when the reader was moved up alongside the detective and given the opportunity to match wits with the great man. To make the game fair, it was incumbent upon the author to present the reader with all the clues available to the detective. Granted the author could try to hide the clues, misinterpret them, and mix them in with false clues (red herrings), but he had to present them.

Here's Agatha's view of the subject (from Gwen Robyns' *The Mystery of Agatha Christie*):

> I have a certain amount of rules. No false words must be uttered by me. To write, "Mrs. Armstrong walked home wondering who had committed the murder" would be unfair if she had done it herself. But it's not unfair to leave things out. In *Roger Ackroyd* I made the narrator write: "It was just on ten minutes to nine when I left him." There's lack of explanation there, but no false statement. Whoever my villain is it has to be someone I feel COULD do the murder.

She's right as far as she goes. And we will certainly grant her the right to have the villain someone she's neglected to include on the suspect list, as in *Ackroyd* and, as another example, *The 4:50 From Paddington*. And we will also agree that it's not fair, as Sayers pointed out on page 60 with the bit about Dr. Thorndyke, to require the reader to be possessed of esoteric knowledge if he's to match wits with the detective. The skill is to hide clues that the average reader can interpret.

Personal Notes

The Disappearance of Agatha Christie

But now back to Agatha. It was in December of 1926, not long after the publication of *Ackroyd*, that her famous and never fully explained ten-day disappearance took place. She had lost her mother, to whom she was devoted, earlier that year, which might have been a factor. More to the point was the fact that her husband had fallen in love with a Nancy Neele, whom they both knew.

When Agatha disappeared, *Ackroyd* was already a best-seller so her disappearance made headlines. There are those who will argue that her disappearance made *Ackroyd* famous, but the evidence is that it was *Ackroyd* that made her disappearance famous.

Her abandoned car was found a quarter of a mile from a lake called Silent Pool and there was the thought that she was in it, the victim of suicide or foul play.

In that regard, it's worth mention that Dorothy Sayers paid a visit to the pond during the disappearance and promptly said, "She isn't in it."

She wasn't. She was found, registered under the name of Mrs. Teresa Neele, at a resort hotel in Harrogate. The whole affair was as mysterious as any of her plots, and remains so to this day, for her motivations and behavior have never been satisfactorily explained, including by her.

Agatha divorced Archie in April 1928 on grounds of adultery. Archie then married Nancy Neele and they lived happily ever after. As for Agatha, she married archaeologist Max Mallowan, 14 years her junior, in 1930, and they too lived happily ever after.

The Private Person

A few notes about Agatha Christie, the woman. She was an extremely shy, reclusive person (Daphne DuMaurier was another — is shyness concomitant with great talent?). She would only accept the presidency of the Detection Club on condition she did not have to do anything, let alone run a meeting.

As a side note, when she was chosen as a recipient of the Mystery Writers of America's first Grand Master Award for contribution to the mystery in 1954, Dorothy Gardiner, MWA's executive secretary, visiting

England that summer, called at Agatha Christie's home, hoping to deliver the Edgar Statuette into her hands in person. Dorothy had to hand it to the maid at the door instead. Agatha Christie, no offense intended, declined to appear.

And, if memory serves, the only way she would consent to attend the Palace ceremony to be made a Dame by Queen Elizabeth, was on condition she enter and leave immediately by a side door.

Perhaps it was her personal fame that frightened her for, according to friends who knew her from the archaeological digs she attended and worked at, side by side with Max Mallowan, she was neither unfriendly nor distant.

Agatha did try, so the reports go, to accommodate her archaeologist husband and develop an acceptance — if not a taste — for sherry or some similar mild, pre-dinner alcoholic beverage, but she never could manage it.

According to Robyns, Agatha Christie tired of Poirot — ultimately to the point where she wished she'd never invented him. That's not surprising. It's an inevitable consequence of the non-hack writer, of the writer who grows and develops. The games of our youth are the boredom of our maturity. Cannot one sense that Jane Marple was an escape from Poirot? Cannot one sense that Agatha Christie favors Miss Marple in the long run? (And this is not sexist. Agatha Christie would not have known the meaning of the word.) She needed an out. Doyle tried to kill off his hero. Agatha tried to replace hers. It's to the same end.

Agatha Christie remained president of the Detection Club until her death on January 12, 1976. Once elected, it's a lifetime honor.

Thus, her life.

Christie's Novels

As for her writing, which is our concern, in 1930, Agatha Christie introduced Miss Jane Marple, her second great detective, in *Murder at the Vicarage*.

Then there were her plays, most notable of which, of course, is *The Mousetrap*, which opened in London on November 25, 1952. It is still running, and, because it has become a cult classic, bids fair to last as long as Great Britain.

But let us attend to her novels, for this is where her contribution to the field of the mystery lies.

Characterization

Though there are those who applaud her characterizations, this is, in reality, a field in which she was weak—which was more fortunately than unfortunately so.

Charles Higham, in his biography of Charles Laughton (W.H. Allen, 1976) writes: "Given the difficult challenge of making a real human being out of Miss Christie's pasteboard figure of Poirot, Charles gave an excitingly detailed performance."

The unfortunate part of producing a cast of cardboard characters is that it's hard for the reader to tell them apart, aside from their names. And when, as in the beginning of *And Then There Were None*, Agatha throws ten characters at the reader one after the other, it's a major task trying to keep them separate, since, and this is the flaw with cardboards, you can take the words out of one person's mouth and put them in another's and no one will ever know the difference.

This, inevitably, draws us back to Agatha's claim, stated earlier on page 65: "Whoever my villain is it has to be someone I feel COULD do the murder." One then has to ask, in her terms, who could NOT do the murder?

Here is her view on the creation of characters: "Sometimes you get involved with a character and can't see how to manage him or her and throw them out and start again. It's like auditioning actors."

To this, I think any writer can attest, but it is difficult to deduce what problem she might have had, other than which sex, what kind of appearance, which occupation?

Cardboard characters have a value, however, from a mystery writer's viewpoint—and certainly from Agatha Christie's. In a cast of cardboard characters, the criminal is exactly like everyone else. Picking him out is akin to "Which cup is the pea under?"

If the heroine, for example, turns out to be the killer, there will be nothing in her dialogue or behavior which will reveal her to the reader. Only a proper interpretation of the clues will give her away.

In the real world, of course, or with well-drawn characters, there would be inferences in her manner and approach to life which would reveal the possibility that she is not what she appears and that danger lurks within her.

Plot

So let us forget characterization and turn to plot. Cyril Hare, discussing the Christie "formula," says (in Robyns' *The Mystery of Agatha Christie*): "It resembles one of those connected series of equations by which a mathematician can prove conclusively that nought equals one. Each step in the series is clearly stated and is manifestly correct. The end result is impossible. It is only when you make the closest inspection that you can detect the tiny fallacy which falsifies the equation."

What we have to realize in her books, and in others of the Classical Age, is that Puzzle is All. Let us note, when we consider the various titles and plot lines of Christie novels, that they bear no relationship to reality. *Ten Little Indians* (*Ten Little Niggers* or *And Then There Were None* — the title was changed to avoid the suggestion of racism, of which Christie would have been entirely unaware), for example, purports to show the death of ten people together in an isolated environment, the stated fact of the situation being that no one outside of the group could be involved. Not only do they die, but they die in sequence according to the nursery rhyme of the title. If that isn't bizarre enough, Dame Agatha has to show how this could happen without outside intervention.

That none of this could occur in real life, however, doesn't matter. What matters is another Christie poser — who is the murderer? And here she, once again, shows her adeptness at leaving the reader confounded. When it's all explained at the end, the reader must concede that Fair Play has been done, but one must also acknowledge that it was done at such a price to any understanding of the workings of fate, of chance, of plot and plan, and the motivations of the human animal, as to reduce the whole story to its one basic element: Puzzle — and to Agatha Christie's forté, creating puzzles which defy solution.

So we play the game with Agatha, seeking ways to undo her, to read her mind (far too nimble to be read), and see if we can't fathom the solution she'll come up with next.

All too often, the murderer is produced with too little evidence given to the reader. I remember approaching her *4:50 From Paddington* with interest because its beginning made it appear to be a departure from the almost inevitable country house and the rural life of the English upper-middle class wherein she was not only so much at home, but almost unable to leave.

Disappointingly, from that expectation, the plot promptly reverted to the familiar milieu. Nevertheless, on we go and, at the end, the murderer is unmasked and is, as usual, the last person the reader would suspect. Except that, in the denouement, much is revealed about the murderer that the reader had not known before. Agatha was not always Fair.

Not always Fair, did I say? But let us be wary. To claim Agatha Christie is unfair, is a charge one has to be very careful about making, for she is extraordinarily subtle and the moment one says she left something out, it's likely that a more careful search of the text will reveal that she didn't.

To analyze a Christie plot requires a lot of work. She so buries her clues that, even when one ferrets them out, usually by backtracking, one can protest that, though they're there, the esoteric quality of the clues is insufficient to justify Poirot or Miss Marple claiming they knew the answer from the first, or that they could know it at all. There is, in the element of Fair Play, the expectation that, if the reader had seen the clue, he too could have deduced the killer. In short, the ability of Poirot and Miss Marple to glean from, say, a host of rumors about someone in the story the only single rumor that has relevance, betokens an ability beyond the norm. Who can compete "fairly" on those terms? (Is this not Dorothy Sayers's protest against Dr. Thorndyke?)

However, let us not quibble too much. Agatha Christie's genius lay in surprising the reader with the identity of the killer and she could conceal it better than anyone else. *Who will it be?* one asks: *The heroine, the detective, the detective's best friend?*

The reader is aware that in a Christie novel — and this was her plan — one must omit no one from suspicion. And usually she could lure the reader into forgetting that *this* particular person, in *this* particular novel, is not above and beyond suspicion — and this is when she trapped you. She lulled and then surprised. More than any other writer, she could lure you into overlooking a member of the cast. Not so, the others. This was her advantage, and she used it to maximum effect.

In 1922, A.A. Milne, who later became better known for his "Winnie the Pooh" stories than for his mysteries, turned out a novel called *The Red House Mystery*, named by Alexander Wollcott as "one of the three best mystery stories of all time." It deals with Mark Ablett, the owner of the Red House, deciding to impersonate his brother Robert, 15 years absent in Australia. His secretary encourages Mark and, when the impersonation succeeds, murders him. As a result, the body is believed to be Robert's, Mark is thought to have disappeared and is assumed to be the murderer. Clever secretary, and clever mystery sleight of hand, for, of course, the reader (and the police) are also to believe it's Robert who's been murdered.

That's a great plot gimmick — the apparent murderer being the victim. It's the kind of trickery that was done in the Classical Age of the detective story, a sample of those particular flavors and savors of the mystery novel which set this period apart from the before and after. It we want to bamboozle the reader, how better?

Enter now, Raymond Chandler and his essay entitled, "The Simple Art of Murder," which appeared in the *The Atlantic Monthly* in December 1944.

In 1944, the world of the detective story had undergone marked changes, Chandler's contribution to those changes being significant. *The Red House Mystery* a great mystery? Not by Chandler's reckoning, and he is quite testy about it.

He leaps upon the absurdities of the plot: the idea that Mark can be passed off as his unknown brother by shaving off his beard and roughening his artistic hands with sandpaper, a ploy which wouldn't fool even an acquaintance, let alone the police. And, of course, the tale must fudge over police requirements for identifying bodies.

It's a fraud, says Chandler: "Not a deliber-

THE CLASSICAL AGE

ate fraud, because Milne would not have written the story if he had known what he was up against. He is up against a number of deadly things, none of which he even considers."

Chandler lists them:

1. "The coroner (in the story) holds formal jury inquest on a body for which no legal competent identification is offered." (Identification of the body is by hearsay—totally unacceptable.)

2. The testimony of Mark's secretary as to Mark's movements are totally without corroboration and automatically suspect until proved true.

3. Police findings that Robert was not well thought of in his native village, fail to produce anyone to testify to this at the inquest.

4. The police haven't tried to trace Robert's movements to explain his presence in England. (They couldn't for he'd been dead for three years.)

5. The police surgeon, on the basis of a shaved beard and roughened hands, can't tell that the body isn't the rough-hewn brother from Australia.

6. The clothes have had their labels removed, yet no one questions the fact, and, instead, accepts the body's identification.

7. Mark is missing, the body in the morgue closely resembles him, yet nobody considers the possibility that the dead man might be Mark.

Chandler, having dispatched *The Red House Mystery* as ridiculous, goes on to point out the flaws in a number of other highly regarded mysteries of the era, including *Trent's Last Case* (another accepted classic)—as well as lodging the complaint against Agatha Christie, quoted on page 64.

What does this mean?

Do we say that the writers of the Classical Period were a bunch of idiots, that their tales were nonsense?

No. That is not the case. Chandler is being ruthless—but Chandler was not averse to speaking his mind—and one has to say, whatever was on Chandler's mind was worth attention.

In this case, however, we must remember where he's coming from. We have to consider the type of story he wrote and the era in which he wrote. He came after Hammett. His approach to the detective story was to its reality—write about murder as it is, not as the Classical Age writers presented it.

Reality—and the lack of it in any and all detective stories—is a subject to be dealt with later. The Classical Age detective story was not that much more unreal than the later hard-boiled tales of Hammett, Chandler, and those who followed. (If you want unreality, read Spillane.) Nor are Classical stories any more unreal than the later Police Procedural tales which were supposed to reach the epitome of realistic detective story writing.

None of them are "real" in any ultimate sense. All of them cater to the urge of the reader to be entertained by a story—a story about murder and its solution. The readers' tastes change with the times and what was acceptable as "real" in one day and age, is not what is "real" to a later generation.

Chandler is absolutely right in his critique of *The Red House Mystery*. It would fall apart in the face of even the most superficial investigation by the "real" police. But that is not what the readers of that era cared about. They didn't want real policemen bolixing up the scene and spoiling these deliciously contrived puzzles. They wanted to go with the make-believe world of "idiot" policemen and "brilliant" (inevitably young and charming) amateur detectives who "dabbled" in crime as a hobby, with far greater success than the professionals who made a career out of it. Those were, after all, the days of the amateur: Bill Tilden, Red Grange (at Illinois), Bobby Jones.

No one with any wit is going to believe this could really happen, that the dilettante amateur could beat the accomplished professional in any field of endeavor. And the readers of the exploits of the detectives in the Classical Age didn't believe it either. The point was, it was fun to *dis*believe.

The readers of those tales didn't want to slog along with the police in their very difficult, dreary task of solving a crime. They wanted to be entertained, to identify with the charming, elegant, upper-crust gentleman detective (never mind how he got to be that way) and walk with him through the rose gardens of fashionable crimes that were laid upon his doorstep.

The Detective Story as Game

So Chandler is both right and wrong in his critique. He's right in pointing out the ridiculousness of the plots which the authors in the Classical Period designed. Where he's wrong is in failing to appreciate what those stories were *really* about, and why they were so eagerly received.

There was a mystique in that era—fostered by the ignorant author, and accepted by the equally ignorant, willing reader.

The detective story of that era was a game. The game had rules, just as mah-jongg, canasta, chess, bridge, baseball, and football have rules. A rule in baseball is that a ball hit outside of the baselines is a foul. You may claim, if you wish, that it's a ridiculous rule, and who can deny you? But if you want to play baseball, that is a rule that is a part of the game. If you don't like it, don't play.

The game of the detective story was constructed by the authors of the Classical Age. First and foremost was the rule of Fair Play, which required that every piece of evidence supplied to the detective must be supplied to the reader. That was because the author and reader were competing on equal ground. There were additional ground rules, however, which the reader had to accept and go along with if he wanted to play the game with a chance of winning.

These rules were laid down by the authors in all ignorance of what true crime was all about, and the authors accepted as *fact*, for the purposes of the Classical Detective Story, certain conditions. These included such things as:

1. A body could not be surely identified if the head was missing. (If the head was gone or the face disfigured, never mind what else was going on, watch out!)

2. Fingerprints could be obtained from *any* object, most especially including guns. (Watch out for fingerprints — and ways to forge them.)

3. Fingerprints can be "saved" by wrapping the source in a handkerchief. (This is nonsense, but was accepted as a part of the game. Once that gun was wrapped up in a handkerchief, whoever had handled it was trapped.)

4. We've gone into this before. The expression on the face of a dead man is a nonexpression. However, in this game, the reader accepts that a "placid" expression means the victim didn't know he was about to be killed, while an expression of "horror" means he realized his fate. These are some of the rules.

That these "rules" have no reference to "real life" is irrelevant. They're like the foul lines in baseball. Either you accept them and play the game, or you reject them and you don't. In the Classical Age, these WERE the rules and Chandler's objection only means that he didn't want to play this particular kind of game. So be it. He came later, after the game had not only been played, but enjoyed.

The Players

We've talked about Dame Agatha and her way of dealing with the rules. What of the others? The number of mystery writers of that era was legion, as is true today. And, as is true today, they ranged the gamut from a few giants to a host of able practitioners, to the ranks of the ordinary and little skilled. (As Chandler puts it, "The average detective story is probably no worse than the average novel, but you never see the average novel. It doesn't get published. The average — or only slightly above average — detective story does.")

Dorothy L. Sayers

The other giants of the era include, first of all, Dorothy Leigh Sayers. We say "first" not only because her maiden mystery, *Whose Body?*, appeared in 1921, the year after *The Mysterious Affair at Styles*, but also because she, like Christie, remains prominent today though her last mystery was published in 1937 and her total output was only twelve.

Her Views on the Mystery

Dorothy L. Sayers (she insisted on that middle initial, so let us not quibble) was a very opinionated woman and she expressed very strong views on the mystery form and its various aspects. Most other writers merely followed the procedures and made their mark in the form of their particular impact upon the genre. Ellery Queen has views and has analyzed the nature of the field in depth. So has Willard Huntington Wright (S.S. Van Dine) and a few others. The major contributors to the genre, however, were quiescent as to how they wrote what they wrote, or what it was they were writing. Agatha turned out mystery novels, but did not go into any deep analysis as to what the form was all about, other than to discuss the ingredients of Fair Play.

Dorothy L. Sayers, however, was not to be kept silent on the subject (or on any subject for that matter). Ergo, it behooves us, in any discussion of the mystery, to give countenance to her views and opinions and explain where and why and how we either agree or disagree.

She notes, in the *Omnibus of Crime*, on the subject of "Watsons" (those chroniclers of the Great Detective's doings): "It is not surprising that this formula should have been used so largely, for it is obviously a very convenient one for the writer. For one thing, the admiring satellite may utter expressions of eulogy which would be unbecoming in the mouth of the author, gaping at his own colossal intellect." Further, she points out, it is all a device of the writer to delude the reader into believing, because he's smarter than Watson, that he sees deeper into the story than the writer intended. Thirdly, she says: "by describing the clues as presented to the dim eyes and bemused mind of Watson, the author is enabled to preserve a spurious appearance of frankness, while keeping to himself the special knowledge on which the interpretation of those clues depends."

That, too, is true, but a Watson is not necessary for the purpose. Ellery Queen, for example, had no Watson. All he did, while presenting the clues, was keep to himself his interpretation of their meaning.

She has little to say in favor of the female detectives of the times (the 1920s): "Why these charming creatures should be able to tackle abstruse problems at the age of twenty-one or thereabouts . . . it is hard to say. Where do they pick up their worldly knowledge? Not from personal experience, for they are always immaculate as the driven snow."

"The really brilliant woman detective," she concludes, "has yet to be created." Sixty years later, this may be coming about.

Regarding Poe's contribution to the detective story, she says of "The Murders in the Rue Morgue": "In this story also are enunciated for the first time those two great aphorisms of detective science: First, that when you have eliminated all the impossibilities, then, whatever remains, *however improbable*, must be the truth; and, secondly, that the more *outré* a case may appear, the easier it is to solve."

We have already discussed this view, accepting the first, but denying the second. We still deny her second claim, albeit in the face of Chandler's statement from "The Simple Art of Murder": "The boys with their feet on the desks (the real cops) know that the easiest murder case in the world to break is the one somebody tried to get very cute with; the one that really bothers them is the murder somebody thought of only two minutes before he pulled it off."

We're going to challenge that claim too. In perhaps 95 percent of murders, the police know who did it five minutes after they arrive on the scene. It's a relative or friend, and the motive is obvious. If it was, in fact, committed on two minutes' thought, the evidence will be abundant. These are the simple cases. John Jones suddenly needs the twenty bucks his uncle owes him so he goes and demands it. He's testy because of his need. The uncle, resenting the approach, refuses to give it to him. Belligerency increases as both men get their backs up. Finally, John pulls out a knife and says, "You're going to pay me right now or I'll kill you." Uncle dares him. Neither can back down. Result: John kills Uncle. It's as simple as that and it happens all the time. (But it doesn't make a good story.)

The case that really all but defies solution is the one involving strangers. Robber kills victim for his wallet. The motive may be obvious, but the list of suspects is city-wide. This is what Chandler is talking about when he remarks about spur-of-the-moment killings.

But the elaborately planned murders aren't all that easy to solve as Poe, Sayers, and Chandler would have you believe. A man murders his wife and puts her remains through a wood-chipping machine. That's not going to be easy to prove even with a motive and a suspect.

Or the case of the man who dissolved his wife's body in acid in the bathtub. What ultimately nailed him was the recovery of the fillings of her teeth from the drain trap. But suppose he'd thought to clean the trap?

Here's what Sayers has to say on "The Most Unlikely Person" murderer (*The Omnibus of Crime*):

> At first, while readers were still unsophisticated, the formula of the Most Unlikely Person had a good run. But the reader soon learned to see through this. If there was a single person in the story who appeared to have no motive for the crime and who was allowed to amble through the penultimate chapter free of any shade of suspicion, that character became a marked man or woman. "I knew he must be guilty because nothing was said about him," said the cunning reader. [Christie used this ploy a number of times.]
>
> Thus we come to a new axiom, laid down by G.K. Chesterton in a brilliant essay in the *New Statesman*: "The real criminal must be suspected at least once in the course of the story. Once he is suspected, and then (apparently) cleared, he is made safe from future suspicion."
>
> Other developments of the Most Unlikely Person formula make the guilty person a juror at the inquest or trial; the detective himself; the counsel for prosecution, and as a supreme effort of unlikeliness, the actual narrator of the story (*Ackroyd*). . . .
>
> The possibilities of the formula are becoming exhausted, and of late years much has been done in exploring the solution by the unexpected means.

Here we have to disagree. That article was written in 1928. Those of us writing today, are still using the "Whodunit?" formula. We grant that every conceivable character in a mystery has turned out to be guilty over and over again. That doesn't spoil the game for the next time around.

Any competent mystery writer, by introducing as few as four suspects in a story, will succeed in fooling at least 75 percent of his readers.

But enough of Dorothy L. Sayers's views of the mystery. Let us pay attention to the life of the woman whose works maintain the interest of readers still today.

Sayers's Personal Life

What is the most interesting aspect of Dorothy L. Sayers, herself and her writing, is her impact upon the field of the mystery novel. She is, in the Classical field of mystery writing (with all due respect to the other giants of the era, Earl Derr Biggers, S.S. Van Dine, Ellery Queen, and Rex Stout), second only to Agatha Christie.

Yet, on what claim to fame? Her first novel, *Whose Body?*, appeared in 1921, the year after Christie's first. She wrote but twelve novels, compared to Christie's eighty-five. Her last, *Busman's Honeymoon*, appeared in 1937. Christie's last Poirot and Marple novels came out nearly fifty years later. Nevertheless, her novels are still in print and read today. Charlie Chan, Philo Vance, Ellery Queen, and even Nero Wolfe are, today, somewhat quaint—relics of a bygone era. Yet Dorothy Sayers, for all her slim and antiquated output, still commands our attention.

Who was this woman, that she should still beget our interest throughout all these years?

Dorothy Leigh Sayers was born June 13, 1893, the daughter of the Reverend Henry Sayers, headmaster of the Choir School belonging to Christ Church College, a religious connection which would come to dominate her later life. She was educated at Oxford, where she formed, interestingly, a group called M.A.S. — Mutual Admiration Society. (One can sense, in this, the essence of Dorothy L. Sayers.) After college, she taught, got brief jobs, published *Whose Body?* in 1921, and settled in St. James Street where she lived for twenty years.

Pictures of Dorothy Sayers show her with prim face, glasses, and bobbed hair. The possibility that Sayers was a lesbian has been discussed, but says James Brabazon, in his biography of Sayers, ". . . this is the time in her life when such tendencies, had they existed, might well have emerged. . . . Nothing of the sort was even considered" (*Dorothy L. Sayers: A Biography*, Avon/Discus, 1982).

With the entry of Peter Wimsey into her novels, a man named John Cournos came into her life. He was wriitng a book called *The Wall*. If he was the prototype of Wimsey, the dream figure outlasted the real man and their affair ended in 1922. On the rebound, she got "accidentally" pregnant (she was eager to have a child) by a motor mechanic she then went with, and gave birth to a baby boy in January 1924. She named her son John Anthony and gave him to her cousin to raise, pretending to him that she was an aunt.

In 1925, Oswald Atherton Fleming, known as "Mac," a man twelve years her senior, who had been gassed and shell-shocked in the World War, entered her life. He was a newspaper correspondent, divorced, with four daughters. They were married in 1926. Quite apart from her secret illegitimate child, Dorothy, a convinced Anglo-Catholic, was aware that in the eyes of the Church her marriage was invalid and she was living in sin.

Brabazon describes Dorothy as a "woman with a strong streak of self-indulgence — in food and drink, probably in sex, and certainly in the intoxication of using rich, evocative language and in the delights of defeating other people in argument."

As for "probably in sex," there seems to be no "probably" about it for, as one of her fellow members of the Detection Club described her to me, Dorothy was "quite a lay-about."

As for arguing, he continues, it is remarked that "The trouble with Dorothy had always been that she had to be right, she had to be above questioning. At any suggestion of criticism, her hackles rose." She loved to argue for the sake of demolishing the foe, to vanquish rather than discover. As for fools, whom she did not suffer gladly, if at all, she claimed, "Stupidity is the sin of sloth." (Whatever that means.)

The Detection Club

A word here should be said about the Detection Club, which was an important part of Sayers's life. She took her membership in it very seriously. It was founded in 1928 at the suggestion of Anthony Berkeley for the purpose of enabling fellow detective story writers to dine together periodically, enjoy each other's company, and talk a little shop. From the first, Dorothy was an enthusiastic and energetic member, having a considerable hand in drawing up its bizarre initiation ceremonies and those for the installation of its presidents, the first of whom was G.K. Chesterton, who held the office until his death in 1936.

Today there are about fifty members; membership is by invitation, and the club is selective, fastidious and snobbish. Original members included Freeman Wills Croft, Berkeley, E.C. Bentley, Hugh Walpole, Baroness Orczy, Sayers, ("then at her most assertive"), A.A. Milne, Clemence Dane, A.E.W. Mason, Helen Simpson, Gladys Mitchell, and Agatha Christie.

Brabazon describes the meetings: ". . . members sat around drinking tea or beer and listening to Dorothy L. Sayers expound her view on life in general and detection writing in particular. Dorothy was a great one for talk."

E.C. Bentley followed Chesterton in the presidency, and Dorothy Sayers then held the office from 1940 until her death, treating her position with such solemnity as to take all the fun out of it. But that would be Dorothy. It was largely her baby and she was a motivating force from the Detection Club's inception. (Upon her death at the end of 1957, Agatha Christie was prevailed upon to accept the office and did so only on condition that she not have to run the meetings.)

The Importance of Religion

Though she wrote no more mystery novels after 1937, Dorothy L. Sayers was far from inactive. Religion was always a deep urge within her despite her "deliberate sins," a fact which is best revealed through a piece she wrote for publisher Victor Gollancz as a Christmas message after the start of World War II which expresses her views on kinds of Man:

1. Theological man (a whole being), followed by

2. Humanist man (complete in himself, but without a relationship to God) leading to

3. Rational man (embodying the intelligence of the eighteenth century), then

4. Biological man (Darwin)

5. Sociological man (the herd-member)

6. Psychological man (his response to environment)

7. Economic man (his response to the means of livelihood).

Says Brabazon, this whole process, in her view, "Represented the gradual whittling away of the essential wholeness and dignity of man; and since it was not possible to return to the Church-made vision of theological man, a new conception of man was now needed to rescue him from spiritual impoverishment — this was to be creative man."

This piece, entitled, "Begin Here," ran 160 pages and made her regarded in the eyes of Churchmen as a spokeman for liberal Christianity. She became very active in that capacity.

Sayers's Best-Loved Characters

Though she is most remembered for Lord Peter Wimsey, undoubtedly the books she wrote during these years of the war, *The Mind of the Maker* and *The Man Born to be King*, went deepest and were the works that meant the most to her.

But there was and always will be Lord Peter Wimsey and the books about him are the ones for which she will be remembered. In her own professed view, she had little use for Wimsey. She denied she was ever "besotted" with him and relegated him to the role of "breadwinner." She even claimed she wished she had never invented him.

Come now, she's putting us on. She was in love with her creation. He was her ideal man. Listen to her in *The Unpleasantness at the Bellona Club* (1928): "Lord Peter, having set the springe for his woodcock, slept the sleep of the just until close upon eleven o'clock the next morning."

"Sleep of the just"? That's a telltale symptom if ever there was one. And what about the six-page "Biographical Note" detailing Wimsey's life that precedes the same novel, purporting to be written by an "uncle" of Wimsey's? There's even a "Who's Who" for Wimsey in the front of the book, including the "family coat of arms." You don't do all that for a "breadwinner," and it's doubtful one would go to such lengths if one were *not* "besotted."

But if Wimsey was Sayers' dream man, Harriet Vane, his lady love and ultimate wife, was Sayers herself. Harriet, in her first appearance — *Strong Poison* (1930) — is introduced as a writer of detective stories who lives in a flat at 100 Doughty Street (which happens to be around the corner from where Dorothy lived).

So Wimsey falls in love with Dorothy Sayers. Shall we say her feelings have now been reciprocated?

But watch what happens. Once Harriet Vane enters the scene, she starts to hog the stage. As Dorothy uses Harriet Vane to express herself there is more and more Vane and less and less Wimsey. In *Have His Carcase* (1932), Vane occupies the first forty-seven pages and in *Gaudy Night* (1935), virtually the whole book is about Harriet, and Wimsey only comes in at the end.

That was Dorothy L. Sayers. Nobody, not even Wimsey, was going to upstage her. Nobody else was going to dominate a situation while Dorothy was around.

A Final Word on Sayers

How do we summarize this remarkable person? Dorothy L. Sayers was a feminist — if such be a proper word for her, which is doubtful — for she was a feminist before such a term was invented. This was a woman about whom one is tempted to say "intellect was all." That doesn't happen to be the case. Intellect belonged to her and came out of her as rays come out from the sun, but, in her own mind, that was not where she lived. She thought she was a romantic. She dreamed romantic ideas and sought to make them come true. And she succeeded to a degree—perhaps as well as a responsible person has a right to expect—but she was a woman of intellect and it is for her intellect, which interfered with and dominated all her other aspirations, that she is known.

Charlie Chan

Charlie Chan is probably the most striking example of the well-known detective and the unknown author. Had the title of this section been "Earl Derr Biggers" most readers wouldn't have a clue as to whom was to be talked about. Call it "Charlie Chan" and the whole world knows. "Charlie Chan" is, still today, a household name, though Earl Derr Biggers wrote only half a dozen Charlie Chan novels and died over half a century ago, in 1933.

As Christie made her Hercule Poirot distinctive by calling him Belgian and sprinkling his conversation with classroom French phrases, so Earl Derr Biggers created his own distinctive detective by naming him Charlie Chan, calling him Chinese and exchanging l's for r's in his speech. Have him say, "Velly solly," instead of "Very sorry," and no one is going to confuse him with the other members of the cast.

This is, of course, more of the Sherlock Holmes syndrome, the effort to create an "unforgettable detective." Sayers, with her Wimsey, created a more "human" detective than either Poirot or Chan, which is to her credit. She was doing what E.C. Bentley did in *Trent's Last Case*, trying to make the detective "recognizable as a human being," and she acknowledged her debt to him. Chan, however, like Poirot, was a stick figure detective, portrayed as gentle and kindly. "Sinister and wicked Chinese are old stuff," Biggers maintained, "but an amiable Chinese on the side of law and order had never been used." Nor, of course, had ever been used the speech characteristics which were employed to make Charlie distinctive.

Biggers' first Charlie Chan novel, *The House Without a Key*, was published in 1925, but to nothing like the acclaim that would, the following year, attend the arrival upon the scene of Philo Vance. After two or three of his adventures got into print, however, Charlie Chan hit his stride and has been going on ever since. Much of his popularity resulted from the score or so of movies relating his adventures—far more than the half dozen actual books — Warner Oland becoming the prototype Charlie Chan until his death, with Sidney Toler emulating Oland in the films thereafter.

With all due respect to Biggers' novels, which were, of course, of the puzzle variety, one has to suspect that Chan's wide exposure to the movie-going public is the real reason for his enduring renown.

Philo Vance

1926 was the year that saw the arrival of Philo Vance upon the detective scene. These tales were written by Willard Huntington Wright (1888-1939), dilettante and critic, who used the pseudonym S.S. Van Dine and represented Van Dine as Vance's associate and chronicler.

Philo Vance, detective, was, like his creator, a dilettante and dabbler in the arts — not only the arts, but the esoteric arts, fourteenth century music, Sanscrit manuscripts; that sort of thing. (Wright describes Vance as a "young social aristocrat and art connoisseur." This pretty well describes Wright himself.)

Such cultural expertise has a great deal of snob appeal, but it can easily be overdone. In fact, it becomes almost impossible not to overdo it. After all, to carry on the pose, Wright had to keep injecting ever more odd corners of culture into the story for Philo Vance to be absorbed in, since he never seemed to be investigating the same field twice. In time, as could be expected, Vance became so precious as to become a parody of himself.

Early on, however, the Philo Vance novels were such a smashing success that, for a time, he was (barring Sherlock Holmes, of course), the best known detective in the world. The Vance books were made into movies almost as soon as they came off the presses, with a number of actors playing Vance, most notably, William Powell, who did so many of them that Carole Lombard, his then wife, nicknamed him "Philo."

Of Van Dine's detective story "formula," Gilbert Seldes is said to have remarked that he could readily pick out the murderer in a Vance novel because he always entered the story on the same page.

As for the character of Philo Vance, Ogden Nash's poem, "Philo Vance, needs a kick in the Pance," says it all.

In toto, S.S. Van Dine produced twelve Philo Vance novels, the first six of which are felt to be his best. All, of course, were of the puzzle category, which was what detective fiction was all about in those days.

Puzzle Mysteries

In that regard, let us turn to Willard Huntington Wright, using his own name instead of "S.S. Van Dine." In his Introduction to his anthology, *The Great Detective Stories* (Scribners, 1927), he goes into a detailed history of the development of the detective story, lists a great number of its able practitioners and critiques their work.

Near the end of the essay, he remarks that the habitual reader of the detective novel has become a "shrewd critic of its technic and means . . . and is thoroughly familiar with all the devices and methods of his favorite craft. He knows immediately if a story is old-fashioned, if its tricks are hackneyed, or if its approach to its problem contains elements of originality. . . . Because of this perspicacious attitude on his part a stricter form and a greater ingenuity have been imposed on the writer; and the fashions and inventions of yesterday are no longer used except by the inept and uninformed author."

Wright then lists the following as hackneyed devices:

1. The dog that does not bark (indicating the intruder is a familiar personage).

2. Establishing the culprit's identity by dental irregularities.

3. Finding a distinctive cigarette or cigar at the scene.

4. The cipher message containing the crime's solution.

5. Murdering the man in the locked room *after* the police have broken in.

6. Commission of the murder by an animal.

7. The phonograph alibi.

8. Firing a dagger from a gun to avoid proximity.

9. The seance or ghost to frighten the culprit into a confession.

10. The word association test for guilt.

11. The dummy figure to establish a false alibi.

12. The forged fingerprints.

He then says: "These, and a score of other devices, have now been relegated to the discard; and the author who would again employ them would have no just claim to the affections or even the respect of his readers."

What is interesting about these comments is how much they serve as a symptom of their times. The name of the game in those days was "puzzle" and the tactic was tricking the reader. In commenting on the tricks that had been overdone, Wright is, wittingly or unwittingly, presaging the end of the detective story. If the only direction the detective story could take lay in devising new tricks which, in their own good time would also become hackneyed, how long would it be before authors ran out of tricks? And when that happened, there would be nowhere for the detective story to go.

But, of course, the demise of the detective story did not ensue. For it turns out that puzzle stories don't have to rely on tricks and gimmicks. There are other ways of presenting the puzzle, as modern detective stories amply demonstrate.

And of course, as the hard-boiled school of detective fiction would soon demonstrate as well, there would be other ways of telling stories that had little to do with the puzzle.

Ellery Queen

Two young cousins, Frederic Dannay and Manfred B. Lee, both born in 1905, worked in advertising in the mid-twenties. Fred was art director of an ad agency; Manny did publicity and advertising for a motion picture company. They happened to read the announcement of a detective story prize contest, decided to enter and, being in advertising, devised the great gimmick of having the "author" of the book bear the name of the detective in the story—Ellery Queen. By making the name of the author and the detective synonymous, they could eliminate the confusion in readers' minds as to "Who wrote Sherlock Holmes?" "Who wrote Charlie Chan?" "Who wrote the Hercule Poirot stories?"

(Astute as that ploy was, Fred, much later, professed his and Manny's naivete. In choosing the name "Queen," he said, they had no idea of its meaning in the homosexual world.)

The detective story they created and submitted, entitled "The Roman Hat Mystery," to their surprise won the contest. But the magazine sponsoring the competition ceased publication and they never got their prize.

However, a book publisher became interested and produced it and, in 1929, America's most prestigious detective was born. Never mind Philo Vance and Charlie Chan, who preceded Queen, and giving full marks to such as Nero Wolfe and Perry Mason who followed, Ellery Queen holds a special place in the pantheon of Detective Story Greats.

Anthony Boucher, the esteemed critic of *The New York Times* said of him: "Ellery Queen *is* the American detective story."

Read Queen—and I'm talking about the early Queen books—for intricacies of plot. They are devilishly clever in their workings and their meanings.

One must, of course, overlook the unfortunate addendum to "The Roman Hat Mystery," written before Dannay and Lee had any idea of what an on-going series they had created. Fred blushed at its ending, which had Ellery living happily ever after somewhere in Italy. It's like Sherlock Holmes arising from the dead. Fred and Manny thought they were finishing off a one-time novel, an entry into a contest, and they wrapped it up—or thought they had.

Given the demand for more Ellery Queen novels, they had to overlook that unfortunate ending and pretend it never happened. Ellery was forever back in New York ready to tackle the next extraordinary murder case. As Holmes survived Reichenbach Falls, so Ellery survived that retirement to Italy.

For intricacies of plot, the early Queen novels are hard to match. I mention "early Queen" and this needs some explanation.

Fred and Manny, in creating their detective hero, did what everyone else had done in response to the impact of Sherlock Holmes. They tried to design a "unique" detective. What they did was create a detective who was effete, rather than manly. He was totally intellectual, wholly unphysical. He wore a pince-nez, he was afraid of firearms. To give him a reason to be involved in a case, they made his father an Inspector in the New York Police Department. In that way, his appearance on the scene could be countenanced. In that way, he could now go to work and solve the cases that baffled the NYPD.

And those cases were of a nature that only an Ellery Queen could solve. This was the era when fictional murders were at their most adroit, when elaborate planning, plus the accommodations of Fate gave cunning murderers the advantage that only the amateur supersleuth could decode. And no one could contrive better plots of a compound-complex nature than the Ellerys Queen. Their murderers, in step with the mystery of the period, were more devilishly clever in contriving and concocting crimes that no one but an Ellery Queen could solve, than any others in the history of detective fiction.

A Change of Character

There came a time, as it must to us all, when this particular plot ploy was no longer feasible and, it's interesting to note, Ellery Queen, courtesy of

Dannay and Lee, adjusted to changing fashions and the later Ellery Queen changed character. The new Ellery no longer needed a pince-nez — in fact, not long into the series, it was forgotten that he'd ever used one.

There came a time when it was forgotten that he quaked at violence. There came a time when he was made more "human" and even felt attracted to members of the opposite sex. One might say that Ellery Queen was growing up, but the real reason was that he was being updated.

Never mind that. Those later books about the "new, updated" Ellery Queen still were marked by those Dannay-Lee elegant plots, but they aren't quite as elegant as those of the original Queen stories. Flaw the original Queens as you will, those tales are as intricately created puzzles as you will ever find in mystery fiction.

And the one thing that Queen did — the one innovation that showed Dannay and Lee knew and understood the problems and expectations of the mystery — was to present their unique "challenge to the reader."

At a given point in a Queen story (early Queen, when puzzle was all), the author would announce, in effect: "At this point, *you* have all the information available to Ellery." The challenge to the reader was, "Ellery Queen can now solve the case. Can you?"

How much more Fair Play could one ask for?

Perry Mason

I once contacted Erle Stanley Gardner to say that Mystery Writers of America was awarding him its Grand Master's Edgar and it was incumbent upon him to attend the ceremony to receive the award. He replied that he was flying over Baja California in a helicopter at fifty dollars an hour (this was back when fifty dollars was fifty dollars!) researching a book and he didn't know if he could make it.

As I recall, I said he *had* to make it because no one else could get a Grand Master's Edgar until he did. Fortunately for all of the Grand Masters who have followed, Erle Stanley Gardner made it to the ceremony, and was so rewarded.

The thing I remember most about Gardner, which has nothing to do with the success of his creation, lawyer Perry Mason, was a remark he made when he was, early in his career, grinding out cent-a-word stories for the pulp magazines. (I would suggest you don't read what he was writing back then.) In one of his stories, the Hero aims at the villain and fires: "Bang, bang, bang, bang, bang, bang!"

A friend said to him, "You mean your hero can't kill this guy with *one* shot?"

Gardner's reply was, "At one cent a word, do you think I'm going to write just *one* bang?"

How Gardner went about writing his stories is interesting. He had several dials, so the story goes, one listing places, another listing plot ideas, and so on. When he had finished a book and was ready to start another, he would spin the dials, set whatever story line came up in whatever location came up, and go to work. His method of writing was dictation and he kept three or four secretaries busy, dictating one story to one, then switching to dictate another to another. And the books came tumbling forth. (He, early on, did something the rest of us could profit by. He disciplined his mind to concentrate solely upon the issue at hand. Wandering thoughts wasted time, he had decided. In that, he was right. In succeeding in such a self-discipline, he exceeded most of the rest of us. It takes a hard taskmaster to force one's thoughts away from the siren songs of our daydreams.)

When told of his Grand Master's award, he denied that he merited it. He didn't regard himself as a "hack," but he felt he was just someone who ground out multitudinous books of no particular distinction.

In this, he was too modest. If he didn't turn out great literature, he did turn out fine detective stories. They were of even quality and the quality was so good that his books have sold in the hundreds of millions. As "Sergeant Cuff," pseudonym of the critic for *The Saturday Review of Literature* said, his detectives "DETECT." Gardner's books have a pace and, since he was a lawyer himself, his courtroom scenes — even if unlike real life — crackle with authenticity. One could pick up any Perry Mason story with the assurance that he was in for a good read.

Nor did Gardner merely utilize his knowledge of law to write books; he used it to make points.

In his first Bertha Cool-Donald Lam tale, *The Bigger They Come*, written in 1939 under the *nom de plume* of A.A. Fair, he invoked a flaw in California law as a key in his plot, the result of which was that the law got changed — which was obviously his intention.

Rex Stout

One of the detectives who belongs in the Pantheon of the immortals is Rex Stout's creation, the obese, orchid-loving gourmet, Nero Wolfe, and his fresh-as-paint assistant, Archie Goodwin. The pair made their debut in 1934 in *Fer de Lance*, and while the series did not break new ground, Stout brought to the mystery literary talent, wit, and a breezy narrative skill. Stout is, in fact, one of the few authors whose name is as well-known as his detective.

Archie Goodwin is a good reflection of his creator and, for this reason, is a Watson who upstages his Sherlock. For that's the way Rex was.

I once got Rex to moderate a panel on the mystery story on WNYC radio in celebration of "Mystery Month," the panelists being George Harmon Coxe, Ruth Fenisong, and myself; the subject, "Should Mystery Writers Play Fair?" The question of Fair Play came up and Rex promptly stated that he doubted he'd ever played fair in his life. That happens not to be so, for he was just as scrupulous about the rules of the game as the rest of us, but to admit it would be trite and true, whereas a denial would have flair. Rex preferred the flair. Only Rex, in the article he contributed to the Baker Street Irregulars, would come up with the outrageous conclusion that "Watson was a Woman." One can see him chuckling with delight as he wrote it.

Dorothy Gardiner, who was Executive Secretary of Mystery Writers of America in those days and who knew all about all the members, referred to Rex as "an old goat." She used the term fondly and it's the best way to describe Rex — to call him an "old goat" — fondly. He went out of his way to be "different," but that was part of his charm, for he was entertaining, witty, and interesting. And, though he appeared to treat matters lightly, he took important things seriously.

Rex and his wife, Pola, lived in a comfortable home on the side of a hill in Brewster, New York, overlooking the distant rolling landscape. It was there that he held court. You went to see Rex, he didn't come to see you. Outside of the MWA Edgar Awards dinners which he attended, I don't know that he ever left his aerie. He worked sixty days a year — writing one book — and the rest of the time was his own. And he was very much his own man. There was a time when Hollywood was interested in doing a TV series of mysteries in connection with MWA. But they needed to sign up the Big Names in the organization if they hoped to sell the idea. Rex Stout was one of those Big Names. Rex, however, was not interested.

Many, and well known, were the guests who joined Rex Stout on his patio overlooking the distant hills. Nevertheless, it came as a surprise to me to discover that he was a great name-dropper. "Arthur and Marilyn," he remarked as we sat on his patio, were living nearby, and he hoped that they'd be happy. (We're talking about Miller and Monroe, of course, when they were newly married.) And he told of the wedding that had been held on the lawn the week before — his daughter's, I believe. He spoke of the beauty of the occasion, then added how special he thought it was that, when the ceremony ended, Marian Anderson got up and sang.

I found this name-dropping intriguing. Because, after Rex, George Coxe, Ruth Fenisong, and I had finished taping the radio broadcast, Rex gave us all a ride uptown, only to be stopped for passing a light by a policeman who was sufficiently ill-tempered to bellow at George for throwing a match out the window. But when he saw Rex's driver's license, he asked if he wrote the Nero Wolfe stories. Rex got out to talk with him and returned with the news that the violation had cost him $1.60. He had to send the cop a book. (I said, "Are you going to sign it?" He said, "If I can find a pen.")

The point of this tale is that Rex was such a celebrity in his own right, it seemed strange to me that he'd bother mentioning the other celebrities he knew.

What do we say about Dashiell Hammett? He was a drinker (not to be confused with drunkard); he was profligate — well-off one moment, broke the next; he was a womanizer — as he once wrote to Lillian Hellman during one of their break-ups, "they come and they go. You just go." And, yes, he was a writer — a writer who changed the shape of the American detective story.

But he only wrote five novels. And, of the five, only two could be called detective stories in any proper sense of the word. The other three not only don't qualify, they aren't even very good novels, despite the fact that they made him a reputation. And of the two that do fit the detective form, the one that is his most famous work, and rightfully considered a classic, is very interestingly flawed and its real value lies in something other than its being an example of the detective story.

Lastly, his other detective novel, which is generally regarded as his most minor work, is one of the finest examples of detective fiction ever written and truly deserves the rank of classic.

All in all it is a meager output for a man of great talent; but the booze and the success and various other aspects of his nature did him in.

But let's start with the man. Who is this strange person who, so almost accidentally, had such a profound effect upon the field of the detective story? Where did he come from? What was he like?

DASHIELL HAMMETT

His Life

Samuel Dashiell Hammett was born in St. Mary's County, Maryland, May 27, 1894. He entered Baltimore Polytechnic Institute in September 1908 but quit after one semester to help his father run a small business. After a variety of odd jobs, he became a Pinkerton detective in 1915. He quit to join the Army in 1918. That's important to note — his volunteering in World War I. For he did the same in World War II. He rejoined the army in 1942 at the age of forty-eight when his health, permanently impaired in the influenza epidemic of 1918, was frail.

Hammett became a Pinkerton detective again after the First World War, was hospitalized for six months with TB, married his nurse in July 1921 and had a daughter the following October. He quit detecting at the end of that year, tried his hand at writing and advertising, and had to give up his good advertising job in mid-1926 due to poor health. At that time, he also moved away from the family to avoid infecting his second daughter with TB and thereafter, outside of a brief reunion, his wife and daughters no longer figured in his life, and his wife got a Mexican divorce in 1937.

Meanwhile, writing became his career and he honed his skills writing short stories, mainly for the pulps, and reviewing mysteries for *The Saturday Review of Literature*. With the publication, by Knopf, of his first novel, *Red Harvest*, in February 1929, followed by *The Dain Curse* six months later, and *The Maltese Falcon* in February of 1930, his reputation as an author was made. Hammett became a literary lion, the toast of Hollywood and New York.

With success came money, and with money, which he strewed recklessly, came sex and booze, those two emblems of a deeply disturbed, unhappy soul.

It was at that time, in 1930, at the age of thirty-six and at the height of his success and concomitant debauching, coming off a five-day drunk, that he met Lillian Hellman. Hellman, then an aspiring young playwright, was twenty-four. He helped and guided her through her first hit, *The Children's Hour*, and for the next thirty years, until his death, their lives were entwined, either together or apart, but mostly together.

Their life together, despite their mutual successes in their chosen fields, was no fairy-tale existence, however. Instead of enjoying their achievements, it seemed they hardly reckoned them. They drank, they quarreled, they split up and came together again. Though Lillian can speak of the happy times that they shared on her farm, her tale of one argument they had — she drunk, he drunker — when she found him grinding out the stub of his lighted cigarette against his cheek, and she asked, in horror, what he was doing, he replied, "Keeping myself from doing it to you," bespeaks a relationship nourished by misery (from Lillian Hellman's *Unfinished Woman*, Little, Brown & Co., 1969).

They were alternately rich and poor. Their spending was profligate and while, like true artists, money was not important to them, almost anyone but Hammett would pay a little attention to where it went and wonder about tomorrow. But with him it came and it went and the spending of it did not seem to bring him happiness. Nor did he seem to gain satisfaction and pleasure, excitement and gratification from work well done.

The rewards of his success did not long last. Heavy drinking and his reckless lifestyle took its toll. Dashiell Hammett, after finishing *The Thin Man* in 1933, was never able to write another novel. Nor, as time went on, could he meet screenplay deadlines nor come up with adequate story ideas, and his once-brilliant career dissolved into nothingness.

Strangely, though he'd lost either the desire or the ability to write, he had not lost his interest in the world and world events. He and Lillian became involved in left-wing causes which, while they might have been *au courant* at the time of the Spanish Civil War and the rise of Nazism, they became un-American once Stalin's Iron Curtain fell upon post-war Europe. Hammett and Hellman nevertheless pursued these causes to such an extent that Hammett spent 155 days in jail for refusing to testify about the Civil Rights Congress bail fund, and was later called before the McCarthy committee.

Thereafter, Hammett's health was gone, he was in debt, and he lived out the rest of his life, with Hellman, as a virtual recluse. He died January 10, 1961, at sixty-six, and such an advanced age is something else to be noted about a man of ill-health and frail body, who drank so heavily that he suffered delirium tremens in 1948. This is a strange, and in many ways remarkable, person.

If one were to define Dashiell Hammett in one word, that word would be "integrity." There was about him a sense of honor, a sense of self, a sense of living by a private code of personal behavior which could not be touched by anyone or anything. By my personal definition of the measure of a man, which is, "Those things he holds dearer than his own life," I would have to call Hammett quite a man. He didn't pander; he did not curry favor; he did not bend to the will of others; he did not compromise. In some respects, he was *too* unyielding and there were times when his sense of honor seemed slightly askew, but it was *his* and he lived by it whether or not anybody else could understand it.

A case in point: He went to jail, according to Hellman (*Unfinished Woman*), rather than reveal the names of contributors to the Civil Rights Congress when he didn't even know the names. When asked, "Why not tell them that," he replied, "No I can't say that." Asked why, he said, "I don't know why. I guess it has something to do with keeping my word. . . . Maybe I better tell you that if it were more than jail, if it were my life, I would give it for what I think democracy is, and I don't let cops or judges tell me what I think democracy is."

He was a man who did not suffer fools gladly. He wouldn't suffer them at all. Nor would he suffer the gifted and the great if he did not find them worthwhile. When Lillian was entertaining Mrs. Litvinov, the wife of the Russian ambassador, for the weekend, Hammett, on the second night, refused to come down to dinner, calling her the "biggest waste of time since the Parcheesi board." Another time, he left the room and wouldn't come down to dinner when a famous writer held forth on existentialism, about which he knew little. "He's a waste of time," Hammett said. "Liars are bores."

And whenever Dorothy Parker, with whom he shared a mutual dislike, came to visit, he moved out.

If this seemed ungracious and unmannerly, which it was, he didn't care. One might expect a man who behaved in such a fashion to be shunned, especially in those periods when his wealth and fame were in eclipse and there was no point in seeking his favor. Yet, on the contrary, people were very eager to have Hammett think well of them. Hellman quotes Richard Wilbur as saying that, "As you came toward Hammett to shake his hand in the first meeting, you wanted him to approve of you."

Perhaps the point is best made by a tale Hammett himself told: When he was fourteen and had his first job, with the B&O Railroad, he came in late every day for a week. His employer told him he was fired. Hammett nodded and started to leave. When he got to the door, his puzzled employer called him back and said he could keep the job if he'd give his word it wouldn't happen again. Hammett said, "Thank you, but I can't do that." After a silence, the man said, "O.K., keep the job anyway."

This is more of that integrity Hammett had. He would not give his word if he didn't intend to honor it. The classic example concerns his 1948 attack of delirium tremens. The doctor said to Lillian, "I'm going to tell Hammett that if he goes on drinking he'll be dead in a few months. It's my duty to say it, but it won't do any good." Then he reported, "I told him. Dash said O.K., he'd go on the wagon forever, but he can't and he won't."

But Hammett did and, half a dozen years later, when Lillian told him the doctor had said he wouldn't stay on the wagon, Hammett said, "But I gave my word that day."

One has to conclude that it was that inner core of steel, which all too few of us have, that affected people, made them want his favorable opinion, gave him that quality that made people want to call him, "Sir."

Rightly or wrongly, he held to his own standards. William Faulkner irritated him in claiming that his *Sanctuary* was a potboiler and he'd only written it for the money. Hammett's answer was that nobody ever deliberately wrote a potboiler, that "you just did the best you could and woke up to find it good or no good."

That might have been true for him, but if he really believed it for others, he deluded himself. There are many writers, some very successful, who turn out junk and know it's junk, but do it because it sells. There are writers who farm out series books to other writers, and put their own names on them.

But that was not for Hammett. When he wrote, he wrote as well as he could.

His Work

Enough about the man. Let us now consider what he wrote, its qualities and flaws, and why he had such an impact upon the literary scene and upon the detective story.

To begin with, for a man accorded Hammett's stature in the field, his oeuvre is small, consisting, as mentioned before, of only five novels published over a space of only five years: *Red Harvest* and *The Dain Curse* (1929), *The Maltese Falcon* (1930), *The Glass Key* (1931), and *The Thin Man* (1934). And three of the five are forgettable.

What, then, gains him his reputation which — make no mistake about it — is well deserved? Three reasons come to mind offhand: 1. He knew how to write; 2. He introduced a new dimension to the detective story; and 3. He broke the bonds of the mystery form which, even today, is still considered by many to be second-class literature, and showed what can be done in the field by a first-class author.

Breaking Taboos

Attention should be paid to the term "gunsel" which is what Spade calls Gutman's bodyguard, the two-gun boy killer in *The Maltese Falcon*. Many years ago, a writer remarked on Hammett's use of the word. It meant a homosexual, he said, and writers in those days weren't supposed to mention such a thing. Reference to homosexuality was a taboo. But, of course, writers, fretting under the restrictions laid upon them by Society try, as people always do, to slip one past the censors. So Hammett inserted the term, figuring editors, interpreting the word as some variation of "gunman," wouldn't bother to look it up and Hammett would get his point across to those with a wide vocabulary range and, even if the reader didn't know what he meant, he'd still have made his point and he'd still have put one over on the editors.

As he anticipated, the word got through. And, as he probably also anticipated — or should have — almost everybody interpreted the word as meaning a "gunman."

As a result, it's interesting to note, the word has now taken on that meaning and *The Random House Dictionary of the English Language, The Unabridged Edition* (Copyright 1966), defines gunsel as: "1. A catamite. 2. A criminal armed with a gun." Only when one looks up catamite (definition: A boy kept for pederastic purposes) do we see what Hammett meant. He not only slipped one past the censors, he effectively changed the meaning of the word.

That was one time when Hammett was able to come right out and break the taboo directly. However, in earlier books he hinted at homosexuality through describing one or two members of a gang as blond young men. Nobody could challenge him on that, for youth and coloring are not symptoms of sexual orientation, but it was obvious what he meant. Doubtless, though, he chafed until he could be explicit.

Character Traits as Clues

One of the new qualities of Hammett's tales was his use of character traits as clues. Theretofore, most figures in detective fiction were cardboard characters, moved around in the story like pieces on a chessboard according to the exigencies of the plot. Each talked and behaved as everyone else talked and behaved. You could take the words out of one character's mouth and put them in another's and the reader wouldn't know the difference. (Well, one should note that Charlie Chan's speech was distinguishable through the expedient of substituting *l* for *r* to make him Chinese, and Poirot's was distinctive through the inclusion of classroom French phrases to make him Belgian.)

Clues in those stories were factual: the mysterious stain, the necklace hidden in a shoe. (Van Dine does use a reported trait of violent temper as a clue in *The Greene Murder Case*, but the temper isn't in evidence, front and center. We are told about it, but it's never shown.)

Hammett, then, was the first to introduce character as a clue. Mimi's "Queen of France" attitude in *The Thin Man*, mentioned twice, and then actually shown by her epileptic attack upon Nick Charles when she can't have her way, proves to be the motive for Julia Wolf's murder. (It's a little hard to fathom all this from the text — for the reason stated in the next paragraph — but it's all there.)

Another, and cleverer example was his use, in *The Maltese Falcon*, of Miles' lechery and experience as a detective as clues by which Spade deduced the identity of Miles' murderer. It's a better example because Hammett could create better male than female characters.

Female Characters

Apropos the above, let us interrupt here for a moment to discuss Hammett's female characters. There aren't many, and they may seem fewer than they are — because they aren't memorable.

Consider Brigid O'Shaughnessy (a horrible name for a *femme fatale*) in *The Maltese Falcon*. The reader has to regard her as a "sexy siren." This is not because Spade sleeps with her (undoubtedly a *first* in detective fiction), for he's not that hard to please (witness Iva Archer). But we have to deduce that Captain Jacobi was totally enthralled by her inasmuch as he delivers the black bird to Spade on her behalf rather than betake himself to a hospital. And there's also mention of Cairo (homosexual) and being "beyond her reach."

Nothing, however, in Hammett's rendering of Brigid, evokes in the reader this sense of her sexual appeal.

That is one weakness Hammett had. He was not good at doing women. One might suggest as an explanation that he did not understand women. They were "objects" — viewed, but not comprehended.

We note one exception here. Nora Charles is a well-drawn character. But he was patterning her after Lillian Hellman, which means he didn't have to "create" so much as "modify."

The others have to be taken more for what Hammett *says* they are, than for the way they appear to the reader.

The Movie

As an aside on the subject of Mimi, Nick, and Nora; Fred Dannay and Manny Lee, the "Ellerys Queen," once told me a fascinating story about the making of *The Thin Man* movie. They were in Hollywood at the time on Ellery Queen business and could report it firsthand.

It seems that the careers of William Powell, who'd descended to playing Philo Vance in detective movies, and Myrna Loy, whose modest film success was notable mainly for her roles as an oriental villainess, were in eclipse. They each had one more picture to do for MGM and then they were going to be dropped. At the same time, the husband and wife screenwriting team of Albert Hacket and Frances Goodrich had one more film to do before they quit Hollywood to move to Europe.

The powers that be at MGM therefore decided to lump them all together in one last film and wrap up the whole thing. So they pulled out *The Thin Man*, a mystery story that had been collecting dust on their shelves, and gave it to them, figuring to kill all their birds with one stone.

Since it was to be their last picture and they didn't have to worry about pleasing their employers, Hacket and Goodrich decided to write the kind of script they wanted to write instead of the kind they were supposed to write. So they did, and since this was a minor film being shot on a back lot, nobody paid any attention to what they were doing and none of the top brass bothered to look at the daily rushes.

The film was shot and the first the bigwigs got to see of it was the finished product. What they saw brought forth howls of outrage. This was not the way to make a mystery movie!

The outrage, however, only lasted until the public got a look at the film and raved.

As a result, Powell and Loy were signed up to long-term contracts, Myrna enjoyed a universal reputation as the perfect wife, both became top stars, made something like seventeen pictures together, including a whole series of *Thin Man* films, and any number of additional films on their own, and both enjoyed long and memorable careers.

Red Harvest and The Dain Curse

But enough of the asides. Let's tackle Hammett's novels one by one and discuss what's good and bad about them. In his first two novels, *Red Harvest* and *The Dain Curse* (both 1929), Hammett uses as his detective hero, the Continental Op, the protagonist of his pulp short stories. The Continental Op, a detective working for the Continental Detective Agency, is reputedly an amalgamation of a couple of Pinkerton detectives Hammett knew. The Continental Op has no other name in Hammett's stories, if we discount the names on the business cards he hands out according to the role he wants to play. This is well and good, and a distinct departure from anything that had appeared in detective fiction before.

Hammett's major impact upon the genre of detective fiction was due to the fact that he was the first writer in the genre to have been a real detective. And the kind of detecting he introduced, which hadn't been done before, was that of the private investigator.

Hammett also introduced an element of "realism," meaning blood, guts, and gore, which, while prevalent in the pulps, hadn't been seen before in the detective novel. It came as a surprise, for the readers of detective stories weren't readers of pulp magazines and didn't know what was being done in that field. If detective novels were viewed as "second-class" literature, the pulps weren't literature at all and nobody among the cognoscenti who admitted to reading detective novels had any idea what was happening there. Hammett brought that form into public view and, in the doing, changed the nature of the American detective story.

This new approach was presaged by Hammett's review of S.S. Van

Dine's first Philo Vance novel, *The Benson Murder Case* (1926), done for the *Saturday Review of Literature*. Says Hammett:

> This Philo Vance is in the Sherlock Holmes tradition and his conversational manner is that of a high-school girl who has been studying the foreign words and phrases in the back of her dictionary. He is a bore when he discusses art and philosophy, but when he switches to criminal psychology he is delightful. There is a theory that any one who talks enough on any subject must, if only by chance, finally say something not altogether incorrect. Vance disproves this theory: he manages always, and usually ridiculously, to be wrong. His exposition of the technique employed by a gentleman shooting another gentleman who sits six feet in front of him deserves a place in a *How to be a detective by mail* course."

This is as blistering an appraisal as any author could receive on a first novel. That Philo Vance, unhindered by Hammett's judgment, became *the* detective of his era, was due to the popularity of that form of the detective story at that time, a time before Hammett had published his own alternative viewpoint novels. In fact, it was the erudite Willard Huntington Wright's (S.S. Van Dine) opinion at that time that the purpose of the detective story was Plot — to provide the reader with a puzzle, the necessary clues to the solution and, ultimately, the answer to the puzzle. His claim was that emotions had no more place in a detective story than in a crossword puzzle and violence should be minimized. His aim was to elevate and refine the form. Philo Vance was his means to this end.

Quite obviously the immense popularity of the Philo Vance series showed him effective in his aim and Hammett's negative response out of step. Hammett, however, had his own ideas of what should be done with the detective story. When he submitted *Red Harvest* to Knopf in 1928, he told Blanche Knopf that his ambition was to elevate mystery fiction to the level of art. It was a different kind of art than what Wright had in mind. Once his novels began appearing, however, attitudes changed. The Classical form of the detective had a newborn rival. The Hard-Boiled School of detective fiction had been born.

Richard Layman, in *Shadow Man* (Harcourt Brace Jovanovich, 1981), his biography of Hammett, says, regarding Hammett's desire to raise mystery fiction to the level of art: "Six years and four novels later, it was widely acknowledged that he had done just that."

Raymond Chandler, on the other hand, questions Hammett's aims in his assessment of the mystery, entitled "The Simple Art of Murder" (1944). Says Chandler, "I doubt that Hammett had any deliberate artistic aims whatever; he was trying to make a living by writing something he had firsthand information about. He made some of it up; all writers do; but it had a basis in fact; it was made up out of real things."

This, of course, is what gave Hammett his impact — this and his taut, brisk style. For the first time, a detective novel was written by a real detective. As H.R.F. Keating puts it (in his *Crime and Mystery — The 100 Best Books,* Carroll & Graf, 1987), "Hammett is portraying a new man for new times — at the beginning, incidentally, of a new decade, the 1930s."

Whatever Hammett's purpose, and one suspects that Chandler underestimated him here, his importance must be conceded. Hammett's is one of the great names in detective fiction and deservedly so. Yet his greatness must not be too facilely and unquestioningly granted. He deserves a thorough analysis.

Flaws in the First Novels

Consider his books. The first two, *Red Harvest* and *The Dain Curse,* both published in 1929, record the adventures of his nameless Continental Op. Both are of a piece. Both are replete with mindless violence and awash with such slaughter as makes Mickey Spillane look like a choirboy. Chapter XXI of *Red Harvest* is, in fact, titled, "The Seventeenth Murder" and Keating says there are twenty-five deaths "directly described." (I didn't count.)

There are less, but still a plethora of killings in *The Dain Curse* and the Continental Op comes through as a one-man gang, spreading death and destruction among the bad guys in all directions. Meanwhile, everyone who shoots at him misses, and he emerges with nothing more than a nick or two.

Now there's nothing wrong with having a hero come through the battle in one piece, but when it's luck rather than skill, the reader can't help wondering what would have happened to the story if one of the bad guys' bullets was as well, or luckily aimed, as his own. In other words, one has to wonder at the wisdom of the Op in announcing to the crooks (which includes much of the police force) that he's going to clean up the town. One wonders how he could have made it back to his hotel without being ambushed.

There are, unfortunately, a number of additional complaints to be aired. One complaint that makes these books fail if viewed as mysteries rather than novels, is that Hammett does not present a single problem. In a proper detective story, no matter how many murders are committed (usually too many), there is only one murderer and the identity of that one murderer is the puzzle to be solved. And this is as true today as back in the days of the classical puzzle tale.

Consider *Red Harvest*. The Op goes to a town called Personville (known as "Poisonville") to meet a Donald Willson, only to discover he's been murdered. That's an excellent start for any story and the way Hammett builds up suspense in the opening pages is worth noting.

However, not too many pages later, after being hired to clean up the town, the Op solves that killing — with good deduction by the way — but the story and the other murders, by other murderers, have hardly begun.

One might ask whether his breaking of the rules by having more than one killer for more than one murder is due to inexperience, or an attempt to break new ground. The conclusion has to be that he was writing his own story and wasn't interested in rules. If some of the elements of the detective story are present in this novel, it's because he was a detective and he wrote about detection. The novel itself isn't a mystery, it's a melodrama.

The same is true of *The Dain Curse*. He has good deductions there too — the kind I like — such as concluding on the basis of what's wrong with Leggett's suicide note that he was, in fact, murdered by his wife. But again Hammett has a murder solved midway through a story with more killings and killers yet to come.

A few more complaints and then let's get on to the good points about Dashiell Hammett and what merits him his reputation.

He does tell complicated tales here so he can't waste too much time in the telling, but he does spell many things out in *A-B-C* fashion as if for first graders. In his defense, this could be because he feared that the public, unacquainted at that time with the way real detectives worked, might not follow what was going on. But there is an awful lot of talk — telling, not showing.

Also, and this is true of *The Glass Key* as well, he goes into over-elaborate detail. The hero makes a phone call, gets no answer and has to call back — that sort of thing. This is the way life really is, but it's unartistic. Good plotters contrive to have every action and event significant, each following on the heels of another. The fact that, in real life, there are substantial dead spots between significant events, is skipped over. In plotting, as in arranging a group for a photograph, reality is sacrificed for art. It's a sacrifice the reader is pleased to accept. In fact, that's the purpose of art: to call attention to the relevant; to be selective.

And also, in these novels, there is repetition. As a case in point,

Hammett has the Op explain to Dinah (*Red Harvest*) what we just saw happen.

Hammett's Strengths

With all of these flaws — and more can be found — we might well ask what makes the guy good? Two things. His style and certain of his characterizations. And, when he's on — as he is in *The Maltese Falcon* and *The Thin Man* — his stories. Style includes description (e.g., "Long oyster-colored lines of rain slanted down into China Street.") and dialogue that crackled (e.g. Ned Beaumont, in bed: "Well, it wouldn't hurt to talk it over with him." Whiskey: "You're damned right it wouldn't. Pin your diapers on and we'll go now.")

Where Chandler's dialogue gets sometimes cutesy, Hammett's dialogue is crisp. Chandler's writing style is lazy-romantic. Hammett's is taut and quick. You can tell he was a real detective; the authenticity crackles.

And there are Hammett's characters. Perhaps he doesn't do women well, but what he does do is create characters who operate on each other. And the way they operate provides clues and motivations for his stories.

The Maltese Falcon

After *Red Harvest* and *The Dain Curse*, for his third effort, *The Maltese Falcon*, Hammett shed his Continental Op and created one of the most memorable detectives in mystery fiction, Samuel Spade. One thing Hammett could create was tough guys. His Continental Op was tough, so were any number of the hard-boiled characters who inhabited his tales, but I daresay no one in literature was tougher, in a realistic sense, than Sam Spade.

There's Mike Hammer, of course, and there's the Continental Op himself, but their toughness isn't impressive. For one thing, it's not developed through bravery in the face of peril. Like the Saint, neither of them knows fear because they know the author won't let anything happen to them. All bullets will miss, all villains will let them live a little too long, all dungeons will produce a beautiful maiden with a key.

Spade, on the other hand, has to reckon with reality. He has to measure the pros and cons of every action. When he puts himself at risk, he has weighed the consequences.

Spade is dynamic. In every situation, no matter who's supposedly in charge, he dominates. The only person in *The Maltese Falcon* he has trouble dealing with is Iva, his murdered partner's wife.

What is particularly charming about Spade is that he's not only tough, he has a little boy's pride in being tough. Nobody's going to be tougher than Sam Spade. Nobody's going to push Mrs. Spade's little boy, Sam, around, not even a little bit. When Lieutenant Dundy and Detective Tom Polhaus awaken Spade at 4:30 in the morning to query him about his partner's murder, and Dundy, overriding Spade's objection, says, "All right, sit down and listen," Spade's instant response is, "I'll sit or stand as I damned please."

When he has lunch with Tom Polhaus, and Tom, referring to Spade's quarrels with Dundy, says, "He's as bullheaded as you are," Spade promptly replies, "No, he's not, Tom. He just thinks he is."

Tom goes on to say, "I suppose you don't never pull the same stuff on anybody that we pulled on you?" and Spade says, "You mean that you tried to pull on me, Tom—just tried."

When the D.A. calls Spade in for questioning and suggests, "I only mean that you might have been involved in it without knowing what it was," Spade comes back with one of the great retorts: "I see," he says. "You don't think I'm naughty. You just think I'm dumb."

These are the touches that make Spade human rather than superhuman. There are other human touches about him too, that show off his feet of clay and set him apart from all the detective heroes who had preceded him. He was, for one thing, playing around with his partner's wife, which hardly casts him in the heroic mold.

And there is, to mention it again, the way he dominates every situation no matter where he's at, no matter with whom, no matter what the circumstances. At his first meeting with Casper Gutman, the obese and ruthless ringleader, surrounded by his bodyguards, it's Spade, outnumbered and totally in the dark as to what's going on, who issues the ultimatum to produce or else.

And it's Spade who calculates just how far he can go. Disarming the two-gun "gunsel," he hands the guns to Gutman who promptly returns them to the seething kid. This isn't reckless daredeviltry, *a la* the Continental Op, this is the bullfighter knowing how and when to turn his back on the bull.

Then there's what must be, perhaps, the greatest "tough guy" scene in literature. Spade, who has (can lay his hands on) the Falcon, is facing Gutman and his gang who, Gutman points out, "have *him.*" Gutman wants the Falcon and reminds Spade that, since they can torture him to get it, *they* have the upper hand. Spade counters, reminding them that torture is no good if the threat of death doesn't lie behind it. If they try to torture him, he'll put up such a fuss they'll either have to kill him or quit. Since, if he's dead, they'll never get the Falcon, that gives *him* the upper hand.

Gutman points out that, in the heat of emotion, people sometimes forget where their best interests lie and might do things they would later regret (i.e., kill Spade). So Spade, in this unenviable position, says (and this marks the difference between the "heroic" pseudo-tough guy and the *real* tough guy): "That's the trick from my side, to make my play strong enough that it ties you up, but yet not make you mad enough to bump me off against your better judgment."

That is the essence, but not the whole of the scene. Read it. It is a classic.

The Plot

It is the measure of the man, Sam Spade, that makes *The Maltese Falcon* great. Also great is the story behind the falcon. This is not a hoard of gold that everybody's after, nor the Hope Diamond nor the Star of India. This is an unheard of treasure, the concept of which Hammett has researched and made believable. That Gutman would reveal its worth to Spade is questionable in story terms, but it's great for giving motivation and understanding to the people pursuing it.

Not great, however, is the plot of *The Maltese Falcon*, which is seriously flawed from a plot point of view. Many of the things that take place are obviously contrived. Consider the extraordinary event of Captain Jacobi delivering the Falcon into Spade's hands and dying on the spot. Spade, without having to lift a hand, without having to do any detective work at all, has the "McGuffin" given to him. And, to ease the situation, the messenger drops dead on the spot, conveniently removing him from the scene. Questions as to the why and how are ignored. All that is important is that Spade have the Falcon in his possession for the climax scene when he bargains with Gutman and his gang.

Another serious plot weakness—as deftly handled as Hammett could manage (so that no analysis of *The Maltese Falcon* I've ever encountered, has noticed it)—is the introduction into the story of Gutman's daughter, whose only purpose in being in the book is to send Spade on a wild-goose chase. Who was this girl? Why was she drugged? Why did she come up with this false address?

The reason is evident when Spade at last returns to his apartment and finds all the bad guys are gathered there to wait for him. In short, Hammett, to create his final scene, which he wanted to take place with Spade walking into an ambush, had to invent a way to keep Spade out of things until the setting could be arranged.

These gimmicks are weak. But we forgive them. They aren't what Hammett was about. He used them as he used his whole story—to tell the tale of a man called Spade, as tough and memorable, and as different a detective as the mystery story had seen before. *The Maltese Falcon* isn't about a jewel encrusted bird of untold value being sought by a band of memorable cutthroats, nor about the solution to the murders of Archer and Thursby (note again that Hammett has different killers for each killing), nor about a detective's effort to track down his partner's killer.

It is the story about a private detective named Sam Spade and how he operates.

And for that story, we forgive all plot deficiencies, all irrelevant digressions and all flaws. We will forgive anything for the sake of having Sam Spade introduced into the annals of literature.

The Glass Key

Hammett next published *The Glass Key*, which we have mentioned and dismissed, in 1931. It's an education in political corruption, which mystery writers didn't get into back then, and which might have been its impact. It is not, however, a detective story in its proper sense and, in my view, rates with *Red Harvest* and *The Dain Curse* as one of Hammett's lesser works. One thing does stand out. Everybody drinks as if "tomorrow we die." But drinking is heavy in all Hammett's novels—again something new in mystery fiction—and one has to suspect that Hammett is the one who created the image of the hard-drinking private eye.

The Thin Man

Now we come to *The Thin Man*, published in early 1934, which is Hammett's finest detective story from the standpoint of meeting and making the most of the requirements of detective fiction. Here again, as with the Continental Op and Sam Spade, we are presented with a detective who knows what the detecting business is all about. This detective, Nick Charles, happens to be a retired detective, back in New York and into his old stamping grounds because he and his wealthy wife have come East for a vacation. Nick and wife, Nora, drink a lot, but that's because they're vacationing, not working.

What makes this a proper detective story is that it obeys the requirements of a proper detective story. Here, all the murders are related and are committed by the same person, all the necessary clues are presented, and the puzzle facing the reader is "Whodunit?"

Two things are worth noting here. The story has been criticized (in Richard Layman's *Shadow Man*) because "Nick lazily solves the three murders . . . withholds clues from the police as well as the reader." The last two points are challengeable. He is frank with the police to the point of giving them privileged information they couldn't have come by in any other way and there's nothing Nick produces at the end of the case that the reader can complain has been pulled out of a hat.

It is true that Nick "lazily" solves the case. He gets into it against his will, in fact, and then only because he himself becomes a suspect. But his attitude is part of what makes the story so good. A first-rate detective story is one in which the case is played out as a backdrop behind an interesting tale which engrosses the reader on its own merit. And the engrossing tale which involves the reader in *The Thin Man* is the doings of Nick and Nora Charles on vacation in New York at Christmastime in the year 1932.

Which brings up the second point. Vincent Starrett asked how, if we were granted the wish, we would choose to spend a day from the irrecoverable past and concluded, who would not want, most of all, to find himself in late nineteenth century London with its gaslights and fog and carriages, and be at 221B Baker Street with Sherlock Holmes when he'd cry, "Come, Watson, the game is afoot!"

The aura of the times that Doyle created around Sherlock Holmes, we noted, is a part of the mystique that surrounds his character. It is my persuasion that sociologists of the future, if they would understand the past, should read the mystery novels of the era. For mystery novelists are not making comments about the society in which they live, they are merely recording it. The social milieu of which they write affects their stories because it's there. Why and how it's there is not their concern and sociologists will, therefore, gain a reporter's uncolored picture of what things were like at a given time and place.

Such a picture Conan Doyle gave us of Holmes's London. It's gone now and will never come again, but it springs to life each time we open the pages of a Sherlock Holmes tale, and we feel we know what it was like back then, though we were never there.

Likewise, *The Thin Man* gives us a vivid picture of prohibition New York, the speakeasies, the gangsters, the thugs, the way of life, upper and lower. That again is an era that is gone forever, but it has been as vividly and as unwittingly created by Hammett as Holmes' nineteenth century London was vividly and unwittingly created by Doyle. Better than in any of his other novels, Hammett gives us the aura of an era. The book is worth a reading for that alone.

Flaws in the Novel

One does have to note an odd habit of Hammett's. In the middle of *The Thin Man*, in response to a question Gilbert asks Nick about cannibalism, Hammett fills several pages of the novel with the direct quote of an article on the subject. It is totally irrelevant, adds nothing to the story, and is an all too obvious attempt to fatten a thin novel.

He does the same kind of thing in *The Maltese Falcon* when Spade interrupts the course of the story to tell Brigid O'Shaughnessy a long tale about what happened to a man named Flitcraft. It has been suggested that the Flitcraft story was told in order to explain that Spade wasn't afraid of death. Even if true, it is not a valid excuse for the dissertation, for Spade shows his views of death through his behavior (which is the proper way to acquaint the reader with a character) and the dissertation belabors the point out of all proportion even if that were the aim.

We have to fault Hammett for these lapses. They do not represent the art of storytelling.

So much for the man and his work. As a man he was strange. As a writer, he was sometimes very fine, other times quite mediocre. His *Maltese Falcon* is notable because, in it, he created one of the great characters of fiction. His *The Thin Man* rates praise as an example of a first-class detective story.

His enduring fame, however, must be viewed as due to his impact upon the field of the detective story. He broke the mold. He showed it could be done another way. He created the hard-boiled, private-eye form of the detective story, and for this we must all be grateful.

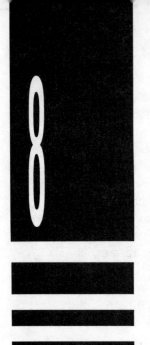

8

ON RAYMOND CHANDLER

The following article was originally written as the introduction to a proposed Bantam edition of Raymond Chandler's The Big Sleep. *The edition never materialized and this is the first time this introduction has been seen in print.*

Raymond Chandler was not a prolific writer. He didn't publish his first work of fiction until he was forty-five, and his total output consists of twenty-three short stories (only fifteen of which are generally available to the public) and seven novels. The first short story, "Blackmailers Don't Shoot," written for the pulp magazine market, appeared in *Black Mask* (the most famous of the pulps), in December 1933, and his last novel, *Playback*, which, sad to report, was only an echo of the real Raymond Chandler, appeared in 1958. By then he was on his way out (he died March 26, 1959) and I was told that the manuscript he was working on at the end (*The Poodle Spring Story*) was unpublishable. He was already gone.

Seven novels and a scattering of short stories (he published only one collection) is such a small output as would be expected to doom a writer to obscurity. Hundreds of forgotten writers have published ten to twenty times more. Few writers of note have published less.

Yet Raymond Chandler — forget his short stories, for they only made the writer, not the legend; and forget, too, his last literary efforts when his underpinnings had been torn away and his disintegration showed in his work — has had an impact upon American letters that has not yet been finally evaluated.

That impact stems directly from his novels, the *big* novels he wrote when he was at the height of his talents. One can list, in order, *The Big Sleep* (Alfred A. Knopf, 1939) — my first introduction to Chandler and my favorite; *Farewell, My Lovely* (Knopf, 1940); *The High Window*, (Knopf, 1942); *The Lady in the Lake*, (Knopf, 1943); *The Little Sister*, (Houghton Mifflin, 1949); *The Long Good-*

bye, (Houghton Mifflin, 1954) — for which he won the Mystery Writers of America's Edgar Allan Poe Award for best mystery of the year but which, to me, seemed to say he was, regrettably, already past his peak; and *Playback*, (Houghton Mifflin, 1958), which we can forget.

The power of Chandler, in my view, lies in the first Big Four. If we go beyond that very far, he begins to unravel. Not that his way with words wasn't still sharp. Chandler's prime power was his way with words. But his strength and impact is diminishing. *The Long Goodbye* wanders too much. The title says it all. The Goodbye was too long, and it was Good-bye.

In *Playback*, Philip Marlowe even rolls in the hay with a girl, and one feels that his integrity is being compromised, that Chandler is succumbing to the tenor of the times and wants to bring the pristine — or at least discreet — Philip Marlowe abreast of an era, bring him up-to-date, so to speak. There's a sense of Chandler pandering to popular taste here. And he didn't need to. But this was in the last days of his life, after his wife, Cissy, had died and he was cast adrift. And he was cast more adrift, I think, than people realize.

Notes on the Man

I didn't know him until those times, after Cissy, and there was a sense of groping about him, of reaching out. We hadn't yet met, and there'd been only a smattering of correspondence, not enough to establish a friendship, but I would receive occasional notes written as the mood struck him, at all hours of the night. And on some, he would remark that he was wearing cotton gloves because a painful skin infection made it hurt to type.

I don't think Cissy's contribution to Chandler's career is yet appreciated. Much is made of the fact she was eighteen years older than he and that, before he married her, he had lived with his mother until she died. The strangeness of such an age gap is remarked upon but never analyzed, leaving one to speculate on what abnormal afflictions may have affected them both.

But let's get back to the beginning and try to make the man. Where did he come from? What shaped him into the kind of writer whose all-too-few works demand our attention?

Biographies are dull, so let's dispense the amenities painlessly. Ray Chandler was born July 23, 1888, in Chicago, Illinois. His parents divorced in 1896 and he was taken by his mother to London to live, and there he went to school. Attempts are made to attribute his way with the American language to his training, in Britain, in the English language. One can hardly deny that environment does have its effect, but one cannot ignore the quality of the material upon which the environment works. Leave it to others to debate that point.

After schooling, Ray passed civil service exams, which should have assured him a passport to oblivion, but he avoided that fate by returning to California in 1912, just in time for the World War.

In that war, he enlisted with the Canadian Cordon Highlanders and went to France with the First Division of the Canadian Expeditionary Force. In 1918, he joined the Royal Flying Corps. (The first time we met, I recall us huddled over drinks against the bar of the Overseas Press Club, talking about the planes we flew, he in World War I, I in World War II, comparing notes.)

After the war he returned to California with his mother and, upon her death, married, in February 1924, Pearl Cecily (Cissy) Bowen, nee Hurlburt, who had been twice divorced and was eighteen years his senior. Meanwhile, he went into business, became director of a number of oil companies, lost his job in 1932 during the Depression, and turned, finally, to a career in writing. From 1933 and his first published story, and for the rest of his life, that is how we know him.

The Writer

What gives Chandler his stature as a writer? Of course, there is his turn of phrase, his way with description: "I came out at a service station glaring with wasted light." It's spare, but it's one I like. Usually, he's lusher: "The light had an unreal greenish color, like light filtered through an aquarium tank. The plants filled the place, a forest of them, with nasty meaty leaves and stalks like the newly washed fingers of dead men. They smelled as overpowering as boiling alcohol under a blanket." That's his description of General Sternwood's greenhouse. James M. Cain thought Chandler overdid that greenhouse bit, but Cain wrote a stripped-down prose, as telling as it was economical, and such a greenhouse would not be for him.

A Sense of Time and Place

There's more than just his descriptive power, however. There's his sense of place and time. Raymond Chandler set Philip Marlowe in the Los Angeles of the 1930s and 1940s as firmly as Conan Doyle set Sherlock Holmes in the London of the 1880s and 1890s.

Here is Marlowe in the rain at night: "Ten blocks of that (walking), winding down curved rain-swept streets, under the steady drip of trees, past lighted windows in big houses in ghostly enormous grounds, vague clusters of eaves and gables and lighted windows high on the hillside, remote and inaccessible, like witch houses in a forest."

Or there's Taggart Wilde, the District Attorney, who: "lived at the corner of Fourth and Lafayette Park, in a white frame house the size of a carbarn, with a red sandstone porte-cochere built on to one side and a couple of acres of soft rolling lawn in front. It was one of those solid old-fashioned houses which it used to be the thing to move bodily to new locations as the city grew westward. Wilde came from an old Los Angeles family and had probably been born in the house when it was on West Adams or Figueroa or St. James Park."

Plotting

On the negative side, there is Chandler's plotting. In his essay, "The Simple Art of Murder," (*The Atlantic Monthly*, 1944), he stakes out his territory thusly:

> I suppose the principal dilemma of the traditional or classic or straight deductive or logic and deduction novel of detection is that for any approach to perfection it demands a combination of qualities not found in the same mind. The coolheaded constructionist does not also come across with lively characters, sharp dialogue, a sense of pace, and an acute use of observed detail. The grim logician has as much atmosphere as a drawing board. The scientific sleuth has a nice new shiny laboratory, but I'm sorry I can't remember the face. The fellow who can write you a vivid and colorful prose simply will not be bothered with the coolie labor of breaking down unbreakable alibis.

There you have it. The plotting's not what's important, it's the sense of pace and style. In Chandler's view, you can't have both. We can quarrel with him, but that was his position and the course he followed, giving the back of his hand to the intricately convoluted, impossible plots devised by the creators of the likes of Poirot, Wimsey, Philo Vance, Queen, and the rest, in favor of an "ace performer," like Dashiell Hammett, who "took murder out of the Venetian vase and dropped it into the alley," and put "people down on paper as they were, and he made them talk and think in the language they customarily used for these purposes."

Granted that the creators of Poirot, Wimsey, et al were lacking when it came to characterization, suspense, and activity, but they were, indeed, consummate plotters. They had to be for the slightest error in the location of the wastebasket, or the discarded sweater, could destroy their book.

So Chandler allies himself with Hammett's action tales, wherein plotting is simple and sometimes scarcely relevant. In *The Maltese Falcon*, for example, Captain Jacobi delivers the black bird into Sam Spade's arms, Jacobi's own so covered with blood that the reader fails to realize that the great treasure everyone is after has, by the most monumental good fortune, been handed to the hero without him having to lift a finger. Such a coincidence could never be countenanced by the plotters. (But finding the black bird isn't what Hammett's story is about.)

Chandler favored Hammett's way, the way of the storyteller. He created great tales of derring-do and presented them unforgettably, but his plot lines were only casually interwoven and he was known to become irked when a curious reader pressed him too hard on details. As a case in point, late in *The Big Sleep*, when Marlowe, on a rainy night, with "two flats and one spare," knocks on the doors of Art Huck's repair garage wanting help, he's first told to go a mile down the road to another garage, then, when he persists, is welcomed with a gun. Granted Huck and his crew are bad guys, but there's no reason for them to blow their cover treating a stranger in such a manner. It leaves them no operating room.

The Moral Man

To return to the positive side, there is a moral quality in Chandler which has not been remarked upon. Philip Marlowe is more regarded as a "romantic" figure than a "moral" figure — a romantic in an age when romanticism has died, a chivalrous knight in a time when nobody knew what chivalry meant. Chandler's definition of a hero ("The Simple Art of Murder"): "But down these mean streets a man must go who is not himself mean, who is neither tarnished nor afraid," makes both Marlowe and Chandler romantics.

But probe deeper than that. Consider the "dirty book" racket that plays a role in *The Big Sleep*. Listen to Marlowe's description of a customer who comes in for one such book: "The door opened and a tall hungry-looking bird with a cane and a big nose came in neatly . . . The tall bird went to the door in the paneled partition and opened it barely enough to slip through . . . He left as he had come, walking on the balls of his feet, breathing with his mouth open, giving me a sharp side glance as he passed." That's not exactly a description of the All-American boy.

Then we have Marlowe's (Chandler's) reaction to the books themselves. "I knew about what it would be, of course. A heavy book, well bound, handsomely printed in handset type on fine paper. Larded with full-page arty photographs. Photos and letterpress were alike of an inde-scribable filth."

Admittedly, in the 1930s, pornography was not as generally ac-cepted as today when neighborhood theaters show more explicit sex than the old-time stag movies, possession of which could have resulted in arrest. Even so, Chandler's revulsion seems excessive. In fact, Carmen Sternwood, posing nude on a throne with her knees together, presumably the kind of "arty photographs" being taken, could hardly be labeled "indescribable filth" in any age. Chandler seems very down on smut.

And there's his reaction to homosexuality. There are some who query his sexual interests, pointing to the vixen quality of his female characters and an almost caressing description of the big he-men who beat Philip Marlowe's head in. And, of course, there's the fact he lived with his mother till she died, then married a woman eighteen years his senior.

But he does show a distance from such activity: "I took my dark glasses off and tapped them delicately on the inside of my left wrist. If you can weigh a hundred and ninety pounds and look like a fairy, I was doing my best." That doesn't display much knowledge of the subject.

And there's Geiger's house the morning after Carmen has had her picture taken: "The place was horrible by daylight. The Chinese junk on the walls, the rug, the fussy lamps, the teakwood stuff, the sticky riot of colors, the totem pole, the flagon of ether and laudanum — all this in the daytime had a stealthy nastiness, like a fag party."

If one wants to believe he protests too much, there is this analysis by John Houseman, who worked with Chandler on several movies: "In life he was too inhibited to be gay: too emotional to be witty. And the English Public School system which he loved had left its sexually devasta-ting mark upon him. The presence of young women — secretaries and extras around the lot — disturbed and excited him." (*The World of Ray-mond Chandler,* ed. by Miriam Gross, A & W Publishers, Inc., 1977).

Chandler not only had morals — Victorian morals if you will — but he also lived by them. Billy Wilder reports that when he and Chandler were working on the script of *Double Indemnity* together, Chandler walked out, complaining about Wilder's rudeness, his drinking, his constant phone calls to women. All kinds of promises had to made to get him back.

There was the movie Chandler wrote, *The Blue Dahlia.* It had a deadline, for Alan Ladd, the star, was to go into the army. When a worried Paramount offered Chandler a $5,000 bonus to make sure he met the deadline, Chandler quit in outrage at the insult to his integrity. Ultimately he returned and completed the movie, but at a risk to his health that only his sense of honor would have allowed.

His Greatest Strength

Raymond Chandler was a man of many parts, and nobody can fully understand him. Nor did he understand himself for, I'm sure, he didn't do what he did or behave as he did through analysis, but from emotion. And maybe that's what makes the superior writer and the great writer — emotion.

A professor once opined of a writer that he would not become great because he didn't hate his parents. He was saying, in effect, that gut responses are what count. It's not what you think, but what you feel that people care about.

Ray Chandler gives the reader some of both. He tells what's in his head, but he presents it through the heart.

Very few can do it so well.

One cannot pass over the field of the Hard-Boiled mystery novel without reference to Mickey Spillane's one-man-gang, private detective Mike Hammer. Hammer represents the ultimate — or perhaps the post-ultimate — denouement of that type of tale. I say post-ultimate, because the extremes to which Spillane took the private eye detective story went far beyond the imagination of any writer other than Spillane.

There was, interestingly, a great antipathy toward Spillane by his fellow mystery writers. It was not jealousy, let it be quickly stated. Nor was it because Mike Hammer was stupid, nor because he was rougher and tougher than any detective anyone else had devised (or could have devised?). Nor was it because he lusted (what private detective secretly didn't?) nor because he actually made out with the story's cast of beautiful blondes right there in the book. It wasn't because Mike Hammer took justice into his own hands (*I, the Jury* was the appropriate title of his first novel). It wasn't because he could Out-Saint "The Saint" in overcoming the forces of Evil single-handedly. The objection was that his hero was really a *villain*.

Mike Hammer was not Philip Marlowe, a man who walked down "mean streets" who was, "not himself, mean." Mike Hammer was very much, himself, mean. Mike Hammer was not a Hero, he was an Anti-Hero, and *this* is what put other mystery writers off.

In one Hammer book, a memorable occurrence took place in the parking lot outside a nightclub. Mike encountered someone whom he thought was after him, so he jumped him, broke the guy's jaw and left him half dead, only to discover the victim was an innocent patron going for his car. Says Mike, on this revelation, "Gee, did I feel like a dope." (What happened to the guy left half dead isn't revealed.)

Some points should be made. Spillane could write, and write well. He told stories. His

MIKE HAMMER

stories may not always have been good, but he told them with impact. One of his books deals with the old "twin brothers" theme—one is good, one is bad. The "bad" one is killed, the "good" one survives. The reader thinks to himself, "Now Spillane *can't* possibly be pulling the old chestnut that it's the other way way around!" Oh yes he can, and he does.

The writing is good, the plots are bad, the hero is unredeemable. So much may be the case, but back in the days of his popularity, in a list of the ten top-selling books of all time, which included a certain cookbook which is forever number one, and the *Bible*, which is number two, three of those top ten books were by Mickey Spillane.

So, what did he have? Impact is one word for it. Shock value is another. Spillane's books *shocked*. Their like hadn't been seen before.

There's a problem, however, in writing books that shock. They'll sell, but "shock," unlike such themes as "romance," "suspense," and "mystery," doesn't wear well. What is "shocking" in a first book, becomes "ordinary" in the second, and "banal" in the third. (In my own case, I read Spillane's first novel in a matter of hours. His second took me three days. I never finished the third.)

Spillane, in my view, is not someone who will go down in the history of the mystery for his contribution to the field. His "impact," to use the word again, was because he had something to say for the times. Someone, I think it was Joan Kahn, described him as a "gutter Monte Cristo." Mike Hammer was a man who took it upon himself to right the wrongs of society, which society seemed so unable to accomplish, and which the people could not do themselves. He was the essence of their dreams— Superman in paperback instead of the comic books. As such, his crudeness, witlessness, and cruelty could be overlooked because, by brute force if nothing else, he got the job done. And it was a job we all wanted to see done.

This article first appeared in The Mystery Story, *published by University Extension, University of California, San Diego, 1976.*

Let me, improperly, begin this article with a personal reminiscence. In early September of 1949, when I was a young writer with three private-eye-cute-young-couple novels behind me, I chanced upon a slim paperback entitled, *They All Died Young*, written by Charles Boswell. It was a collection of ten true murder cases in which the victims were young women.

I went through those stories, one by one, and was never the same thereafter. They had a vividness, a chilling horror to them that no fiction I had ever read or written could approach.

Immediately, I wanted to get the same kind of impact into my own books, and I pondered what made those stories hit the way that they did. The obvious answer was that these murders weren't make-believe, they had really happened. One of the victims, in fact, had been a nurse in my home city, who had had her throat cut and who had collapsed and died at the entrance of her hospital.

QUESTION: But how does one *know* they happened, other than by the author's say-so?

ANSWER: Because they *sound* that way.

What I fixed upon as giving these stories their aura of horror was not the brutal ugliness of real murder, but the sense of authenticity of the reports. The stories shook me not because the author *said* they really happened, but because they *read* that way.

I thereupon determined to write a fictional murder mystery that would *sound* as if it had really happened. Since it is not private-eye-cute-young-couples who work the real homicides, but sheriffs, police chiefs, and police detectives, this meant a totally new approach — by me at least — to the whole art of mystery writing.

To finish this account, I did sit down and

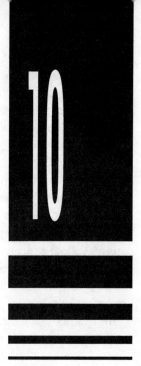

THE
POLICE
PRO-
CEDURAL

do such a book. The year was 1950 and the story was about the murder of a young college girl, solved, as in real life, through the efforts of those whose business it is — the professional policemen. So far as I knew, no one had ever done anything like that before then.

There was a lot going on, however, that I knew nothing about, including a ferment, of which I must have been a part, bubbling just below the surface and which burst into being between the time I wrote my book and the time it appeared in print, in late 1952. It was something that came to be known as the "police procedural."

Lawrence Treat is acknowledged as the first mystery writer to have professional policemen, shown in their natural habitat, solve a crime using authentic police methods. This was his book *V as in Victim*, published in 1945 and followed by *The Big Shot*, using the same characters.

While Larry was first, I doubt that it would be correct to call him the "father" of the police procedural, for this would suggest that a host of other writers were inspired to follow his lead. This did not happen; Larry was ahead of his time and a number of years passed before others began to follow suit. In fact, to quote Larry, "I didn't know I was writing procedurals until somebody invented the term and said that that was the kind of thing I was writing."

If there was a father of the procedural, I think it would have to be the radio program "Dragnet." Perhaps its success was what created the field, or perhaps the *time* of the procedural, which Larry Treat's books foreshadowed, had finally arrived. In either case, I think the "father" title is deserved, for while it is true that no procedural writer I have talked to points to "Dragnet" as a source of inspiration — most not having written their first procedurals until well after "Dragnet's" demise — I would still regard it as inevitable that the potential of the police-station background was first brought to their attention by Joe Friday and company.

In any case, the police procedural, as yet still unnamed, came into being between the writing and publication of my own first procedural so that, when it appeared in print, it was reviewed as an attempt to translate "Dragnet" to novel form. Though erroneous, such critic reaction is, perhaps, further evidence for the "father" figure.

The police procedural represents the second major change in the nature of the mystery story since it achieved its present "whodunit" form with the advent of the classical detective story. The invention which established the classical period and the "whodunit" form was the shifting of the reader's role from that of observer — i.e. standing at Watson's side watching the great man operate — to that of participant — standing at the detective's side, trying to beat him at his own game.

As a result of this change of viewpoint, the classical detective stories became puzzle tales wherein a detective of outstanding intellect matched wits with a murderer, while the author matched wits with the reader.

The first change in this method of handling the mystery story occurred in the forties and early fifties with the establishment of the private-eye school. Tales in this new approach to the genre retained the puzzle form of the plot, but shifted the story emphasis from thought to action. Prowess took precedence over wits. The detectives in these adventures were for the most part loners, knights errant, fighting a desperate battle for Good against Evil. In the beginning days they were private detectives solving murders to save their clients or themselves. Later they became spies and their problems involved the safety of nations.

Though the classical detective and the private eye/spy operated in radically different ways, both shared certain common traits. Both, for example, were virtually free of legal restraint; both were laws unto themselves; both operated alone and kept their own counsel.

The police procedural changes all that. The police procedural thrusts the detective into the middle of a working police force, full of rules and regulations. Instead of bypassing the police, as did its predecessors, the procedural takes the reader inside the department and shows how it operates.

These are stories, not just about policemen, but about the world of the policeman. Police Inspector Charlie Chan doesn't belong. (There're no police.) Nor does Inspector Maigret. (There are police, but Maigret, like Chan, remains his own man.)

When we speak of police procedurals, we are talking about the 87th Precinct books of Ed McBain, about the Elizabeth Linington-Dell Shannon-Lesley Egan, Glendale and Los Angeles police novels. There are John Creasey's Gideon and Roger West stories, there is the Martin Beck series by Maj Sjowall and the late Per Wahloo. These are tales about big-city police departments. In the small-town police procedural genre, there may be none other than my own Chief Fred Fellows.

This business of moving toward the police instead of away from the police is a radical shift in the character of the mystery story, and the nature of the procedural can best be understood by comparing it to the other two city forms. Let us study them in this manner.

I. Realism and the Suspension of Disbelief

"Suspension of disbelief" is one of those awkward phrases that is both hard to say and hard to understand. All it means is: How much *unreality* will the reader endure? How far can a writer go before the reader says, "This is ridiculous!"?

The degree of permissible unreality depends, quite obviously, upon the book. Readers will accept magic spells, witches, and gingerbread houses in fairy tales, but would reject, in disgust, machine guns and electric lights in Civil War novels. The same holds true in the mystery. A great deal more attention to realism is demanded in the police procedural than in the earlier forms. And with reason.

Consider the classical detective story. The moment the reader was brought in on the case and given a chance to solve it, the mystery became a game of wits between author and reader. Authors, therefore, devoted their attention to exploring the possibilities of the puzzle, of finding ways to fool the reader. The result was some of the most elaborately complex plots ever put on paper. Villains, to be worthy foes of the detective, became incredibly clever, incredibly painstaking and, upon occasion, incredibly lucky. The puzzles were exquisite pieces of intellectual architecture.

Such mysteries, naturally, could not pretend a resemblance to reality. Real life murders aren't that elaborately planned. Most actual killings, in fact, are spur-of-the-moment impulses with no more advance thought than will justify the term "premeditation." In real life, the hardest crime to solve is not the one in which every detail has been worked out months in advance, but the unwitnessed, spur-of-the-moment rape or robbery encounter wherein the victim was unknown to the villain.

Such real-life cases, however, would not fit the puzzle mold of the classical mystery. Since puzzle was the aim, reality had to be sacrificed.

As a result, the classical detective story was structured in a language of its own. A large number of wholly artificial devices were accepted as proper baggage. Probably most notable was the traditional denouement wherein all suspects were gathered together and the detective pointed a finger at first one and then another, keeping suspense at its ultimate until, finally, he pointed to the villain and explained in detail how he had found him out. No matter that this is the last thing a real detective would do, the requisites of the puzzle story demanded this kind of approach.

Another was the detective's habit of keeping all the threads of the mystery in his own head, committing nothing to paper, confiding in no one. Keeping the reader in the dark made such behavior obligatory. It also customarily made the detective a tempting target for the murderer and the reader would forgive the lack of reality in favor of the puzzle and the suspense.

Certain artificialities in the form of clues also came to be accepted.

These, however, were not born of necessity, but stemmed from gross errors of ignorance due to the fact that the mystery writers of the era worked aloof from the police and did not bother to research that aspect of their novels.

One of the most notable was the gospel that fingerprints abound and are readily discoverable on guns. As an adjunct, it was also accepted that fingerprints would be protected rather than smudged if covered with a handkerchief. In point of fact, an identifiable fingerprint is very hard to come by, even on receptive surfaces like mirrors, and the chances of getting a print from a gun are, if not zero, very nearly so.

Other clues of misinformation which these stories circulated were that the expression on the victim's face revealed his emotion (surprise, fear, etc.) at the moment of death; that pathologists could tell almost to the minute how long the victim had been dead; and that headless corpses could readily be misidentified.

None of this is true, of course. The best description of the expression on a corpse's face is that there is none. As for times of death, so many variables affect the onset of postmortem changes that an accurate determination is a virtual impossibility without the help of additional evidence. And, of course, the means of identification of bodies by other than facial characteristics are amazingly many. However, for purposes of the puzzle, these gospels of ignorance helped the authors with their clue-planting and readers learned to accept them. The astute reader would, for instance, reflexively know that any body with the face damaged or the head missing belonged to someone else, and that the supposed victim was, in reality, the murderer.

Nor, finally, did murderers ever take the Fifth or deny the accusation, confident that they could never be convicted. Such a concession to realism would make for messy, inconclusive endings and that would not do. When the puzzle was solved, the book had to end.

Mysteries of the classical school might be summed up as follows: Realism is all right so long as it does not interfere with the puzzle.

The private-eye school of mystery fiction is generally accepted as coming to the fore as a revolt against the fantasyland of the puzzle story. It was as if a new breed of author were saying, "This is ridiculous! Let's bring reality to the mystery."

So the stories became more real. The corpses weren't so pretty and death was a matter taken seriously by all concerned, not merely by the detective.

The puzzle could not be as intricate, of course, but that was readily compensated for by having the plot line complicated by an overlay of action rather than one of intellectual obfuscation.

For all that, reality did not really come to the fore. Instead, it became subservient to action. The private eye of these tales behaved in an extraordinarily unrealistic manner. He customarily arrived on the murder scene ahead of the police, tampered with evidence, pocketed clues, and broke laws with a recklessness that was only justified by the fact that the police in these stories were such bumbling idiots that, had the private eye abided by the rules, the mystery would never have been solved. It was only because of his law-unto-himself behavior that the villains were ultimately caught.

As time went on, the stories got wilder, reaching the ultimate in the works of Mickey Spillane. Reality was as absent from the mystery as ever.

One might interpret the advent of the police procedural as if a new breed of author were saying, "This is ridiculous! Let's bring reality to the mystery." Except that one might now ask the ultimate question: How much reality can be brought to the mystery? Can it ever be total? And, if it can, is the police procedural the vehicle? Is the police procedural that ultimate form of the mystery that can combine puzzle, action, and total reality into one? My personal guess is that total reality can never exist in mystery fiction and my definite conclusion is that it certainly can't exist in the procedural.

Consider, first, the narrow field of the small-town police procedural. There is no way total reality can be brought to a series of this kind. In certain areas the reader is obligated to suspend large amounts of disbelief.

Suppose, for example, an author can produce two small-town police procedurals a year—hardly a staggering output. In each there must be one or more confounding murders, problems that strain the resources of both the reader and the police department.

In reality, a town of, say, ten thousand inhabitants, insulated and self-contained, unassaulted by the outside world, would not have a real, honest-to-goodness murder once in a dozen years. That's eight murders a century.

Of these eight genuine murders per century, the chances are that seven of them would pose no problem at all. The police would know who did it ten minutes after they reached the scene and would have the case wrapped up in twenty-four hours.

Inasmuch as the author of the small-town procedural isn't going to write about easily solved mysteries, the stories he will tell are Crime of the Century tales. Except that, in the small town he's writing about, they will take place twice a year.

If this seems against the odds, add in the fact that the small town in question is fortunate enough to have a high-powered resident detective capable of cracking these seemingly insoluble mysteries, and we have to pay another homage to Dame Chance.

What about the other side of the coin? What about the big-city procedural? If we want to portray realism, is this not the locale that offers maximum opportunity? In 1966, there were 700 homicides in New York City. Ten years later, the number was almost 1,500. A writer in this big city could not turn out books fast enough to cover the one-in-eight hard-to-solve cases a single homicide detective might handle in a year.

That part of the story might be true to life. Accurate, also, might be the rules and regulations by which the police abide. The jargon can be learned, the difference between street cops and book cops can be understood. In time, an interested writer who has entree can so familiarize himself with the world of real detectives that he will know their dangers and their territory, guffaw at their "in" jokes, understand the way they think and why. His books may be, therefore, rigorously accurate in all details, except . . .

The real-life detective does not do his detecting à la Sherlock Holmes. He may observe the way Holmes observed; he may well put the pieces of a puzzle together the way Holmes put them together, but this is not the way most real-life crimes are solved. The real-life murder is solved, not by ratiocination, not by the exercise of Hercule Poirot's little gray cells, but by the accumulation of information. Dozens of people are questioned—hundreds may be questioned—and, bit by bit, pieces of information are gathered which, ultimately, reveal what happened.

That's the hard way.

The easy way is to have the information brought in. Ask a chief of detectives how cases are solved and he won't answer, "clues," he'll answer, "informants." (The term informers carries ugly connotations and isn't used.) There is an adage that a detective is only as good as his informants and it is, rest assured, true.

To the mystery writer, this poses certain problems. Consider the following (based upon a true case). There is a shooting in Harlem, one man dead in the hospital, a second man wounded. The wounded man, interviewed by police, tells the story that he and the victim were walking along the street when a man came out of a bar, gunned them down, and ran around the corner. He never saw the man before, he doesn't know why the man shot them. The family of the victim swears he had no enemies, the people in the bar saw nothing, witnesses to the actual shooting don't know who the man was. There is no gun, no clues, no anything.

To an outsider it sounds like a motiveless, unsolvable crime. Even Charlie Chan and Philo Vance would be up a tree.

The police, who are familiar with the local scene, will not be so confounded. They will speculate that it had to do with drugs, that the victim was either a pusher who sold bad junk, or he had robbed a pusher—either act being a killing offense. This gives them motive, but it does not tell them "who." They are not unduly distressed, however, for they anticipate that, later that night—maybe three o'clock in the morning—an informant will slip into headquarters, up to the squad room, and tell the detectives who did it and why. The detectives would then check out the information and, a few days later, make an arrest.

That's the way it usually happens, but it makes for a very bad story. Certain adjustments have to be imposed upon such a tale to put it into salable form, to wit: the detective would have to solve the case without the aid of the informant.

But the moment we start doing this, we are moving away from reality again.

II. The Hero

Let us now turn our attention to the heroes of these tales. What are they like and why are they that way?

The detectives of the classical period are all patterned after Sherlock Holmes. They are created as men of giant intellect, towering over their fellows. The only man, in fact, who can come close to matching the hero's intellect is the villain.

Generally speaking, the detective is also separated from the crowd in other ways. Father Brown wears a habit, Nero Wolfe is an obese gourmet, Poirot and Charlie Chan are foreigners, Vance a dilettante, Wimsey a Lord, the early Queen, effete. Every effort is undertaken to make these detectives memorable, to give the kind of lasting identity that Holmes has. And the ones mentioned above have certainly achieved this distinction.

The homage paid to these detectives and their virtual freedom from the bothersome restrictions imposed on other mortals give them an enviable position. Not for them are there problems about money. They do not have to worry about their jobs, about wives and children. They, like Holmes, are free of all encumbrances, able to devote their great mental prowess exclusively to the murders at hand. It is not difficult for an author to establish reader identification with such a hero.

Let us move on to the hero of the private-eye school. This is a different species of being entirely. This man is a puzzle-solver too, but he is not content to sit and ponder. He is a man of energy and he solves the puzzles through action.

The Saint, James Bond, and Mike Hammer are extreme examples of the type, but they serve as illustrations. These private-eye heroes have more than a touch of Superman about them. They are tough, brave, resourceful, and — as we have noted before — a law unto themselves. They tend to be cavalier, even flamboyant. The qualities that separate them from the rest of the cast are their abilities to operate in excess of everyone else, be it the alcohol they can absorb, the beatings they can take, the laws they can break, the women they can handle.

These men are heroes in the genuine sense of the word, meaning that they go out and battle for Right against Wrong, and WIN. They represent the Walter Mitty dream of the frustrated average man whose world has grown too large for an outcome to be affected by his own efforts. The hero's reckless disregard of authority and his success at overcoming obstacles are therapeutic to the reader. He identifies with such a man. He is eager to read more tales of his derring-do.

What happens, though, when an author seeks to create a hero for a police procedural? Immediately he's in trouble, for the attractive superman hero is denied him by the nature of the genre. Not only does realism require that the hero of procedurals be human rather than superhuman, but also the restrictions of his job and the society he is sworn to uphold.

Consider, first, the small-town procedural. Who can be the protagonist of such a story? Certainly not some handsome young cop who drinks a quart of Scotch for breakfast and has to fight his way past the blondes who camp outside his door — not even a handsome young cop who doesn't drink, smoke, or date — not a young cop at all, even if he's homely.

When it comes to solving serious crimes, the responsibility goes to the top men on the force, which means the chief of police, the detectives he's got, and the officer in charge of detectives. We're talking about older men, men who are probably married and raising families, men who wouldn't find a blonde in every bed, even if sleepy blondes abounded, because they have too little to offer. They are just struggling, balding, graying, unromantic, plain-looking, ordinary Joes.

It is much harder, obviously, for an author to create a memorable character, one the reader will want to keep reading about, if the character can't do or be anything memorable: if he can't attain positions of authority until he is past his handsome, dashing youth; if he can't dine on gourmet foods and know the right wines because he lives on a policeman's salary; if he has to get to work on time, obey the law, go through all the red tape that real policemen do; if he has to turn over significant parts of the investigation to others and stay in the good graces of the public and the board of police commissioners.

Such a man can't help being a rather gray, colorless character, leading a gray, colorless life. No single-handedly walking into the nest of thieves for him; no sneaking into the bad guy's apartment to find crucial evidence; no keeping to himself bits of vital information so that he can hog the limelight when he really socks it to them at the end.

In the small-town procedural, the solution of a case is not a one-man operation in any case. It can be accomplished by a team of two, but no fewer. Nor can the two be Mutt and Jeff, Johnson and Boswell, or Sherlock and Watson. The disparity must not appear too great. It cannot be me and my shadow; it must be a legitimate team of two.

What about a big-city procedural? In a big-city police force, the number of detectives in a squad will run between twenty and thirty. The problem of creating a hero is not multiplied, however. While many of the detectives may help in various phases of a serious crime—interviewing everybody in an apartment building, for example—and while lab technicians, pathologists, photo, emergency service, and other functionaries may be resorted to, these are information-gathering operations from which information will then be delivered to the detectives in charge, and these would probably again be a team of only two. In a New York City homicide, for instance, the two would be the squad detective who "caught" the case and is therefore responsible for its disposition, and the member of the homicide squad—specialists in this kind of crime—who would be assigned to work with him.

This would appear to make the big-city procedural the same as a small-town procedural, with a pair of detectives carrying the ball. In fact, however, the author of a big-city procedural can go with an individual hero if he wants. If his hero is a member of a specialty squad, like homicide, the detective he'd be assigned to help would be different in each new case and he would remain as the sole, continuing character. In such handling, the rest of the detective squad and the other cases under investigation would be background.

Given this material to work with, what are the tactics for producing memorable detectives? It's not as easy a job as when a writer has the license to invent as he pleases, but the opportunities are still plentiful. The family life of the detective can be explored—a possibility that was never entertained in the classic and private-eye forms. The relationships of the men with each other can play an important part in the story—an aspect of the mystery that didn't exist when detectives stood head, shoulders, and waist above their associates and communed only with themselves. In fact, the interior of the squad room can become the equivalent of a daytime serial setting — meaning that the readers get to know the people, their personalities and their problems so well that they look forward to the next book as a chance to rejoin old friends.

The hero aspect of the procedural is radically different from the other two forms, but it offers, probably, a much richer vein to mine.

III. Background

Despite the difference in the hero form, it is in the area of background that the greatest distinction occurs between the police procedural and all other forms of the mystery. In the classical and private-eye forms, an author could get away with minimal research, or none at all. Some authors did do research and enhanced their books with information on special skills or backgrounds, giving their stories an added fillip. The research, however, was inevitably directed toward exotic subjects of intellectual interest. The one area that was not researched was the crass, mundane, very nonintellectual subject of how real detectives operated and what the business of solving murders was actually all about.

Of course, there was little incentive. The creators of the classical detectives did not need to know how the police operated, for the only function of the police was to take the murderer away at the end of the story.

Nor was there any particular reason why the writers of private-eye stories should do background research into the way real crimes were solved. If their heroes operated above the law, there was no need for the authors to know what the laws were. In fact, the only effect a knowledge of law would have upon an author would be to inhibit the freedom he was seeking to give his character.

With the police procedural, of course, the situation is totally reversed. Since it sets itself to show realistic-appearing policemen encountering realistic crimes and solving them in a realistic manner, a knowledge of how police forces are actually structured (they vary greatly from city to city) becomes essential. Not only must procedures be known and understood, but also the law. Even a rookie cop has been drilled in criminal law and knows what he can and cannot do, as well as the requirements he must satisfy. The writer, therefore, had better give himself a similar background and know such things as the rules of evidence and how to cope with the Miranda decision.

The writer of a procedural must be true to life in other ways. Since his readership will grant him scant suspension of disbelief, he cannot have his hero overdrink without getting drunk or sick. His hero can't get bashed unconscious without going to the hospital for observation. Everything must be true to life. All kinds of little bits and pieces of annoying trivia will have to be checked and verified, lest readers start complaining.

The problem, then, for the procedural writer is not merely to come up with a compelling story. He has the added obligation and chore of researching.

IV. Puzzle and Fair Play

Lastly, we come to the story that takes place against this procedural background. Here one encounters a situation which poses interesting questions.

In both the classical and private-eye type mysteries, there was a puzzle to be solved, a villain to be caught and, since the reader was engaged as a participant, an element of fair play to be included. The reader had to know everything the detective knew. The reader went through the case at the detective's side.

The puzzle was in greatest evidence in the classical tale. It was the whole point of the story. In the private-eye genre the puzzle played second fiddle to the action, but it was still there.

Does it exist in the procedural?

The answer is, of course, yes. But, depending upon the type of procedural, it can be foremost, as is likely in the small-town procedural where nothing else is happening, or as low as third fiddle in the big-city type of tale, coming in behind both action and background.

It still, however, must be there. The problem cannot solve itself nor, as mentioned earlier, be solved via the unsolicited arrival of an informant. The detectives must work at a solution and the solution must result from their work. And, of course, the reader again is taken along with the detective — at least on the major case — and is apprised of all the information that the detective is privy to.

These qualities, the solving of a puzzle with the reader given all the clues, are the hallmarks of the mystery story and must be present. Omit them and the tale, no matter how mysterious, how murderous, how police-oriented, is not a proper mystery.

Now comes an aspect of the police-procedural tale which, while it has been a matter of moment to me, does not seem to concern anyone else, with the exception, perhaps, of Ed McBain. (See his deaf man, El Sordo, in such as *Let's Hear It for the Deaf Man*.) This is the element of the "Fair Fight."

Sherlock Holmes had his Moriarty, a man whose talents were a match for his own. In like manner, the mighty-minded detectives of the classical age had to be similarly tested. In order to don the mantle of super-genius, they had to best the best. This is why the puzzles they had to unravel were so elaborate, why the murderers were so clever, why all the odds had to be stacked in their opponent's favor. Chance could not solve the case for the detective. It could only operate on behalf of the villain, making the detective's problem ever more difficult. The detective, to earn his victory, had to prove his supremacy over both the foe and the odds. There could be no sere leaf on the laurel.

In like manner, the private eye had to outsmart the gangleader, the nightclub owner or, in the case of the spy, the arrayed forces of the enemy country. The odds always had to be on the side of the opposition, to be overcome along with the foe.

Now we come to the police procedural and we find there is a change in the battle line-up.

Given: One murderer.

And what is there against him?

We can count on at least two detectives devoting full time to his apprehension while, behind them, at beck and call, lie the total resources of the police, medical, and legal systems of the community. Let the villain hole up in an abandoned warehouse and the hero will not go in and shoot it out with him in a one-to-one showdown. There will be dozens of men, all more heavily armed and protected than their quarry. They will have tear gas, searchlights, walkie-talkies, helicopters — an awesome array of tools — creating a maximum mismatch (quite properly) in order to reduce the element of danger to the "good guys" to a minimum.

The disparity is even greater than that. The police detective will be as observant as Sherlock Holmes by virtue of his training and years of conditioning. If he cannot match Holmes's brilliant mind, he has learned, through long experience, what to look for and where to look, which is almost as good. And the available laboratory facilities can produce, from clues, information the like of which Conan Doyle would never have dreamed.

Meanwhile, against this super-Sherlock stands no Moriarty. The average murderer in real life is below average in mentality. He is motivated by emotion rather than brains. His responses are less planned, his motives less well thought-out. As a physical specimen he would rarely be capable of holding his own against a detective in an even fight. He is more than likely to be one of life's losers. He is outgunned, outmaneuvered, and outwitted every step of the way. The fight is anything but fair.

Does anybody care?

Interestingly enough, I sought, in my own small-town police procedurals, to cope with the problem of the Fair Fight as follows: The murderers were of better than average intelligence — middle- and upper-middle-class in background (not unreasonable in the small-town genre). Then, due partly to their cleverness, the rest to the luck that fell their way, the whole police apparatus would fail to uncover them. An impasse would be reached, at which point the battle became a one-to-one fight between the chief-of-police hero and the villain. The chief would have to come up, on his own, with the one move or idea that would break the case.

This may well have been a wasted concern on my part, however, for nowhere does there seem to be anyone — reader, critic, or other procedural writer — who has given the matter a thought. Do readers feel a certain sympathy for the outgunned and outnumbered murderer? Do they root for the underdog?

Apparently not. In these realistic days where bodies smell and victims spill blood instead of ketchup, perhaps the readers' desire for justice (or is it vengeance?) is such that they don't care how the killer is brought to bay. Perhaps, as another author suggests, the interest in the police procedural lies not in story but in the fascination of this strange world of the policeman and what it is that sets him apart from the rest of mankind, that makes him advance where others retreat, that makes him the helper instead of the helpless.

Or, perhaps what counts is the satisfaction we feel at seeing a great power for Good overthrow the forces of Evil. Perhaps the police procedural excites that emotion within man that is so evident in war: the desire to annihilate the enemy, and the more overwhelming the victory, the more satisfying it is.

V. Conclusions

A comparison of the police-procedural mystery with its predecessors produces eye-opening results. What comes through most strongly is the close relationship between the classical and private-eye forms, and the separateness of the police procedural. This is evident in the areas we have discussed, but the very difference creates a message of its own.

The classical detective story and the private-eye novel were inevitably described as "light reading." One picked up the former for the puzzle, the latter for the action and the accent was on fun. (The lack of reality helped. Who can take the unreal seriously?)

Reviewers of police procedurals, however, don't talk in terms of "light reading." "Social message" is more commonly the measure of evaluation. The police procedural, by showing policemen as they are, shows, by definition, the social ills they contend against as *they* are. Sometimes the social commentaries revealed by procedural authors are deliberately intended, sometimes the revelations are unconsciously done. In either case, the very nature of the procedural provokes a type of story totally beyond the aim of the other forms.

The puzzle — all-important to the classical story — can sink to the depths of being nothing more than the glue that holds a procedural in the genre. There is little else the new form has in common with the old.

One can only ponder the meaning of the changes in the mystery genre. Perhaps the switch from classical to private eye seemed, at the time, as enormous as the new switch from them to the procedural. Perhaps we should, therefore, pay more attention to the common ground the procedural shares with its predecessors than the differences.

Where does the mystery go from here? Can it go anywhere? Do the changes in the mystery point a direction? The future will produce answers to these questions, but as to what they will be, this writer does not feel equipped to venture an opinion.

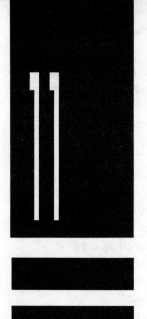

THE REAL DETECTIVES

This article originally appeared in I, Witness, *edited by Brian Garfield, and published for the Mystery Writers of America by Times Books, 1978*

Some years ago, an arrangement was made for Patrick Murphy, then Police Commissioner of New York City, and officers of the Mystery Writers of America to meet together at a press conference for the purpose of making a startling announcement: Mystery writers were going to lend their brains, plotting skill and deductive ability to the police to help them solve crimes!! The press conference was held, the Police Commissioner made remarks thanking MWA for the help, MWA officers made general statements about crime, and the impression left hanging in the air was that mystery writers would soon be meeting with police officials on a regular basis to help them with their problems.

Whose idea was this? It was purportedly spawned by a movie star whose mystery film was at that moment opening in New York theaters. The movie star, however, did not appear in person to promote his great new weapon in the war on crime. He did not want, so his press agent explained, his own presence to intrude upon the merit of the idea.

It did not take great detective ability on the part of the mystery writers present to deduce that this had all been concocted by the press agent to promote the movie. It can be assumed that the same conclusion was reached by the Police Commissioner. It was certainly reached by the attending members of the press who asked pointed questions as to who had rented the suite and made the arrangements — answers to which no one seemed to know.

There is no denying that the idea was at least novel. To the public at large, it might even seem like a not-implausible suggestion — if the police could be made to hold still for it. Has not the public been conditioned by stories headlining every uncovered instance of police corruption, scandal, brutality, and false arrest? Then there was the vicious "Police are pigs" campaign by the rioters of the sixties. Nor let us forget the story lines of the old B movies, to wit: "All cops are dumb; only Boston Blackie, Bulldog Drummond, the Saint, the Falcon, and Philo Vance can solve crimes." Add to that the soaring crime rate, and it would not be surprising if the conclusion were reached that the police needed help.

What about mystery writers as Galahads to the rescue? Would this not be a natural? Mystery writers are the inventors of those great detectives whose genius is to the police mentality what the elephant is to the flea, whose intellectual prowess unsnarls the most tangled web and unearths the darkest secret. And are not these writers even smarter than the detectives they create? They not only solve the detectives' puzzles, they design them as well, a feat even more ingenious. Surely, mystery writers are among the cleverest of people. They must be far smarter than the average criminal—who has already proven himself more than a match for the police. If we want to improve crime-solving, would this not be a good route to take?

That, I am afraid, is as far as I can make myself pursue this flimflam. I was a participant in the aforementioned press conference as one of the invited mystery writers. I had also spent a lot of time with the New York Police Department, riding with the Homicide Squad, Manhattan North, and meeting the squad detectives of Harlem. I, therefore, well knew the other side of the coin and I had to wonder, as we went through the farce that had been foisted upon us, "Why does the Commissioner put up with all this nonsense?" His presence gave an import to the proceedings that they did not warrant, yet he remained pleasant, gracious, and sincere. Part of it might, of course, be argued as public relations: Once there, he could hardly walk out in a fit of temper. However, I suspect that another motive was the operative factor, a tactic that professional policemen develop which would be illustrated by the following.

After I had been with the Homicide Squad long enough to establish rapport with its members, one detective took the trouble to tell me in great detail about an unsolved case he had. It went like this:

A group of models came to New York for a fashion show and were bunked in a clutch of rooms in a hotel. Two girls in one of the rooms heard sounds of a struggle and muted cries from the room adjoining. They went to see if the girl was in trouble. As they knocked on her door, it was opened by a gray-haired man who was breathless and somewhat distraught. He said, "Excuse me, ladies," stepped past them, and went to the elevator. The women went inside and found their fellow-model strangled, her arms and legs taped.

Things went well for the police at first. Investigation showed that the tape could only have been purchased at a certain drugstore in Miami. A description of the gray-haired man fitted an executive in the Organization. More than that, he had just returned from Miami. One of the models, being given a look at this man, definitely indentified him as the one leaving the hotel room. The other model wasn't sure.

It looked like an open-and-shut case and the police were about to move in when another piece of evidence showed up. It was a dinner check from a Miami restaurant that the suspect had signed and which bore not only the date, but a time stamp. And the hour stamped was such that it would have been impossible for the suspect to have caught a plane to New York in time to kill the model at the moment she had been killed.

The only suspect in the case had been cleared; the police had never found anyone else to connect with the crime, and the case lay open on the books, a total mystery.

The detective who told me this story did not do so to give me material for a book. He did not tell it to me because I might mention his name. Nor, certainly, did he tell it because he thought a mystery writer would be more likely than a police detective to fit all the puzzle pieces together in their proper place.

He was telling it to me, instead, because its solution had defied the best thinking of everyone enlisted in its cause. There was no place to go, except to present the evidence to everyone new who came along on the off-chance that somebody, sometime, might come up with an idea, an angle, an answer that hadn't been thought of before. There wasn't any real expectation of this, of course. The attitude wasn't one of hope but, rather, "What is there to lose?"

Which is why, I think, Commissioner Murphy held still for that foolish press conference.

Though I pondered the matter of the murdered model, I did not come up with worthwhile new contributions. I was struck, however, by the difference in approach between the novice (myself) and the pro (the detective). Given that story, my and most people's reaction would be a great reluctance to let go of the gray-haired suspect who fitted the requirements of murderer so perfectly, except for that one pesky restaurant bill. Isn't there some way to get around that tiny, but devastating, stumbling block?

And it is at that precise point that the mystery writer and the professional detective part company. The mystery writer's mind starts clicking in high gear along the lines of how the time stamp could be discredited: error, deception, anything — and then we have our murderer! The mystery writer focuses on how this could be managed — wherein lies the key to his next book. His fictional detective will retire to quarters for three days and emerge with the explanation of how the time stamp alibi had been faked. "Take the gray-haired man away, Inspector."

The real detective operates from a different philosophy. Falsified time stamps which are to serve (if restaurant slips just happen to be checked) as an alibi for a murder fifteen hundred miles away are the stuff of which dreams are made. It's a million-to-one shot and if real detectives expended their energies pursuing such odds, what-ho the crime rate!

Real detectives are too pragmatic to be tempted by such lines of endeavor. The moment that restaurant chit was uncovered, the police kissed off their suspect. How could they combat that piece of evidence in court, even if they wanted to?

What is impressive is that their kiss-off is total. Though I, an outsider, was reluctant to let go of the only suspect, the detective, stuck with an unsolved case, could dismiss him completely. "Think," he said, "how lucky he (the gray-haired man) was that we found that slip. Otherwise he might have been arrested, and even if he were later exonerated, his career could have been ruined." That restaurant check not only convinced the detective that the only suspect was innocent, it concerned him that such a fragile shield separated him from disaster.

We have been discussing, thus far, two traits of real detectives: 1. They will invite ideas and listen to anything, no matter how fanciful; 2. They will dismiss, without a backward glance, their best or only suspect once evidence is found that clears him.

How else do real detectives differ from those of fiction? The ways are many, so let us limit ourselves to a few of the more obvious.

The first and foremost, the most striking distinction between real and make-believe detectives is one that Commissioner Murphy strongly stressed in an article about TV's depiction of policemen and what is wrong with the picture. He pointed out something all policemen do as a matter of course that is completely outside the orientation of the actors, directors, and writers of TV shows, movies, and novels. What real detectives do as the Commissioner put it, is "eyeball" everything.

If one has not been in close association with detectives, it is hard to grasp what this means. It is not as simple as Sherlock Holmes's admonition to Watson, "You see but you do not observe." This was, you will recall, in reference to the good doctor's inability to quote the number of stairs to their lodgings, though he had climbed them a thousand times. Dr. Watson had not noticed the most elementary aspects of his environment, which is true of most of us.

The "eyeballing" problem would not be solved, however, by actors keeping their eyes roving, or by writers having their detectives make periodic comments about their surroundings. The habits that have become ingrained in competent, experienced detectives are lessons in observation that Sherlock Holmes would be hard-pressed to match. A few personal experiences are worth reporting to give a picture:

You get into the back of an unmarked police car. A detective is on either side, another is behind the wheel, and the sergeant is riding beside the driver. It's a friendly, relaxed group, going to get a sandwich perhaps, or to the two-five squad to pick up some files or, in the early days, just to show the visitor around the stamping ground. There is general conversation, there is kidding. It could be any car full of people going someplace with no sense of urgency. Except that, if the visitor in the back seat is paying attention, he will note something unusual about the other occupants in this particular car. Unlike ordinary people, they do not look at each other when they talk. Each is, instead, looking out his window, studying the street. And they don't just look at *things*, they look at *certain* things. And they all see the same things — which are not, generally, the things the rest of us will see if we look out our car windows (which we usually don't).

A couple of illustrations are in order. This first one took place during my early outings with the Homicide Squad, when I was still looking inside the car instead of out. We pulled up in front of a fireplug on Seventy-second Street one evening so that one of the detectives, who hadn't had any supper, could grab a sandwich.

There was general conversation and then, out of the blue, one detective said, "He doesn't know who we are." Another added, "He doesn't know whether to come over or not."

I said, "What? Where?"

"That apprentice cop across the street."

I finally managed to make out the dim, gray-shirted figure on the far side of the heavily traveled thoroughfare. The detectives, however, had instantly spotted him, dutifully tagging cars, and they had detected his uncertainty as to what he should do about the strange black sedan that had stopped in front of the hydrant across the street. He chose to ignore us, but the incident produced dry remarks from the detectives on the inability of foot patrolmen to identify the department's unmarked cars. "Any four-year-old kid in Harlem," one detective said, " — when you turn the corner, it's 'Police car! Police car!' Then you park for a minute and some cop puts a ticket on it."

Then there was a later time, when I was trying to be adept at looking out windows and "eyeballing" everything. I was riding with two detectives up a deserted Madison Avenue late at night and, peer as I might, there was nothing to see. We halted at a stoplight and as I looked around at the nothing, one detective said, "They're sure going at it hot and heavy." And the other said, "Necking up a storm." I said, "Who? Where?" and they replied, "That parked car across the street."

Sure enough, there was a standing car at the other curb. I had seen and ignored it, assuming it to be empty. Now, discovering it to be otherwise, I still couldn't make out what, if anything, was going on inside. But they had. Both of them. They were conversing freely in a language I hadn't even begun to learn.

This is the real difference between the detectives writers create and the police as they actually are. Because a writer has not had a policeman's training and conditioning, the police of his creation do not think, feel, and respond as an actual policeman does. The police of his creation are not tuned in on the wavelength of the actual policeman. They do not speak the language. For the most part, they do not even know the language exists. Thus, while the ersatz policeman of the fiction writer may gain the allegiance of his audience, swallowed if not totally digested, he will not claim the attention of real policemen—who are purported to be notorious nonreaders of mystery stories.

There is an obverse side to the coin. If civilians have trouble making like policemen, the police have equal difficulty making like civilians, which it is sometimes their need to do. One detective summed it up, commenting on the difficulty of infiltrating an area to get information: "You dress up in a white uniform and pedal an ice-cream cart up the street and six blocks ahead of you the word is out, 'Cop coming! Cop coming!' "

I've seen professional detectives mystified by these "makes." They don't know what they're doing wrong, the same way the writers don't know what they're doing wrong, and the fly in the ointment is conditioning. The detective is conditioned one way and the civilian another. The detective looks out of car windows instead of at the person he's talking to. The detective can't help "eyeballing" everything as he pedals his ice-cream cart, and the savvy, streetwise civilians know ice-cream vendors don't do it that way.

What else do detectives do that the average citizen doesn't? What else sets them apart from the rest of us — including the writers who try to depict them?

Fictional detectives on TV and in novels, even when the utmost realism is being sought, treat the public with a certain deferential consideration, a "Sorry to bother you, ma'am, but would you mind answering a few questions?" attitude. This may be done less in ignorance than in an effort to make policmen sympathetic, to show them as friendly, next-door neighbor types, good to their mothers and kind to animals.

Real policemen may be as good to their mothers and kind to animals as anybody else. At home they may even be friendly, next-door neighbor types. On the job, however, they have a totally different orientation and their behavior is going to follow a markedly different pattern.

Consider a homicide in New York City. The squad detective whose turn it is, "catches" it. Likewise, the homicide detective whose turn it is, shares the responsibility with him and the two work on it together. Of course, where necessary, many other detectives will be engaged in the matter as well, but those two are the ones whose case it is. Needless to say, the goal of all these detectives is the swift apprehension and conviction of the perpetrator. To this end, everything else is secondary.

Thus, if a murder victim is found in an apartment in the middle of the night, or a body is lying at the bottom of a stairwell, the investigating detectives are not going to tap on neighboring doors with a "Sorry to bother you" air, or wait until morning so as not to disturb the slumbers of the other residents. It's "All right, everybody out!" and they go around banging on apartment doors in turn saying, "Open up. Police!"

There's also a preparatory action taken — at least in New York — which writers should note. Before the detectives bang on any doors, they fasten their gold detective's shields (real gold, as I recall) to their shirt pockets in plain sight to assure frightened apartment dwellers, peering through their peepholes, that they are who they say they are. It is an unwise Gothamite who unlocks his door and lets in whatever fate lies outside just because that fate calls, in authoritative tones, "Open up. Police!" That shield is a necessary assurance that all the noise and commotion are legitimate.

Nor will the detectives, once the neighbors have opened their doors, pussyfoot around with gentle requests for assistance. For one thing, it's bad psychology to invite the *questionee* to gain control over the *questioner*. For another, the detectives cannot waste time on amenities or expend effort fencing. They have quarry to catch and seconds count. Also, who knows but that one of the neighbors has guilty knowledge?

The above arguments are purely academic, however. Pussyfooting, by its nature, can't happen. Detectives, by dint of training, discipline, and experience, are figures of authority. They have been conditioned to move forward where others hold back. They head toward trouble rather than away. They are the ones who have been there before and know what to do. Add to that the "big stick" they all carry in the form of their shield and their gun and it is axiomatic that when the detective appears on the scene, he will take charge and civilians, like it or not, will instinctively defer to him.

Therefore, when a detective fastens his shield to his shirt, knocks on a door, and says "Open up. Police!" he expects to be obeyed, and the expectation will show in the sound of his knock and the tone of his voice. On the other side of the door, the citizen expects to obey. To disobey is to invite suspicion, which is to invite scrutiny, which is worse than obeying. Most people, even those with nothing to hide, like to remain as anonymous as possible vis-à-vis authority.

These are some of the psychological factors at work when detectives investigate a crime and they speed the investigative process by inhibiting needless impediments. Writers of fiction, intent on the detectives' public image, would produce more realistic figures if they realized that the detectives' motivation is capturing the culprit, not winning popularity contests. This does not mean detectives are deliberately rude or hostile (not if they're smart) for then they are creating their own obstructions. A proper understanding of a detective's psychology involves an understanding of his goals.

This brings us next to the matter of interviews and interrogations. There is a difference between the terms. Interrogation is what a detective does to a suspect, trying to elicit information that will damn him. Interview is what he does with a nonsuspect, to elicit information that will damn someone else.

There may be a difference in the terms but, in my experience, there is very little difference in technique. This is because a detective has become so skilled in asking questions, his techniques for compelling true answers and exposing the false are so honed, his methods so ingrained, that he does not differentiate. He knows only one way to ask questions. Therefore, even the most insignificant figure in a case, questioned about the most insignificant item, is going to suffer the full power of the detective's interrogatory technique.

Consider the following: A Harlem woman hasn't been seen by her neighbors for several days. They appeal to the building superintendent, an elderly black man who can't enter her one-room apartment because of the locks on her door. He therefore gains access through the lone window, this being at some personal risk since he must climb over balconies four floors up. Inside, he finds the woman in her nightgown, face down on the floor, dead. Her face is smeared from a bloody nose but, since nothing's been touched, a plausible explanation is that she suffered a heart attack while preparing for bed and pitched forward, dead. In any event, no suspicion was being directed against this thin, elderly superintendent who found her body. Yet it was an education to hear one of the homicide detectives question him on the stairs outside the apartment.

In books and movies, detectives query people in a neat, logical sequence, each question suggesting the succeeding question. This is a rational, scientific approach which would bespeak a rational, scientific detective. It has the added advantage of enabling the reader or viewer to follow the detective's train of thought and sense his goals. At the same time, however, it also enables the interviewee to follow the detective's train of thought and sense his goals, thus enlarging the interviewee's opportunity to misdirect the detective, which is hardly the course the detective wants to chart.

The questioning of the super on the stairs was not like that at all. Every question the detective asked came from a different angle and related to a different subject, thus forcing the super to undergo a continuous change of orientation. The pattern was patternless and questions jumped erratically: "How long has the woman lived in that room?" "Where do you live?" "What's the name of the people next door to her?" "Do you know any of her friends?" "Who told you you ought to climb in her window?" "How long have you been working here?"

A guilty person, or one trying to propagate a lie, would be under the constant demand to rethink his lie in terms of each new question so that he didn't trip himself up. And this is going to take time — more time than it will take a person telling the truth — which tells the detective who's lying about what.

Even a person telling the truth has to hesitate and think. And the fact he has to hesitate makes him feel he's showing guilt, even though the detective knows better. In this instance, the poor superintendent, innocent of any wrongdoing and trying desperately to answer the detective's questions honestly, nevertheless felt himself sounding guiltier and guiltier. He began to falter so badly that the detective, who couldn't ask questions any other way, had to put a steadying hand on the old man's arm and say, "It's all right, Pop. Don't get upset."

This is, of course, not the only questioning technique by which detectives gain information and spot liars. There are others. The hardened criminal, however, persists in his lies no matter how contradictory he may sound. He knows, barring other evidence, if he does not admit anything, he will go free, for the detective's conclusions on a man's integrity are not admissible in court. Nevertheless, such information is useful for the detectives to have in the general war against crime.

The preceding may indicate some of the inherent ridiculousness in that press agent's dream of having mystery writers help the police. There is more.

For one thing, police detectives are not as dumb as the tastemakers and media manipulators make them out to be. The police force in New York, for instance, numbers some 26,000 members, of whom 2,600, or 10 percent, carry the gold shield of detective rather than the white metal (silver colored) shields (they aren't called badges in New York) of the uniformed force. This 10 percent represents the cream of a crop of a 26,000 man organization which does, after all, have minimum standards of acceptance, so you're going to find a lot of first-class brains at work.

Add to that the kind of training these detectives had been subject to, the years of experience under their belts (the youngest member of the Homicide Squad was thirty-six years old), and throw in on top of that one overwhelming advantage they enjoy—they know their environment. With all that going for them, can anyone seriously believe some green-horn, even if he boasts an IQ of 200, can come in and give them lessons? I was, myself, what the press agent was proposing: a mystery writer working with the detectives. The only difference was, I wasn't helping them, they were helping me. This was because they knew what they were doing and I did not. Nor would any outsider venturing into any unknown field.

Some excerpts from my own indoctrination might best illustrate the matter. My first night with the Homicide Squad, since nothing was pressing (members of the Homicide Squad sit around waiting for murders to happen; no murders, no work), they took me for a ride around their bailiwick, the north half of Manhattan. It was 11:00 P.M. and as we cruised, the sergeant, riding beside the driver, indicated the flitting, ghost-like figures on the streets. "You see those people?" the sergeant said. "They're all junkies. Every one is a junkie."

I thought to myself, "Interesting, if true, but I suspect the sergeant is laying it on a little thick. Quite probably a few of those people actually are junkies, but my guess is that most are ordinary citizens going about their business."

That was the mind of a tyro at work evaluating a strange, new neighborhood in terms of the neighborhoods he had known. Needless to say, I wasn't with the Homicide Squad long before I came to know the sergeant hadn't been exaggerating one iota. Every person on the streets at that hour was a junkie. Harlem evenings were not ateem with returning movie-goers, dog-walkers, gabbing neighbors, or romantic couples. No one but junkies dared venture after dark from their barricaded apartments. But this was something I had to learn.

Another thing I learned was that the production of children in Harlem was not necessarily accompanied by a marriage license. Childbirth out of wedlock may be a commonplace today, but a decade ago it was reasonably expected that where there was a child, there was a husband.

Not so in Harlem, and I quickly noted that when we went to the scene of a child death (usually a crib death, not an infanticide) the detective, in interviewing the young mother, never asked about her husband. He would, instead, say, "When did you last see the father?" or "Where's the father?" and the girl would answer, "Yesterday," or "Last week," or "He's in jail," or some such.

Then there was the case of the abortive holdup. At least one person was killed but the object of the holdup, a young, flashy, swarthy, fast-talking type, was unharmed. When questioned, he knew nothing about anything. People had tried to hold him up, he didn't know them, he didn't know why.

A visiting mystery writer might guess the dark-haired, glib near-victim knew more than he would reveal, but what the more might be was the stuff of which mystery novels were made.

"Where do you live?" the young man was asked, and it turned out he was from New Jersey, quite a distance from upper Manhattan.

What was he doing here?

He said he had friends in the area and thought he'd drop over.

The mystery writer would smell a rat in that one too, but he would need further clues before he could deduce what was really going on.

Not so the detectives. "How much money are you carrying?" was the unexpected (by the mystery writer) next question they asked him.

The man started to dismiss the amount as trivial but changed his mind. He told the police he wouldn't try to kid them, he had $1,500 on him, and produced his loaded wallet to prove it.

Why on earth, the writer wondered, would the man gratuitously reveal this information? And why, for that matter was he carrying such a large amount?

The writer comes to realize, with more experience in the environment, what the detectives knew from the first. The man had arrived in town to make a buy (heroin) — thus the question about the money he carried — and some junkie or double-crosser was laying for him.

As for the interview between the sharp young man and the detectives, it was a charade. The detectives knew his story was a lie, and they knew what the real story was. And he knew that they knew—which was why he didn't bother lying about the money he was carrying. All of them also knew he would not reveal who had nearly killed him, that there was no evidence against him, and that he would be turned loose. There was nothing to do but play out the game. The ritual of the questioning was conducted and the young man was released.

The young man will, of course, be fully aware that he narrowly escaped with his life that night and that certain protective measures should be taken in the future. No matter how fearful he may be, however, he would never turn to the police for help. Nor will he stop coming to Manhattan to make further buys. As one detective said, "You can never wipe out the drug traffic. There's too much money involved."

The sum and substance of all this is that it's the mystery writer who learns from the police, not the police from the mystery writer. In fact, it is disconcerting to discover that the brilliant deduction with which the mystery writer plans to have his genius detective solve the crime turns out, in real life, to be about the first thing a good detective thinks of. In fact, it is a challenge to create a fictional crime that will keep real detectives guessing for long. In my own case, I gave the homicide detectives the clues of the plot I was concocting to see how they would handle them and it was eerie the way they, without knowing it, were homing in on my villain. I had to keep inventing additional complications for, as I said to them, "I want this case to take a week and you'd crack it in twenty-four hours."

Part of the real detective's skill at crime solution comes from the fact that he takes nothing for granted. Consider the case of a man whose body was found hanging above the bathtub. It looked like murder by his worst enemy. The homicide detective, however, collected the water in the tub's drain trap for analysis and, lo and behold, it was ice water, not tap water (there's a difference). The victim had committed suicide using a block of ice, in the expectation that his enemy would be charged with his murder.

That's a prime example of not taking anything for granted, but there are lesser ones. A detective's report never uses the word "gold" in describing jewelry, rings, etc. It uses "yellow metal" instead. "Gold" means the 14-karat stuff and a detective could be in trouble if he described a stolen brooch as "gold" and the recovered brooch turned out to be brass. And if it is your intention, as a writer, to complicate your plot by having the scheming widow omit a couple of items when she lists the jewelry that was stolen, forget it. The detectives will dutifully record the baubles she finds are missing, but they will then match that list against the insurance-company records and if there's a discrepancy, they'll be back, knocking on the widow's door to find out why.

Nor do real detectives go out of their way looking for work. If a bloody body is found in a stairwell, the Homicide Squad will start investigating "just in case," but it's not accepted that the body is a murder victim unless or until the Medical Examiner's Office says it is. People do, after all, drop dead of heart attacks at the top of stairs and end up bloodied and battered at the bottom. Detectives, like other people, don't make their life any harder than necessary, and nothing is much harder than hunting for murderers when no murder has been committed.

One final significant difference between real detectives and the TV, movie, and novel variety. This is the matter of empathy and concern. Fictional detectives are very often portrayed as caring and sympathetic, as getting personally involved with each new case. This may be how the writers feel, or it may be an effort to make their detective heroes appealing.

In real life, however, this degree of emotional involvement could not possibly be maintained. The human system cannot stand it. The number of cases a homicide detective works on in the course of a year, the number of dead bodies he looks at—in all stages of mutilation and/ or decay—requires that he grow a protective shell around his feelings. Constant pounding on a sensitive spot develops a callous and no detective will respond to the hundredth corpse the way he responded to his first, in the same way that no doctor will respond to his hundredth appendectomy as he did to his first, nor the social worker to the hundredth tale of woe as to the first. They may recognize that the hundredth is as important as the first and treat it that way, but the emotional response won't be the same. Detectives, exposed to more of the vagaries of the human condition than the rest of us, become inured to more. They become shockproof. They have witnessed what the rest of us cannot even dream of. I felt the need to acknowledge this in one of my books by saying, "Homicide detectives see, firsthand, such aberrations of human nature as psychiatrists only read about."

One is not to deduce from this that detectives don't ever care. They have to keep their personal involvement at a minimum if they are to survive, but sometimes their deep-hidden concerns do break through. I am reminded of the case of a little nine-year-old Harlem girl whose assaulted and mutilated body had been found in an abandoned refrigerator in a vacant lot. The police knew who had committed the crime. They even knew where the man was—in Puerto Rico. For that or some other reason, they could not touch him. The case, open and unsolved because no arrest had been made, was three to four years old. But the detective telling me about it suddenly went to the file, pulled from it the picture of the perpetrator, and pinned it to the bulletin board. His action was speaking for them all and it was saying, "Let us not forget this man! If we cannot ever get him for what he did to that little girl, perhaps we can get him *hard* for something else."

This article has obviously been written by one who has not only had close contact with the police but has been much impressed by the police. The article sounds, in fact, like a panegyric, and readers with a less charitable view of our law enforcement agents may tend to dismiss it with the conclusion that the author has: 1. Been brainwashed; 2. Been bought; or 3. Been sold.

It is only proper, therefore, to show the dark side of the glass. One member of the Homicide Squad, a fascinating raconteur of entertaining tidbits, was summarily suspended from duty pending a hearing. I did not ask what the charges were, nor did anyone volunteer the information, but the matter must have been serious indeed.

Another detective was kicked downstairs — shunted to a detective squad in the far hinterlands. Hints were given me as to the cause, but they remain only hearsay.

I report these facts by way of indicating that homicide detectives aren't supermen or angels. They have the same foibles and failings in the same proportion as the rest of mankind.

Perhaps this is the biggest difference of all between the detectives of fiction and those in real life. The real detectives are very fallible and very human.

12

FEMALE PRIVATE EYES

The one innovation in the detective story since the advent of the Police Procedural is the rise of the female private detective. These are stories about women detectives written by women, and we don't mean Agatha Christie's Miss Jane Marple. Nor do we mean the female detectives referred to by Dorothy Sayers in her Introduction to *The Omnibus of Crime*, of whom she says:

> In order to justify their choice of sex, they are obliged to be so irritatingly intuitive as to destroy that quiet enjoyment of the logical which we look for in our detective reading. Or else they are active and courageous, and insist on walking into physical danger and hampering the men engaged on the job. Marriage, also, looms too large in their view of life; which is not surprising, for they are all young and beautiful. Why these charming creatures should be able to tackle abstruse problems at the age of twenty-one or thereabouts, while the male detectives are usually content to wait till their thirties or forties before setting up as experts, it is hard to say. Where do they pick up their worldly knowledge? Not from personal experience for they are always immaculate as the driven snow.

No, these are female detectives of a different breed, feminists in their own right, created by feminist writers who in the climate of equal rights for women and the thesis that women can do anything men can do, are out to demonstrate it. This new kind of female couldn't have been thought of before Women's Lib brought the plight of women and the difficulties women face in a male-dominated world to public attention.

But once the situation was brought into the realm of public consciousness, it was only a matter of time before the newly emancipated female not only invaded board rooms, men's clubs, male colleges, and the priesthood, but the private detective agencies of fiction.

Recognizing the Differences

What we have here, fortunately, is not Super-Woman, matching the more bizarre Supermen private eyes of the past—heroes who killed off a quart of Scotch for breakfast and made it to the office without falling in the gutter; got knocked unconscious at least twice a week with nary a headache, let alone a concussion; and bedded down bevies of beautiful blondes—all of whom unanimously found them irresistible—without the slightest qualm about the ability to perform.

These female private eyes are more in the Philip Marlowe-Lew Archer tradition, detectives who are reasonably human.

Granted that these female private investigators emulate the male of the species in their detective ability, they, nevertheless, can't be dealt with and treated in the same manner as their male counterparts. For one thing, they are women, and for another, they are written by women.

Since these detectives are women, and they are being drawn realistically and believably, they cannot enjoy the physical strength and athletic prowess of the hard-boiled male. They can, through quickness, agility, and good physical condition, gain a temporary edge over ordinary males, but their authors don't pretend they can beat up armed assassins.

There are other concessions made to the fact these are women. After a hard day's labors, feeling the need of a drink, they don't pull out a bottle of bourbon from the bottom drawer of the office desk, they come home and pour themselves a glass of white wine.

Sex

Then there is the matter of sex. The male private eyes in the male-authored novels are not averse to casual sex and the women in such novels (with the exception, perhaps, of Iva Archer) do not try to make more out of the relationship than the detective does. That, of course, is the male ideal—sex without entanglement—and these novels are written for men by men who, knowingly, make the ideal come true.

The feminist writers, wanting their female private eyes to be on a par with their male counterparts, must match them in this area too. They can't make their detectives virgins, especially not in this day and age. Virginity in a worldly wise, experienced, knowledgeable female detective would smack too much of what Dorothy Sayers was complaining about. Besides, who would believe it? The reader would wonder what was the matter with her.

So the female detective must likewise be experienced in boudoir antics. And, like the male detectives, along with the hotpants blondes who are always chasing them, the female private eye must not take her romantic dalliances seriously. It would greatly handicap her effectiveness as a detective were she to start yearning for the man she'd just spent the night with and worry about when or if he'd phone. In real life, sexual encounters almost invariably affect the female more lastingly than the male, but this poses only a minor problem. We make the female detective an exception. We portray her as enjoying sex, as does the male, but it no more interferes with her pursuit of the murderer than it does his.

There is, however, a more serious problem with sex that the creator of female detectives faces that the creator of the male is spared. That is the double-standard which, despite Women's Lib, is still with us. That is the old adage that the boys who sleep around are only "boys will be boys," while the girls who do it are "sluts." The creator of the female detective must, therefore, walk a narrow line. Her detective can't be a virgin nor a prude, but she can't jump into any bed at the crook of a finger either.

She is therefore generally shown dallying with a couple of men in a book—good friends, of course, with whom she has a close working relationship. It can't be *many men*, but it must be more than *one*—so the reader doesn't get the idea she's a one-man woman, which would be a crippling handicap.

To establish the female detective as a free spirit and not a "slut," the custom is to have her a divorcée. Thus, having been introduced to the pleasures of sex in proper circumstances—or at least having once made it legal—she is now entitled to carry on as she chooses without condemnation.

All this does the job very well, but it is obvious that the creator of the female private eye has to deal with problems her male counterpart is spared.

Interestingly enough, at least one female private eye, remarking on past sexual encounters, admits to an affair with a married man. (Loretta Lawson in Joan Smith's *Masculine Ending*, Scribner's, 1988.) That, frankly, is a little eye-brow raising. Outside of Sam Spade (with Iva Archer again) I don't know of any other male detective hero who dallies with married women. But Sam isn't really put forth to the reader as a "hero type," the kind you'd set up as an example for your children to emulate.

Details from Life

There are other interesting differences between the male and the feminist writers of private eye stories. These, however, are not so much differences between the way the private eyes go about their business, as they are the differences between men and women themselves; their view of life and what in life is important to them.

There are those who would insist that the differences (nonphysical) between males and females are solely cultural, and they're entitled to propound that thesis. As far as my interpretation of human behavior is concerned, the differences are essentially hereditary and these differences are ineradicably ingrained in the genes.

What is striking, when one compares a female private eye novel, written by a woman, with a male ditto, witten by a male, is just these differences. The woman writer's first-person heroine goes into a great deal of detail about her daily life, for example, whereas the male hero does not. The heroine does her laundry, takes baths, decides what dress to wear, what it's made of and how well the color may become her. And she may even say, as Kinsey Millhone does in *A is for Alibi*, wondering how much a female acquaintance knew about the case and how much she was willing to share, "I also hoped to hell I could look that good in another ten years."

All of these extras are fine. In fact, the women writers do much better than the men at working in little bits of detail such as mentioned above, which enriches their stories.

But that's what differentiates them from the men. What the male detectives do about their laundry, whether they wash it themselves, send it out, or have one of their blonde bedmates do it is unknown. In fact, what they wear is, for the most part unknown. We hear about the bottle in the bottom drawer, what kind of gun is in the shoulder holster, and we know something about the layout of their office, but most of the other details of their ordinary life remain in limbo. (Robert B. Parker's Spenser is the exception that proves the rule here.)

And the reason is simple. By and large, male writers don't think to concern themselves with such things. With the female writer and her detective, the business of living: what to wear, what to eat, what to buy, how to keep the apartment neat, is much in her mind. Philip Marlowe had a pad somewhere, but we don't know where, and we don't know what it looked like, all of which gives the impression it wasn't much of a place to come home to, except to sleep. He did play out chess games there, and that was about it.

It's the difference between men and women again: what concerns them; how they think; and what they think about. A male author, for instance, wouldn't have his hero wonder what he'll look like ten years hence. It wouldn't occur to him.

Variation on Pace

Another difference between the male and female private eye stories is pace. This too is interesting. The female detective tale may let a couple of days go by between the heroine's interview with witness number one, and lunch with witness number two. There's a leisurely quality here, and much less sense of urgency. In the male novels, the hero is chasing down three witnesses in one day and staking out the suspect's house that night. Everything happens one-two-three. There's no laundry to be done, no meals to be described, no soaking in a hot tub while ruminating over the information acquired. It's all catch-as-catch-can, with the hope, sometime, of being able to get some sleep.

Writing True to Gender

These are exaggerations to be sure, but there are points to be made. For one thing, the female private eye is not being presented as a male private eye in drag. The feminist creators of these feminist detectives wisely recognize that there are differences between the sexes and that the female's response to circumstance cannot ever be quite the same as the man's.

Part of this is conscious skill — like making the heroine a divorcée so as to enable her to have sex without any more impropriety (by today's standards) than for the hero.

Most of it, however, is subconscious, the result of that difference between men and women; the difference in the way they view themselves in relation to others, the way they view the world, the way they approach the world, and, certainly, how these factors affect the way they tell a story.

A male, trying to write a first person female private eye story, couldn't do it — at least couldn't do it (even using a female nom de plume) in a way that wouldn't reveal to the discerning reader that it was written by a man. In the same way, though women mystery writers have used masculine pen names (mainly back in the days when manuscripts by women were rejected because the writers *were* women — not bias, really, merely the conviction of publishers of the period that books by women didn't sell) any perceptive reader could tell — and can tell — the sex of the author from the way the book is written — its slant, point of view, everything. (As a case in point, note the male storyteller in Charlotte Armstrong's *The Black-Eyed Stranger* [Coward McCann, 1951]. He thinks like a woman.)

Christopher Morley undertook the acid test in *Kitty Foyle*, and he did as good a job as a male could be expected to do. (The mother of a friend even complained to me, "No man has a right to know that much about women.") But Kitty was a masculine type girl. She was the jacket and skirt type female. There was nothing lacy and frilly, buttons-and-bows and perfumy about Kitty Foyle. Her mind was as male as could be.

In like manner, Peter O'Donnell wrote about a female private detective back in 1965 with his series about Modesty Blaise. As you can tell by her name, she was a male creation, geared to appeal to males. She was as casual in her sex encounters as the male, and as the female private eyes the women writers are writing about today, but there is a difference — slight, but one that marks the difference between male and female.

Males, for one thing, treat sexual encounters in a different way than females do. (My view is that it's due to the biological fact that females are saddled with the results and males aren't.) In any case, Modesty Blaise was created to titillate the male reader and the private detectives created by the female writers aren't. I would suggest that this is for three reasons:

1. The female writers are creating their female detectives for an entirely different purpose: to promote the idea of sexual equality.

2. The idea of writing to titillate the male is not only anathema, but totally contrary to their purpose, as stated above.

3. Women, since they don't view sex in the same way men do, wouldn't know how to write male-erotic prose. They know (read the ever popular, female-oriented, romance novels) how to stir the sexual emotions of the female. But the males don't respond to the same triggers and female writers aren't able to sense what buttons to push to arouse the male.

The Matter of "Offensive" Language

A word about four-letter words. These female detectives sprinkle their language with four-letter expletives. In fact, they and their male acquaintances trade them back and forth. These are words which, once, were not only unspeakable in polite society, but would not be allowed in print. Norman Mailer, in *The Naked and the Dead* (1946), used the word "fugging" in order to express the language of GIs in World War II, at the same time avoiding the unutterable.

And, later, when authors wanted to be more explicit than editors would allow, they used first letters and three dashes to indicate what four-letter word their characters were speaking.

Times have changed and there now exists no word in the English language which is not, today, acceptable in books and is used in most drawing rooms, even if it might shock the old dowager. Certainly, such words are no longer unfit for maidenly ears. The maidens swear like sailors themselves.

What is the purpose of bringing this up? Certainly not in criticism. After all, four-letter words are, today, scattered far more profusely through the books of male authors. So this is not a comparison, nor a complaint about the use of four-letter words in books today. Most people adjust to the tenor of the times. The purpose of these remarks is not four-letter words, but the tenor of the times. I think it was Christianna Brand who, at the Third International Congress of Crime Writers in Stockholm in 1981, stated not only that she couldn't use a four-letter word in one of her books, she couldn't bring herself to utter one.

Passé? Behind the times? Not with it? That is true, but there is an implication. Someone once remarked upon the interesting fact that in the whole of *Treasure Island*, a story of villainous pirates, rogues, cutthroats and murderers, not a single swear word is uttered. Yet the story suffers not. In fact, the lack isn't even noticed.

So the question arises: Today, anything goes. No expletive, no detail of sexual encounter, no atrocity by human upon human is too gruesome to escape a detailed recounting. Nothing is left to the imagination—if anything has been overlooked, it will be revealed tomorrow.

But the pendulum swings. Yesterday, prudery reigned. Today, everything hangs out. We live today, however, at the extreme end of one of those pendulum swings and tomorrow it will start back again, toward the prudery end of the spectrum. And what will happen to the literature of today?

To the degree that it offends, as the laces tighten and the taste of the populace grows away from the grotesque of today toward the purity of yesterday, the books of today will increasingly offend the taste of their new audience and will fall into disrepute.

This is by way of saying that, while the plentiful distribution of four-letter words throughout a manuscript may make the author appear to be "with it" today, it may make that same author "gone with it" tomorrow, his "shocking" language offensive to the new, more sensitive reader.

Meanwhile, on the other hand, the author who took a more universal view as to what would appeal and offend, would find himself with a broader audience. Write for the ages, offend no one with your style, and you bear the chance to remain popular no matter how the pendulum swings.

In Conclusion

This is not to suggest that the feisty female heroine will have but a short stay in the sun. No so. The feisty female has always had it over the fainting damsel in distress. Witness Rachel in *The Moonstone* versus the *Lily Maid of Astolot*.

And, certainly, in the history of literature, females have never been feistier than today, nor, today, feistier than in the mystery novels about female private eyes, written by females.

The prediction is only that the explicit language used by the authors of both sexes today will enjoy but a limited vogue. It's the language of today, not the characters of today, that will suffer eclipse tomorrow.

PART 2

THE MAKING OF THE MYSTERY

This article first appeared in The Mystery Story, *published by University Extension, University of California, San Diego, 1976.*

There is an awareness on the part of most readers that the mystery per se is something separate and distinct from the novel itself. This fact of fiction is acknowledged both by the devotees of the mystery form and by its detractors; the term "mystery" is applied to a specific type of novel to set it apart from the so-called "straight" or "serious" novel.

There is a difference, that is true, but the degree of difference depends upon how we define the term "mystery." Time was when "mystery story" meant "*detective* story"; then the tale was a puzzle and little else. More and more, however, the parameters of the genre have broadened and where they now lie is more a matter of personal viewpoint than of any objective line of demarcation. Nowadays suspense stories have come under the umbrella of mystery fiction so that Harper & Row even labels each book in its mystery line as "A Harper Novel of Suspense." Spy stories are called mysteries, chase and adventure yarns come under the heading. Gothics, those tales of romance and suspense, are a part of the field, and even some ghost stories can be included. Anything that involves crime or the threat of crime is eligible. So is anything that pits the forces of Good against Evil — and Evil can mean anything from Count Dracula to Hitler's minions.

This covers, we might note, a rather broad area. In fact, not much is left over for the field of straight fiction. Mystery writers induct into the fraternity not only the likes of Edgar Allan Poe, but also Dostoevsky (*Crime and Punishment*), Shakespeare (any tragedy with the possible exception of Lear), Victor Hugo (*Les Miserables*), and anyone else who has produced a work of fiction involving criminous activity.

Quite obviously, if we are going to use this

13

THE MYSTERY VERSUS THE NOVEL

broad type of criterion, then we will have to say that the only difference between mystery fiction and straight fiction is that the former involves criminal wrongdoing and the latter doesn't—a distinction too meaningless to acknowledge.

Yet there is a difference, and everyone knows it. Shakespeare wrote about crime, but he was not a mystery writer in the sense that Agatha Christie was a mystery writer. Inasmuch as the mystery novel, especially in America, has traditionally been regarded as second-class fiction and its top practitioners as less worthy of note than the most hapless of straight novelists, the insistence of mystery writers in embracing the literary giants of history as kissing kin may well be nothing more than an attempt to overcome an ill-begotten inferiority complex.

If we are to separate the mystery from the novel and recognize the similarities and the differences, we must more adequately define our terms. We must find the areas of distinction that identify one and not the other. We must construct a discriminatory sieve that will firmly hold the likes of Earl Derr Biggers' *Charlie Chan Carries On* in the mystery genre and turn loose such as Theodore Dreiser's *An American Tragedy*.

Is it a matter of length? Mysteries, in all their recognized forms, are pretty standard in this regard. Generally speaking, the range is from 185 to 225 pages, or 60,000 to 70,000 words. Gothics are longer and a reader expects closer to 300 pages or 110,000 words in that form. The moment a book gets into the 350-pages-and-up range, even if it deals with crime, it will be accepted by editors and public alike as "more than a mystery."

Length, though indicative, is not a valid measure; quite obviously length does not determine greatness and we must not pretend that extra pages are a hallmark of distinction. There are too many gems of classic fiction—*The Red Badge of Courage* for one—that deliver their message in beautiful brevity.

Another totem that is supposed to identify the mystery is that it is read for "entertainment." The mystery is supposed to be light reading, something that doesn't require serious involvement; a piece to be ingested for relaxation, for fun, for pleasure.

But what does this tell us? Are we to conclude that books of merit are literary spinach: "You won't like it, but it's good for you"? That argument won't wash. Shakespeare, Dickens, Austen, Hardy—the list is long—were, and are, enormously popular. Dull novels are bad novels and will not sell, but dull mysteries won't sell either. So it is not a matter of bad writing versus good writing, or fun reading versus dull reading, short books versus long books, or crime stories versus noncrime stories. The subgenre of the mystery is isolated from the rest of fiction by other criteria.

To make the distinction, we need to dig deeper and realize that the mystery has been growing and expanding, maturing, and almost leaving its old self behind. In fact, the more the mystery probes into character and issues and the makeup of the human animal — and it is doing this — the more it is departing from its original format and outgrowing its original aims. If the spy is no longer fighting the forces of evil to rescue the kidnapped scientist, but is, instead, coping with the cynicism of his trade and his own expendability, or learning to live with the realization that his life is a cipher, then we are leaving what used to be the mystery form and entering into the field of the straight novel. Even if the spy is rescuing the scientist while he's having his self-doubts, we are dealing with a different kind of book. The original essence of the mystery is becoming hidden beneath additional layers of what would be called "serious" writing. (How serious the writing actually is, of course, depends upon the talent and insight of the author.)

To lay bare the bones of the mystery itself, we should turn back in time to the point of greatest separation, to the period when the distinction between a mystery story and a novel was the most unmistakable. We must return to the era of the puzzle story, to the fantasyland of mystery — before Hammett and Chandler moved murder out of the prim neatness of the drawing room and into the blood and guts of the back alley, which more closely approximates where actual murders occur and what they are like. We must get away from the subsequent *rapprochement* toward "realism" that led the private eye and the gangsters *cum* nightclub, which gave way to the later world of the detective squad and the police procedural. We should return to the artificial world of Hercule Poirot and Philo Vance, of Charlie Chan and Ellery Queen, to the heyday of the intellectual detective when every murder was compound-complex and ratiocination was all.

We use for our model those long-ago stories and their never-never world because those tales, for all time, represent the essence of the mystery. They were tales from which everything had been distilled. Here lay, for all to view, the artifacts of the pure mystery, the articulated skeleton of the whole art form. Whatever has since happened to the mystery — and much has — is overlay. Flesh, nervous systems, muscles, blood, and clothing of various kinds have been added, but the true mystery today still has the same old skeleton deep down underneath. It's just a little harder to find and therein lies a tale — but there are several tales to be told about this particular skeleton.

In those bygone days of the classical detective story, when the skeleton first stirred itself in permanent form, the puzzle was the thing. The reader was presented with a crime, a handful of clues, a cast of suspects, and a detective against whom to match wits. The object of the game was to beat the detective to the solution. Quite obviously, under those conditions, the difference between reading a mystery story — "detective" story in that context — and a straight novel was equivalent to the difference between doing a newspaper crossword puzzle and reading the columnists. Yet, despite the obviousness of the difference, there is more kinship here — as we shall shortly discover — than meets the eye. It is this kinship that has enabled the mystery to develop to the point where it successfully challenges straight fiction on the best-seller lists and enjoys an everbroadening base of popularity. Let us examine these bones, then, and determine why this form of literature, the mystery story, is to the novel what the sonnet is to poetry.

Let it be recognized first that the skeleton that structures the classical puzzle story is nothing more nor less than a series of ironclad rules. These rules became essential in order to present the puzzle properly and also in the interests of fair play. The book, remember, was a battleground between author and reader — with the reader trying to outguess the detective and beat him to the criminal, and the author trying to waylay, bemuse, and trick the reader so the detective would get there first. Since the author was in control, his efforts to win had to be restricted to make sure that the reader had an equal chance.

The first and most obvious rule of Fair Play was the requirement that *every clue discovered by the detective had to be made available to the reader*. The author could try to discount it as a clue, misconstrue its meaning, or hide it amid a lot of inconsequential garbage — but he had to show it. It had to be there so that at the end of the book, when the detective revealed its true nature, the reader would be able to say, "You beat me that time," but he could not say, "You left out a piece of the puzzle."

Rule two: *Early introduction of the murderer*.

Obviously it would be unfair for the author to introduce a totally new character on page 214 and name him as the murderer on page 215. All suspects must be prominent throughout — known if not shown.

Rule three: *The crime must be significant*.

To elicit reader involvement, the problem in question had to be of sufficient seriousness for the reader to want to see it solved — to want to solve it himself. Since murder is the most serious crime of all, most mystery stories are murder mysteries. By choosing murder as the crime, the mystery writer automatically fulfills that requirement.

Rule four: *There must be detection*.

The crime in a detective story doesn't solve itself, nor does it go away. An effort must be made to solve the crime. In fact, the *raison d'etat* of these early detective stories is the solving of the crime.

Rule five: *The number of suspects must be known and the murderer must be among them.*

This is the fair play element again and the method generally adopted in obeying this injunction was the construction of an enclosed universe inhabited solely by victims, suspects, murderer, and detective. One of the commonest such universes was the mansion full of guests, cut off from the outside world by a storm or other expedient, thus ensuring that when the murder occurs, the killer must be among those present.

So far these requirements, while restrictive, do not seem onerous. But lastly there comes the rule that does draw the binding tight. Since the story is a puzzle and a contest of wits between author and reader, *the reader, as part of the game of fair play, has the right to expect that nothing will be included in the book that does not relate to or in some way bear upon the puzzle.*

This is, incontrovertibly, a logical request and one that cannot be denied. It is, however, a crushing liability to the author. It is demanded of him that there be nothing extraneous in his story. All scenes, all events, all effects (and this includes red herrings) are to relate to and bear upon the puzzle—the creation and solution of which is the story.

The author is not allowed to rhapsodize over Renaissance art or the poetry of Keats—if that be his fancy. He is not to go into irrelevant detail on the workings of the Palomar telescope or the Gatun locks. Relevant details, yes, but not irrelevant.

It is a brutal blow. The author of the highly disciplined detective story is tightly fenced, his limitations severe. Admittedly, to the writer who has the wit and the relish, the strictures offer challenge. First, he must learn how to work within these disciplines and, thereafter, when he has mastered that art, how to maximize whatever opportunities he is afforded. Finally, he must learn to make the disciplines work for *him*.

Nevertheless, the boundaries are narrow. The mystery writer does not have the freedom to digress into his philosophy of life while the action stands still. This does not mean philosophy is not permitted, nor does it mean that Renaissance art or Keats cannot be evaluated, nor that background cannot be given on 200-inch telescopes or canal locks. It only means that the writer must create plots and story lines of such nature that they will be furthered and developed through such discussion.

It is a harsh stricture. But all of the requirements of the detective story are harsh strictures. Certainly, the writer of a mystery novel is working under a much tighter rein than the straight novelist who can roam pretty much at will—or at least he thinks he can—over the whole landscape of his intellect.

These rules then, are the emblems which identify the mystery novel and set it apart from the rest of fiction. Times have changed, of course, and the mystery has changed with them. No longer is it deemed sufficient to present the puzzle in a vacuum. No longer are characters made of cardboard, distinguishable from each other only by name and by sex. No longer do they serve merely as tokens to be moved on the puzzle board. Background can, without betraying the nature of the genre, add spice and purpose to the tale. The stories can come out of their closed universe and take place in the real world. Schools of the mystery can develop: the hardboiled school, the private-eye school, the cute young couple, the blood and sex, and the police procedural. These things can happen. All kinds of flesh can be laid upon the bones.

Many variations of the theme can also be played: Whodunit? Howdunit? Howcatchem? Stories can be told backwards and sideways. Yet, through it all, the same distinguishing bones lie underneath, only slightly modified over the years—and then only in reponse to the changing view of the readership. If the disciplines are not as rigidly restrictive as they used to be, it's because the reader is no longer being approached as nothing more than a puzzle-solver. Today's aficionado is more interested in being entertained than puzzled—perhaps he always was—and a little relaxation of the codes is permitted to serve the aim of entertainment. But the codes are still in force and a mystery novelist who sits down to plot a book today automatically obeys the rules.

One might now ask, since it is time to direct our attention to the straight novel, is there any advantage to the above rules? Let the mystery writer learn his craft; let him become facile in plot manipulation, clue planting, and the rest. Does this serve him any useful purpose above and beyond his own specific subgenre in the field of fiction? If one aims to write novels, is the mystery in any way a training ground?

An obvious advantage in writing mysteries lies in the disciplining of a talent. The greatest genius in any field, from athlete to concert pianist, will, to the degree that he develops and trains his talent, be greater than before. The demands that are made upon a mystery writer, if he is to flex his muscles within that framework, will hone his talent.

A counter reply can also arise. If the field of the mystery is so firmly structured, does one need talent to become competent? Is there not a difference between craftsmanship and talent? And would not craftsmanship be a sufficient commodity with which to work successfully in this medium? On the other hand, does not talent rise above the rules? Would not a great talent be thwarted and stifled trying to cope with such narrow limits?

Let us return to and amplify the earlier statement that the mystery is to the novel what the sonnet is to poetry. The sonnet is a stylized form of poem which makes rigid meter, length, and rhyme scheme demands upon its practitioners. In like manner, the mystery is a stylized form of fiction which makes rigid storytelling demands upon *its* practitioners. To this extent they share the same bed. Does the relationship go further?

The sonnet is a discipline. Those who would meet its demands must shape, manipulate, and refine their message so that it fits into fourteen iambic pentameter lines, totaling exactly 140 syllables, no more, no less. That is no mean task. Add to these limitations the further requirements of rhyme scheme, and the sonnet becomes a honing strop of awesome proportions. Any poet who masters the sonnet form takes with him into the broader field of poetry sharp skills indeed.

What of the mystery story? Does it, in like manner, refine an author's skills for other forms of fiction?

It does, indeed! For, it turns out, the disciplines that govern the mystery are actually the rules — masquerading incognito — which structure the whole art of fiction! Truly revealed, they form the complete training ground in the art of communication through storytelling. Let us view them with their masks off:

Rule one: *All clues discovered by the detective must be made available to the reader.*

In its broader sense, this rule is saying that all stories should be tied together, and the tying requires that coming events cast their shadows before. The clues to the future are planted in the present. The reader is not to be cheated, surprised, or upset by the story's taking a sudden, irrelevant course. In no way can Hamlet and Ophelia walk off, hand in hand, into the sunset. Nor may Petruchio not tame Katharina. The omens promise a different future.

The course of clue-planting is broader and deeper than just mood. The lottery ticket must be bought before the prize can be won, the ice must be known to be thin before the child falls through. The way must be paved. The reader may be caught unawares — and, indeed, it is a part of storytelling to catch the reader unawares — but he should never be caught in *ignorance*. All surprises must stem from within the universe of the story; they may not be introduced from outside. There should be that totality in a tale which pulls it together as a whole so that the reader is always comfortable. His credulity is never strained because whatever happens can be related to what has gone before. *The clues have been fairly planted.*

Rule two: *Early introduction of the murderer.*

This is only another way of saying that the sooner the cast is assembled, the better. It is not required, of course, that all hands be on deck at the launching, but it is required that the way is paved for the arrival of those who aren't. This again relates to the enclosed universe of the story and proper concern that the reader is not unfairly and uncomfortably surprised.

Rule three: *The crime must be significant.*

This is the warning any novelist must heed—that the events and concerns of his tale must be sufficient to grasp the interest of the reader. For all that an author should write to please himself, it must never be forgotten that he is writing to be read. If, in arrogance, a writer takes a "public be damned" attitude, and writes for himself alone, he reveals himself as failing to understand the nature his craft. Writing is communication. The purpose of words and of language is to transmit as accurately as possible what is in the mind of one person into the mind of another. An author must always write with his reader as well as himself in mind. The more successfully he involves his reader, the more successfully he is communicating. He must create interest in his purposes. Therefore his purposes, like the mystery writer's crime, must be significant.

Rule four: *There must be detection.*

In its broader application, this rule means that something must happen. An author, whatever kind of story he may seek to tell, whatever message he may want to deliver, or whatever emotion he may want to share, should couch it in a developing tale. There should be form to the novel, there should be shape and direction. Characters should act and react. They must not drift at the mercy of the fates.

Rule five: *The number of suspects must be known and the murderer must be among them.*

This is the matter of the enclosed universe which we have mentioned before. Every story must operate in such a system. It is necessary, for purposes of orientation, to help the reader feel comfortable and aware of his parameters. To put it another way: Only the characters in a story can have impact upon other characters in the same story. Consequently they've all got to be there.

Rule six: *Nothing extraneous may be introduced.*

This is the final fence that pens the mystery writer so tightly. This is the discipline that makes the highest demand upon such a writer in terms of skill, economy, and artistry.

What it is saying with regard to fiction as a whole is that an author should not wander or meander. He should have purpose and he should stick to his purpose; everything he puts into his stories should relate to that purpose. Quite obviously, the purposes in a straight novel can be quite different from those of the mystery and they will generally embrace far vaster areas. The lesson, however, is the same. Do not be sloppy, do not be verbose, do not be irrelevant. Writing is communication, and it's not enough merely to use the right words to transmit the message; one should also take pains to see that the form of the message is not garbled.

What we have been talking about until now has been, actually, the areas of similarity between the mystery and the novel, and what we have been saying, in effect, is that the mystery makes a good training ground for the novel. The claim has been made, and I would give it much truth, that a good mystery writer can write a better novel than a good novelist can write a mystery. This is because the mystery writer has had to develop the disciplines of the novel form to a far higher degree than is required of the straight novelist. The mystery is a craft within a craft and all that pertains to the art of the mystery pertains to the art of the novel.

There is, however, a whole universe beyond the tightly fenced realm of the mystery, a universe wherein only the straight novelist roams. In this vast otherworld lie challenges not available to the mystery author, and demands of craft that are not imposed upon him. Therein resides the fact that the great names in literature belong to the novel, not to the mystery!

But why? What is this forbidden land wherein the mystery writer may not tread? What is it that makes these straight-fiction books, even if they deal with crime and punishment, more than mysteries? What can a novelist do that a mystery writer cannot? What is the *difference* between the mystery and the novel?

One distinction is pure and simple. The mystery novel does not contain the equipment to carry messages. It is too frail a box to hold the human spirit. It allows an author to speak, but not to explore and instruct. The credo can be expressed as follows: "If you want to write and have nothing to say, write a mystery." If you have other ambitions, the mystery form had best be eschewed.

Why do we say this? Why is the mystery form inadequate?

The first and most obvious reason is that the mystery is, in actuality, a morality play. Though evil threatens, justice emerges triumphant. Goodness is honored, sin is vanquished. Portia wins and Shylock loses. (But, mark you, *The Merchant of Venice* is a vehicle that would burst into a thousand fragments if it tried to encompass a Lady Macbeth!)

The real world does not behave as tidily as the make-believe world of mystery. Justice, all too often, suffers defeat. Right does not always make might, and one who would deal with the ills of the world and the lessons to be learned therefrom, cannot use the mystery as a soapbox.

There is a deeper reason too. Its inadequacy is not merely because it holds up a slanted mirror to nature — for sometimes nature does conform to the image. The roots of the problem are more sinuous and penetrating than that, for the inability of the mystery to deal with matters of serious concern lies the nature of the animal itself.

In the mystery novel, the story is the core, the be-all, the end-all, the Heart of the Matter. This is its glory, and its liability. This is what sets it apart from the straight novel. This is why it doesn't serve the purposes of the straight novelist.

The author of a straight novel has other fish to fry. His aim is not to puzzle the reader or tell him stories. His basic aim isn't even to entertain. He writes for all the other reasons: to save himself, to objectify his life, to express his preoccupations and concerns with the human condition. He writes, more often than not, because he *has* to write, to get the monkey off his back. Sometimes he is consciously trying to send messages, to argue a cause, put forth a concept, or present a viewpoint, but for the most part his statements are not consciously expressed. The insights he puts forth, for however much or little they are worth, lie hidden in the depths of his prose. They are sought for and argued over by critics, if the ore that is found is deemed worth the mining.

Story is not this author's goal. It serves instead as the vehicle through which he expresses himself. If he is wise, disciplined, and makes his talent work for him, he will pay attention to his story and obey the injunctions we have been talking about. If not, he will suffer a corresponding loss of effectiveness. In either case, however, story is a sideline; expressing whatever it is inside of him that must come out is the guiding fire of his book.

How does he present his case, then, if not by story? He does it through character. It is people working upon people that is the heart of his novel. Characters, or a character, form the core of the work and everything else is structured around them. The story is created to show off the characters rather than, as in the mystery, the characters being created to show off the story.

But, one may ask, does this claim lie above challenge? Is it indeed true that, in the mystery novel, the story is the heart and core? Are not the adventures of Sherlock Holmes mere vehicles devised for the purpose of putting Holmes on stage? Isn't Holmes, really, the center, the core, the *raison d'etre*? Don't we read Maigret for the sake of Maigret and never mind what he's up to in this particular case? How can it be said that "the play's the thing"?

It is true that people, generally, write and read about series detectives for the sake of the detective. The point is, however, that the detective is not touched by the series. If Philip Marlowe mellows, it is only because Raymond Chandler mellows, not because Marlowe has been tempered by experience. Perry Mason and Della Street bore the same relationship to each other in 1963 that they did in 1933. They were no more affected by the times and tides of thirty years than Little Orphan Annie.

Admittedly, the Ellery Queen of *Double Double* is a different person from the Ellery Queen of *The Chinese Orange Mystery*, but this is not due to growth of character, it is due to tailoring and updating him to suit the times.

The mystery writer is a storyteller. He may use the same character over and over, but it doesn't change the fact that all he is doing is telling stories.

To an author who tries his hand in both fields, the needed shift of cores from story to character hits with the unexpected impact of an express locomotive. It is not a decision the author makes, it is a realization that is thrust upon him.

To the reader, the essence of the difference is still vivid. The characters in a novel are *affected*. They think, they feel, they are touched. The working of people upon people produces alteration and what happens to these people — not to their bodies, but to their psyches — is where the author lives. In the novel, people grow, people shrivel, people change. Jean Valjean is not Raffles.

Can one not, at this point, broach a second challenge? It has been acknowledged that flesh, muscle, blood, and clothing have been added to the bones of the mystery over the years. Valjean is, admittedly, not Raffles, but do not the characters created by today's mystery authors more closely approximate Hugo's creation than Hornung's? Is not Raffles irrelevant by modern standards?

It is true that the mystery more and more approaches this aspect of the straight novel. It was, in fact, for just this reason that it was deemed necessary to look to the classical age of the mystery form, when it was more appropriately called the detective story, in order to make clear the difference. Over the years the fuzzing of the line of demarcation has increased. More and more, mystery writers are either growing out of that form — like Graham Greene — or being recognized as having overflowed the field even when they were writing within it — like Hammett, Chandler, and James M. Cain.

In fact, there are top practitioners in the field today who will argue that there is no "forbidden land" for the mystery novelist. They claim there is nothing straight fiction can do that the mystery novel cannot also do.

What this is saying, and what it means if it is true, is that there is no longer any difference between the straight novel and the mystery. This is, in effect, suggesting that "Mystery Story" is nothing but a label put on or not put on a book by the publisher according to the public relations department's assessment of its sales value.

The mystery has grown a lot. It has come a long way, but in my own opinion it has not—and never can—come quite that far. Let us hearken back to the core business again. If it is an author's aim to write a mystery novel, it must be conceded that his purpose is to confound, puzzle, scare, bewilder, or horrify the reader and, generally speaking, to keep him in a constant state of suspense. This, by definition, has to be what he is up to, otherwise he is not writing a mystery.

If this be his purpose, then it is up to him to invent a story that will elicit these results. To present this story effectively, he must create characters who will make it happen. Now it is true that he can show these characters in as much depth as he is capable—which is what most modern mystery writers give attention to and the ancients did not—and he can make them work upon each other, penetrating as many of their seven veils as he can manage. To this extent, the mystery writer can match the straight fiction writer and, if the mystery writer has greater insight, can exceed his counterpart. But the fact remains that his characters were created for the purpose of telling a story. The story is central and upon anyone who would fly from it, it weighs like a lump of lead.

If, on the other hand, an author chooses to write a novel for the purpose of studying the impact of avarice, or jealousy, or love upon the human condition, he does not start with a story. He starts instead with a character, a symbol, a means of conveyance through which his message on these subjects will be made manifest. He will then construct a story created for the purpose of delivering this message.

In short, the one ultimate distinction between the mystery and the novel, and the one which, it seems to me, must always mark the difference, is the question of—appropriately—*motive*. If the motive is "mystery," then the story (suspense, of course) is the core, and a mystery it is. If the motive is otherwise, then story (no matter how gory) is not the core, it is the means, and a mystery it is not.

This article first appeared in The Writer *magazine, December 1969, and was reprinted in* Techniques of Novel Writing, *edited by A.S. Burack, published by The Writer, 1973.*

Plot construction is something I suspect many modern novelists pay little attention to. If challenged, they might even insist that a book doesn't need a plot, that the novel has escaped from the prison of a story line. I would also suspect that authors with such views are more lazy than enlightened. Constructing a good, solid plot is tedious work; it's much more fun to play with characters.

But there is pleasure in plotting too, and it's probably the mystery writer who knows this better than anyone else. While plot is no longer sufficient to sustain a mystery novel all by itself, it still is the book's main *raison d'etre* and lays the heaviest claim on the author's attention. As a result, there is no better training ground for the art of plotting than the mystery. And when one has mastered this art and become experienced in its disciplines, he can dominate, control, and handle plots as a skilled musician dominates, controls, and handles his instrument. This is when plotting becomes fun — when the structure of an intricately conceived story can produce the intellectual pleasure of a subtle chess combination.

But let's start at the beginning. A novel is first an entity. All parts bear on all other parts. Thus we can't lift out this thing called plot and expect it to detach itself cleanly. Clinging things will come with it. Background, for one, characters for another. We should cut those free before going on.

Background isn't much of a problem, for it has a relatively minor effect on plot. A story will, of course, follow one line of action if its setting is New York City, and a different one if it's rural England. The problem of transport, the problems

PLOTS AND PEOPLE IN MYSTERY NOVELS

of privacy, of obtaining goods, of terrain, of virtually all of life will vary markedly between such places, and the story will have to vary to solve them.

Motivation and Behavior

Such strictures affect only the surface of a story, however. What is basic to the plot and what will not change is the behavior of the characters. A given man's response to a stimulus will be the same in England as in New York, and the only variable is the means at his disposal to respond with.

It is character that has the affecting influence on plot. A given man may respond the same way to the same stimulus regardless of locale, but a different man will respond to the same stimulus in a different way. Twenty men will respond in twenty different ways.

This business of character is a major stumbling block in plotting, and the way an author handles it separates the would-be writer from the professional. The would-be writer remains a would-be because he makes the mistake of letting his story move his characters. The professional knows it's the other way around. The characters move the story. That's the first big lesson and the first big task, and at the back of a writer's mind at all times should be the cry, "Motivate, motivate, motivate!"

Let's talk about that for a moment. Everything every character says and does must be consistent with his personality. Granted. Next, those consistent responses, actions and reactions must advance the story. It is the only way the story can be told. It is what the story is. But there is more yet. This action that moves the story was triggered by a cause, and the cause should also be relevant to that story. In a good plot there is nothing extraneous.

Suppose the exigencies of the plot require that Jones accidentally bump into Brown as he is leaving his downtown office. There has to be a logical reason for Jones's being downtown at that particular time. Nor will it do to say he went down to buy a pair of shoes or mail a letter. What does he need the pair of shoes for and why buy them now? Or who's the letter to and why can't he mail it in the corner letterbox? And, in any case, what do shoes or letters have to do with the story we're telling?

If his action isn't a relevant factor, then it's a contrivance, and the author is saying to the reader, "I'm too lazy to solve the problem of getting Jones downtown legitimately, so I'm going to rig it."

And what is meant by "legitimately"? Simply: That the reason that brings Jones downtown had, has, or will have some bearing on the story.

The Aim of the Game

Now, having recognized the impact of characters on the motivation of stories, let us get to the business of the story-making itself. The first aim of the game, of course, is reader involvement — that quality that keeps him turning the pages. Some people call it "reader urgency." To me it's simply, "suspense." This doesn't mean the story has to be an action drama. Perilous Pauline doesn't have to be hanging from a cliff at the end of every chapter. All that is required to keep the suspense up and the reader reading is two things: 1. The reader must not know what is going to happen next; and 2. He must want to find out.

Taking up the second point first, the reader will only want to find out if he cares about or identifies with the characters. Thus there must be still another dimension and purpose to the people in the story than merely the motivation of the plot. They must be heroes and villains, liked, detested, feared, or scorned. This is what a book is really all about, and that motivation business we were discussing never should reach the reader's awareness. That's structural support and only the author is supposed to know it's there.

But enough about character. We want to talk about plot, so we'll assume the reader cares about the hero's future, and we'll concern ourselves with the first point, the element of suspense. Let us consider the following: The fair damsel is a prisoner in the moated castle; the hero and his outnumbered band of intrepid men seek to rescue her.

Given this situation, the reader is not sure whether the hero will succeed or fail. Therein lies the suspense, and both reader and author know this. The reader can relax, therefore, during the hero's effort to swim the moat, scale the walls, elude guards, and reach the fair damsel's chamber. He knows the hero will encounter only token danger in this stage of the adventure. (Only an abysmal plotter would have the hero captured *before* he reached the girl.) The real trouble, the reader knows, will arise when the hero tries to escape with her. (There's a 100 percent guarantee that he can't do it without having someone raise the alarm.)

This is a basic suspense setup. It's legitimate, but it's garden variety suspense, very predictable, and very uninspired. That's the kind of plotting I'd have to jazz up in some way. I don't want my readers sitting back thinking they know what my moves are going to be. I'll lull them into sitting back only when I'm ready to pull the chair out from under them. And after I've pulled out enough chairs, the readers will be (hopefully) conditioned the way I want them: to sit on the edges of those chairs.

To go back to that hero swimming the moat and scaling the walls to rescue fair maiden: He eludes the guards. So far so good. He reaches the heroine as promised, and now the reader anticipates those suspense-filled pages while the hero tries to get her safely out of the castle. But now we'll pull a switch and have her flatly refuse to go with him!

A curve like that will not only jolt the reader; it will completely disorient him. Now he has *no* idea where the story is going next. Presumably he now also can't wait to find out!

It goes without saying that the reason for the damsel's refusal must be absolutely valid so that when she explains herself, the reader will acknowledge that her decision was, at worst, logical, at best, inescapable. Ideally—and this is where I like to play games with the reader—a clue has already been planted in the text so that the discerning reader could have predicted that response. The ideal in the plotting game is to keep the reader guessing what will happen next, at the same time secretly weaving into the story all the clues that would tell him. This is where the challenge and the fun lie.

Reader Satisfaction

There's more to good plotting, however, than playing games with the reader or keeping him guessing, interested, or excited. A good story should offer him intellectual satisfaction at the same time. He should feel, when he closes the final cover of a book, that the reading of it has been a rewarding experience and not a waste of time. There has to be meat in a book. It should be packed with content. Thus, no plaudits for plotting can be earned for producing mere one-purpose scenes. Everything that happens in a book should have at least two reasons for being there. And I mean in addition to the suspense motive that keeps the reader reading. (All scenes are assumed to have that or you're not a writer.) Two additional reasons are desired—at least two. And if the author can work in three or four, so much the better.

Here's a sample case. Suppose an author wants to put a bedroom scene in his story. Boy and girl will make love as explicitly as the house rules of his particular publishing company will permit. The purpose? To titillate the reader. This, I have to concede, is a legitimate purpose. The author's aim, after all, is to keep the reader turning pages and titillation will do it as well as suspense. (I suppose my main objection to maintaining reader interest through titillation is that it doesn't require any skill, and even bad writing can get published if it's pornographic enough.)

Now, using this example, assume that a bedroom scene is to be included in the story. If its only purpose is titillation, that is very bad. It has no more business there than suddenly having a man go over Niagara Falls in a barrel to inject suspense. As we said before, there should be at least two reasons besides reader interest to justify every scene in a story.

So we have to give this bedroom bit some meaning. Perhaps we can say that it reveals something of the character of the couple involved. This we can make it do, and now we're on less shaky ground. However, it's a pretty big scene for very little character insight, unless we reveal something about their behavior that will have a future bearing on the story! If we can do that, then this scene becomes a must. Now we're full-fledged legitimate; we have a valid purpose for invading the bedroom and not staying out in the hall.

But that's only one purpose, and we want more than that. What else can that scene do for us? For one thing, if we happen to be writing a mystery novel, this serves as an alibi for the pair. If they're with each other in the bedroom, they can't be killing victim number two. There's a second purpose.

There's no point in using bedroom capers for an alibi unless we can make capital of the fact that it's bedroom capers rather than, say, a trip to the amusement park. So if the amorous duo should have to reveal their indiscretions to save their hides, we're locking this scene in as an integral part of the book.

There is still more we can do. When it's discovered what the couple has been up to, other people are going to be motivated as a result. Perhaps the revelation will move the villain of the piece to embark on a course that will ultimately lead to his destruction. If so, our hot little love scene is indispensable. It has to be in there, and the author can even defend it as artistic if he wants.

Meanwhile, though the reader won't find it out until the end of the book, that torrid little interlude, which he found so enjoyable that he read through it without thinking, really held the key clue to the mystery, and he was conned into forgetting to pay attention!

That is plotting in depth and, to me, is the only way to do it and where the fun lies. The result is a tight, well-integrated story that moves ever forward, and an author, when he has worked out a scheme like that, can say he's got a book. To me, however, that is still not enough. Plot is important but there is something even more important. I mean the characters that make the story happen. They are what I want to play up, not the story.

My tendency, therefore is to strive first for that solid, integrated plot with its box of surprises, then hang it up as a backdrop and have another story—the real story —take place in front of it.

This story will be about the development of a man's character, perhaps, or its degeneration, or the change in the relationship of two or more people to each other or toward life or whatever. In its most elementary form, of course, it's the ups and downs of a boy-girl romance.

There are, besides boys and girls, all kinds of personal relationships which can be explored and presented against the backdrop of the story line, but the writer must take care, of course, that the relationships develop in the context of that backdrop. Though the focus may rest on the relationships rather than on the story line, the two interrelate. They do more than that. They fuse.

As I said earlier, a book is an entity. All things connect with all things.

This article first appeared in Mystery Writer's Handbook *by the Mystery Writers of America, revised edition, published by Writer's Digest Books, 1976.*

Now that you are ready to sit down at the typewriter, plot in hand, to write your first mystery novel, one of the questions that faces you is, what are you going to do about your detective? Is he or she to be an ongoing character making his appearance in future books, or is this to be his only case, the book not just wrapping up the murder, but the detective as well? Since one can go either way, the decision to be made is, which way is better and why?

If money and writing security are your goals — and they usually are — then the series detective seems the best bet. Agatha Christie to the contrary notwithstanding, it can be given as a general rule that fictional detectives are better known than their creators. Agatha Christie is admittedly more of a household name than either Hercule Poirot or Miss Jane Marple, but even Agatha Christie's renown pales before that of Sherlock Holmes. Sherlock, the detective we all wish we had invented, not only dwarfs his creator, Sir Arthur Conan Doyle, he dwarfs most real people as well, both past and present, and, in fact, is recognized as the most famous fictional character ever conceived — with the possible exception of Tarzan. In like manner, as well known as such authors as Rex Stout and Erle Stanley Gardner may be, their detectives, Nero Wolfe and Perry Mason, are even better known. And, for a classic example, who in the world has not heard of Charlie Chan? Yet who besides a mystery buff, can name his creator? The point is that the average mystery reader, when impressed by a particular story, is going to look for more of the same. Same what? More stories about the same detective, of course. It is the detective's name that will stick in his mind. Only incidentally, and as an aid in case

THE SERIES VS. THE NON-SERIES DETECTIVE

the detective's name is not on the book jacket, will he take heed of the author's name.

That being the case, if a writer can create an appealing, intriguing, or interesting detective, there is a definite advantage—both for him and the mystery reader—in his continuing his detective through further adventures. With each new book, the detective's following, and therefore the author's readership (it's not the other way around, mind you) grow. And as new readers encounter the detective for the first time and like him, they will go back to earlier books to acquaint themselves with his previous exploits. Meanwhile, the reappearance of the detective's name with each new book is akin to advertising the whole package. An author develops something of a legacy, as it were. He assures himself and his publisher of a certain sales expectancy. He is producing a known quantity, and that, in the very uncertain field of publishing, is a decided plus.

With all these desirable advantages, one might well ask why any mystery or detective story writer would ever produce anything but series detectives. Why turn out a one-shot story and never use that particular hero or heroine again? What are the advantages of a non-series story, and what are the disadvantages of the series type?

One disadvantage, believe it or not, is that an author can become tired of his series detective, yet be stuck with him. (Conan Doyle tried his damndest to get rid of Sherlock Holmes, but his public wouldn't let him.) Worse than that, an author may outgrow his series detective and find him a hindrance. What is worst of all, is the author who *fails* to outgrow his detective because he stays loyal to him.

Another disadvantage is the likelihood of the author becoming jaded and losing his fresh approach. Familiarity does breed contempt and sometimes, if the marriage continues too long, the detective can start to become a caricature of *himself* and the author an imitator of *himself*. While series detectives have their purposes and their plus sides, generally speaking, it is best if they don't stay around too long.

As for the non-series type of mystery novel, what does it have to offer? What are its advantages?

What is *not* an advantage is the lack of a ready-made audience. Readers, it is true, do at times get to like an author for himself alone. (There is one mystery writer who even has a fan club). Nevertheless, it takes more of a reading connoisseur to fancy an author because of the way he writes rather than because of what he writes. Thus, as a general rule, the audience that picks up a mystery because it's by author A. Good Riter is going to be smaller than the one that picks up a mystery because it's about Detective Derring Do.

On the plus side, these one-shot books offer the author a chance to experiment, to try different ways of telling stories, to try different kinds of stories. Some stories, for example, need to be told in the first person singular, rather than in the traditional third. A different technique is required. If a writer wants to develop himself, he should experiment with and master different techniques. Some stories emphasize action, others, suspense, still others mood, dialogue, or drama. There are wide varieties of tales to tell, and they cannot all be explored if an author is tied to a series detective and to an audience that expects the same kind of book from him each time.

Then there is the matter of the degree of involvement of the characters with the story. This is important, for it triggers and determines the reader's degree of involvement. A novel about a young girl setting out to find the murderer of her brother is going to make a very different impact upon the reader than a novel about a young girl asking the series detective to find the murderer of her brother.

In one-shot novels, a degree of involvement with the characters can be developed and sustained that can't be achieved with a series detective. The series detective is an onlooker. The romances, the love affairs, the heartaches and tears, the tragic or happy endings all happen to others. The series detective (and therefore the reader) remains untouched and unchanged, ready to move on to the next case. All the series detective gets from the heroine is a look of heartfelt gratitude as she melts into the waiting arms of the rescued hero. The detective's arms remain empty— or are entered only at great risk. (One author, who let his series detective marry, had to kill off the new wife to sell the series to the movies.)

Which route, then, is the best to take? Should one follow the safe and sane, but ultimately stultifying road of the series character or try the demanding, less certain, but more satisfying path of the one-shot novel? Or should one try, as I have done several times over, switching back and forth, and become neither fish nor fowl?

A friend who cut his writing teeth on a paperback-original series-character but who now writes hardcover straight novels, says he sometimes thinks of his long-ago detective as sitting in his office somewhere waiting for a next case.

Other things being equal, like tastes, inclinations, needs and abilities, perhaps his is the best route for the beginning writer: start with a series character, learn with him, build with him, and then, when you outgrow him, leave him in his office waiting for that next case, and move on to the new stage of your own career.

16

BACK- GROUND AND RESEARCH

There is an ancient adage (my own) to the effect that: If you want to write a novel about coal mining, and you don't go down into a coal mine, you not only won't fool coal miners, you won't fool anybody else.

That's not because the public knows anything about coal mining, but because the public can tell that you don't either.

The essence behind all this is the fact that the moment a person opens his mouth, he reveals himself. Speak, and you stand exposed before your audience, all virtues and vices showing.

This, of course, is the bane of those promotional agencies hired to make candidates for political office appear ideal for the job. No matter how fine a picture of the candidate their efforts may produce, somewhere, sometime, that candidate is going to have to be seen in public and say something in public that has not been pre-fed to the candidate by the promotion agency. And at that moment, the public is going to see the candidate as he is, not as he's being packaged.

If it's difficult for a speaker to fool the public as to what he is and where he comes from, it's impossible for the writer. For, with the writer, it's not just a few words of self-revelation that must be uttered, but thousands. A writer stands far more naked in front of his readers than does the public speaker. No way can he produce a false image that will subvert more than a few. All of which is by way of saying, if you don't know what you're talking about, keep still.

Therefore, it behooves the writer to be well-grounded in the areas to which he directs his attention. If he fails in that, he has no one to read him. If he succeeds, at least he will hold the attention of those who share his interest and, if he really knows his background, he will elicit the interest of those whom his information and knowledge excites.

What of background? What background

should a writer research to catch the interest of readers?

The answer is Any Background.

I once received a letter from a woman who aspired to write the kind of small-town police procedural novels I was doing. She lived with her mother who ran a boarding house in Brooklyn which, to her, was totally unglamorous and she was looking for what, to her, were exotic backgrounds.

I pointed out in my reply that, while what she was accustomed to might seem mundane, a boarding house background would be fascinating to those of us who knew nothing of such a world.

The point is that one's own background, drab as it must inevitably seem to him or herself, will be a strange new world to everyone else and the details of its operation will be an education for a readership.

Detail

Detail, in reality, is the essence — or certainly an important essence — in the telling of a story. The sense of authenticity that derives from the odd bits and pieces that result from knowing what one is talking about adds immeasurably to the story one tells.

A good writer should obey the precept of the good newspaper reporter: "Check your facts." There is nothing so satisfying as knowing you are correct in what you say, and nothing so contributes to unease as "fudging." In fact, if you're any good, the idea of "fudging" should be anathema.

Here's from my own experience:

Having toured Europe some years before, I thought to use that background for a chase story. Detective hero and target heroine flee evil villains through Italy and France.

Great idea!

So I devised a plot that would take my characters to various of the places I'd been in those countries and started to write.

Then it happened!

I was in the middle of a chase scene. Villains had the hero and heroine in sight and were pursuing them around the docks in Genoa. Usually, when the action speeds up, the typewriter keys speed up as well and the writing goes fast.

Except that suddenly, in the middle of this hot chase scene, I stopped dead. For, as I said to myself, "I don't have the faintest idea what the hell I'm talking about." I'd been to Genoa, but I hadn't been to the docks of Genoa. Nor would it do to make up what the docks of Genoa "might" look like. That would be the acme of phoniness. I'd look like an idiot to anyone who'd been there, or who knew what kind of a port Genoa was and what such a port should consist of. For a writer to attempt such foolishness would be to destroy his credibility forever. Even if I didn't care about such things as credibility, I couldn't have done it because I simply don't know how to write on a subject about which I know nothing.

The result was, my ignorance killed my interest in my high adventure tale. Up it went onto the shelf and there it remained for two years and it might still have been there today, except I interested my editor in the tale and, with money I got from the book contract, I made another trip to Europe, this time knowing in advance every place my hero and heroine would go to and what would happen to them there.

In my own quest for authenticity—and I have a stronger urge for it than most—I pinpointed not only locales, but dates and times. On my first night in Florence, for example, I woke at 3:00 A.M., and after tossing and turning for two hours, it occurred to me that my hero arrived in Florence at 5:00 A.M. and what was I doing staying in bed? "Get up and go see what Florence is like at five o'clock in the morning!" I told myself, which is what I did.

The extremes to which I will go for accuracy is reflected by my realization, when I got to my hotel in Rome, that I'd forgotten, in checking out the Fiumicino Airport on my arrival, to note the location of airport telephones and my hero was to make a call from there. Fortunately, a call to the airport answered the question and saved me having to make a trip back to the airport to get the answer—which I was prepared to make, if necessary.

Upon my return to the States with all details authenticated, I realized that, though I'd done Europe, my story started and ended in Washington D.C. and I hadn't done Washington. So I flew down one morning, tramped all over the Capital to verify the things I needed for my Washington scenes, and flew back that night, mission accomplished.

As an interesting sidelight, since final scenes were to take place in a senate hearing room, I went to the New Senate Office Building to check them out. It was after hours, the place was deserted, and there were no security guards nor police nor anyone to say "You can't go in there." That's the nice thing about this country—the Government belongs to the people—but this freedom granted the people does offer opportunities for those who might wish us ill. For example, while I was in this broad, empty hall standing in the doorway of a hearing room, taking notes, Robert Kennedy came out of an office some doors down and stood for a minute in the middle of the hall, talking to someone inside. He went away, never having seen me. I didn't think anything about it then, but I reflect now that if Sirhan Sirhan — or anybody. . . .

Verifying Your Facts

A few words about verifications. If one writes a book such as this, (*Run When I Say Go*, Doubleday, 1969) your editor will send the manuscript to an assistant editor whose job is to check for discrepancies. Let it be said, one should be sure he knows what he's talking about. The editor who reviewed my manuscript was the most dedicated such editor I've ever encountered. He checked out and queried me on everything I said to make sure I hadn't made a mistake. (I did make one that I know of, called to my attention by a friend. I numbered the plane's seats from back to front instead of from front to back — a minor error, but it rankles. A writer wants total verisimilitude.)

Among the points this editor challenged me on was the fact that, on a street map of Nice, a street is listed by a different name than I gave it. This was true, for I had such a map myself but, in Nice, never mind the map, the name was different.

He also queried me about Washington. According to the street map, traffic was one-way and I had it going two-ways. That was true, for I also had a map, but I was also on that street corner at that precise time and I monitored exactly what the traffic situation was.

One might complain that this particular research editor was being picayune, but I wrote him a letter of appreciation along with my explanation for the discrepancies.

In my own case, the passion for authenticity probably exceeds the norm. Like the dedicated reporter, I must always "Check the facts," and to an extent out of all proportion to the importance of the item. "Have I got that name spelled right?" Look it up. "Does this word I want to use really mean what I think it does?" Look it up. "I'm 99 percent sure this is how a particular word is spelled." Be 100 percent sure. Look it up.

As a result of — shall we suggest, *overdoing* the research angle — this particular chase story, *Run When I Say Go*, could only have happened at a particular moment in history — November 1967. The liner Italia was docked in Genoa, LBJ's picture hung in the American Consulate in Nice, plane and train schedules were valid for that month, and a new, canary yellow 1968 Dodge was on display in the Union Station in Washington D.C. The book is pinpointed in time, which can be a handicap if one seeks a broader appeal.

However, these identifications can readily be made nonspecific. One can mention that the president's picture hung between the French and American flags in the American Consulate in Nice without naming the president; one needn't identify the liner docked in Genoa; and the car being displayed in Washington's Union Station can be "next year's model." Thus such a tale can remain relatively timeless.

Such an approach will allow a book to be "current" for a longer period, but, of course, no book can reflect the times for too long. The times change too fast. The way things were only ten years ago are "quaint" today. Problems are different, mores are different, crimes are different. We cannot, writing a mystery story, write for the Ages. We can only write for today and consider, as our contribution to mankind, the picture of a time and place, preserved in amber for the edification of future generations.

This article first appeared in The Mystery Writer's Handbook, *by the Mystery Writers of America, edited by Herbert Brean, published by Harper & Bros. 1956, and was reprinted in the revised edition,* Mystery Writer's Handbook, *edited by Lawrence Treat, published by Writer's Digest Books, 1976.*

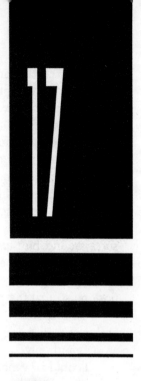

Once I have the idea for the kind of book I want to write, I decide first who is to be murdered, then who kills him and for what reason. In working this much out I have to develop some background on both killer and victim. I know something of their characters and past lives. With that in mind, I can now go on to the problem of how the killer is going to commit the crime, where, and when.

At this point, if I have a gimmick, I know what the key is by which the detective will finally unlock the case, and if it involves the scene of the crime it is included. If there is no gimmick, this is the time to determine how the murder will eventually be solved. Some ideas can be gained through the knowledge of the crime I now have. If that isn't enough I will introduce variations, but at any rate this is where the general plot is thought out. To some extent the plot will be determined by the crime I've planned, but on the other hand the plot idea will alter the murder. Each works on the other, but the whole story develops at this point. In other words, I generally start with the scene of the murder and build from there.

Next comes the detective. The kind of detective he is, private eye or member of the regular force, is part of the original idea, but so far that's about all I know of him. His position will, of course, have an effect upon the plotting I've done since a private detective would work under a different set of rules from a police detective, but now his character has to be developed. To have the plot progress according to plan, the clues will have to be uncovered in a certain order. That will

WHY I
DON'T
OUTLINE

necessitate certain circumstances arising to make that happen, but it will also mean a careful planning of the character of the hero. Different people work in different ways and I'll need a particular type of person to move the way I want him to. Since this one person will have a strong impact upon the story, he must be chosen with a view to having the effect desired.

Once the murderer, victim, evidence and detective have been established, the next step is plot complication. That means the introduction of other suspects with motives and clues that will involve them.

Lastly, since none of the characters will remain static during proceedings, I must now determine how each person will react to the pressures around him and how that can further cast or remove suspicion. Their behavior further complicates the plot, shifting the progress of the story one way or another, and the whole thing must be juggled into position so that the proper end develops.

As is apparent, the whole story until this point has been in a state of flux and outlining would have been completely useless. Everything is in my mind only.

I could now make an outline if I chose. I don't for two reasons. One is that with the whole story committed to memory there is no need of an outline, and the other is that in the actual writing I find the story is still fluid. Though I know about what will take place, I don't know how the characters will behave. It has been my experience that characters tend to act independently from my will and the tight rein of an outline would warp them out of shape. The only way I can keep their behavior natural is to give them as much leeway as possible within the main framework of the story.

This is not to disparage outlining. A good many authors do outline and most successfully. In fact, those who *can* outline have a decided advantage in many ways. With the whole story in front of them, they can write faster and with less need for rewriting. In my own case, and this is a disadvantage, I have to write each story twice, and the first draft could be considered as a super-detailed outline for the second. In the final analysis, whether one outlines or doesn't is purely a matter of individual taste and no one can say that one method produces a better result than the other.

Recommended Reading

Edgar Allan Poe

"The Murders in the Rue Morgue" (1841)

A *must*: The first detective story ever written. In this tale appear nearly all the ingredients which detective fiction writers have utilized throughout the history of the field, including the "unique" and superior detective, his chronicler, the baffled police, and the hero's deductive skills in solving the case.

"The Purloined Letter" (1845)

An additional fine example of the genre in its early stages, particularly in view of Poe's introduction of the "obvious" hiding place.

Wilkie Collins

The Moonstone (1868)

This is only recommended for devotees. Sergeant Cuff is the interesting figure here, being another "singular" detective. His role, unfortunately, is insignificantly small. The novel itself is long and involved by today's standards, having been written before radio and television, back when reading was one of the few ways to spend an evening, and books were therefore cherished for their length. The theme of this novel is romance, rather than detection.

Sir Arthur Conan Doyle

A Study in Scarlet (1887)

A *must*: This is the story that introduces Sherlock Holmes to the world. Unfortunately, it is not a good novel and the recommendation is to skip the flashback section and only read the parts when Holmes is on stage.

The Sign of Four (1890)

This is a worthwhile follow-up only because it continues our acquaintance with Holmes and brings in Mary Morstan, whom Watson marries.

The Adventures of Sherlock Holmes (1892)

A *must*: The first twelve short stories, generally regarded as the best of the tales. All are recommended for their flavor and the essence of Holmes and Watson. One not to be missed is "The Red-Headed League." This might be deemed the best all-around picture of Holmes in a nutshell.

The Hound of the Baskervilles (1902)

Recommended, but not necessary. If you like Holmes and Watson, read on. The tales in the *Adventures* series, however, give you all the "flavor" of the pair you need.

G.K. Chesterton

The Father Brown Omnibus (1935)

This contains all the Father Brown short stories and, certainly, one must read at least one Father Brown tale. If the *Omnibus* isn't available, seek "The Innocence of Father Brown" (1911). But you *have* to acquaint yourself with Father Brown.

E.C. Bentley

Trent's Last Case (1913)

Bentley's effort here is to make the detective more "human" than Holmes and the other prior detectives. Dorothy Sayers, in seeking to make Lord Peter Wimsey a rounded, rather than a stick-figure character, acknowledges that Bentley tried first.

Agatha Christie

The Mysterious Affair at Styles (1920)

Agatha's first mystery, and the introduction of Hercule Poirot to the world. Though a first, it shows that Agatha knew from the start what she was doing. One does not say of this book that it's value is only as an indication of genius yet to come. This, her first effort, stands equal to virtually everything else she wrote.

The Murder of Roger Ackroyd (1926)

A *must*: This is the novel that made her famous. It's also a good example of her cleverness (deviousness?) in hiding clues. If you don't want to be misled more than necessary in her other books, study what she does in this.

Murder at the Vicarage (1930)

A necessary read to gain an introduction to her female detective, Miss Jane Marple. (But it's still the same Agatha.)

Peril at End House (1932)

Hercule Poirot again and one of his and Agatha's best.

Dorothy Sayers

The Unpleasantness at the Bellona Club (1928)

This is Sayers when Wimsey was still her hero and her love, when Harriet Vane still languished in the wings. Actually, any Sayers will do as a sample — well, not *any* Sayers for it's better to read about Wimsey rather than Vane — but at least one Dorothy L. Sayers is a *must*. (She would insist — and rightly so.)

S.S. Van Dine

The Greene Murder Case (1928)

Again, any Van Dine will do as a sample of Philo Vance at work, but this is a good example. It's one of his best. A Van Dine is a *must* if one would gain a sense and understanding of the period.

Ellery Queen

The Roman Hat Mystery (1929)

Any early Ellery Queen will do as a sample. This was the first, so anyone reading it must forgive the ending of the book, which was written before his creators realized they'd started a series.

The later Queens, when Ellery was updated to fit the times, while good, aren't really examples of Queen as originally portrayed, the Ellery Queen that brought fame to Dannay and Lee.

Try *The Chinese Orange Mystery* if you want to see Queen being devilishly clever. Or read *The Egyptian Cross Mystery*. The denouement has been done many times since but was baffling in its time. The tale is marred, however, by ridiculous chase scenes near the end.

In any event, an early Ellery Queen is a *must*.

Dashiell Hammett

The Maltese Falcon (1930)

A *must*. One of the classics. Note the radical difference between this book and the ones above. If you only read *one* Hammett, this should be the one.

The Thin Man (1933)

Highly recommended. *The Maltese Falcon* is more a picture of private detective Sam Spade at work, while *The Thin Man* is a real, bonafide mystery tale. But again note the difference between it and the preceding detective stories.

Erle Stanley Gardner

A *must*. Gardner, a lawyer, was innovative in that he brought the mystery into the courtroom, wherein he could invoke his particular expertise. As for titles, any Perry Mason mystery will do. They are all of a piece, all good, all of equal quality. But an understanding of the mystery is not complete without at least one Perry Mason in your repertoire.

Rex Stout

Any Rex Stout will do, but at least one is a must. Nero Wolfe is the singular detective here, created, as one could expect from Rex, as the antithesis of Sherlock Holmes. Nero may be the hero, but Archie Goodwin represents the twinkle in Rex's eye. If you want a recommendation, try *The League of Frightened Men* (1935).

Raymond Chandler

The Big Sleep (1939)

A *must*. Chandler's first, and probably his best. But any Chandler will do, up until his *The Long Goodbye* which, while it won the Mystery Writers of America Edgar for best novel of 1954, is much too long and involved — at least for my taste. Try one of the prior ones for a proper sample of his work (*Farewell, My Lovely, The Lady in the Lake, The High Window, The Little Sister*), but a Chandler novel is a *must*.

Mickey Spillane

I, the Jury (1947)

Never mind what I've said about him, this man had a tremendous impact (I keep using that word, but it's the only one that fits) upon the reading and non-reading public in the years immediately following World War II and it's important to read him and see why. Significant sociological messages await discovery here. The book listed above is probably his best, but, if unavailable, try one of his other tremendous best-sellers such as *My Gun is Quick* (1950) or *Vengeance is Mine* (1950).

Ross McDonald

Though McDonald started out as an imitator of Hammett and Chandler, his private detective, Lew Archer (named after Sam Spade's partner?), soon developed an identity of his own. McDonald's stories outgrew the genre and became best-sellers as novels, rather than as detective stories. Compare Archer with Spade, Marlowe, and Hammer. Note how different they all are. Recommended: *The Far Side of the Dollar* (1965).

John D. MacDonald

John D. started out writing paperback originals but his work, and his detective, Travis McGee, became so popular publishers started putting him out in hard cover. Since it's usually the other way around, this makes John D. MacDonald not only unique, but particularly good. Help yourself to any one of his books. They're identifiable by the mention of a color in their titles.

Hillary Waugh

Last Seen Wearing . . . (1952)

One of the first, and still one of the best police procedurals. It's listed as one of the one hundred best detective stories ever written and regarded as a classic. Note the difference between this approach to detective story writing and the books that have gone before. *A must.*

Ed McBain

Any one of McBain's 87th Precinct novels will do, but consider him a *must.* He epitomizes the Big-City police procedural. Which book you read doesn't matter, for the quality is uniformly good. If you want a title, try his recent *Vespers* (1990).

Sue Grafton

A as in Alibi (1982)

Introduce yourself to a good example of the modern, feminist female private eye—savvy Kinsey Millhone. Contrast her handling of situations with that of her male counterparts. Note, also, the difference between the male and female approach to the same subject. Very good writing. Her descriptive touches somehow make me think of John D. MacDonald.

INDEX

OTHER BOOKS OF INTEREST

Annual Market Books
- Children's Writer's & Illustrator's Market, edited by Connie Eidenier (paper) $15.95
- Humor & Cartoon Markets, edited by Bob Staake (paper) $15.95
- Novel & Short Story Writer's Market, edited by Robin Gee (paper) $18.95
- Photographer's Market, edited by Sam Marshall $21.95
- Writer's Market, edited by Glenda Neff $24.95

General Writing Books
- Annable's Treasury of Literary Teasers, by H.D. Annable (paper) $10.95
- Beginning Writer's Answer Book, edited by Kirk Polking (paper) $13.95
- Discovering the Writer Within, by Bruce Ballenger & Barry Lane $16.95
- Getting the Words Right: How to Rewrite, Edit and Revise, by Theodore A. Rees Cheney (paper) $12.95
- How to Write a Book Proposal, by Michael Larsen (paper) $10.95
- Just Open a Vein, edited by William Brohaugh $15.95
- Knowing Where to Look: The Ultimate Guide to Research, by Lois Horowitz (paper) $15.95
- Make Your Words Work, by Gary Provost $17.95
- On Being a Writer, edited by Bill Strickland $19.95
- The Story Behind the Word, by Morton S. Freeman (paper) $9.95
- 12 Keys to Writing Books That Sell, by Kathleen Krull (paper) $12.95
- The 29 Most Common Writing Mistakes & How to Avoid Them, by Judy Delton $9.95
- The Wordwatcher's Guide to Good Writing & Grammar, by Morton S. Freeman (paper) $15.95
- Word Processing Secrets for Writers, by Michael A. Banks & Ansen Dibell (paper) $14.95
- Writer's Block & How to Use It, by Victoria Nelson $14.95
- The Writer's Digest Guide to Manuscript Formats, by Buchman & Groves $17.95

Nonfiction Writing
- Basic Magazine Writing, by Barbara Kevles $16.95
- The Complete Guide to Writing Biographies, by Ted Schwarz $19.95
- Creative Conversations: The Writer's Guide to Conducting Interviews, by Michael Schumacher $16.95
- How to Sell Every Magazine Article You Write, by Lisa Collier Cool (paper) $11.95
- How to Write Irresistible Query Letters, by Lisa Collier Cool (paper) $10.95
- The Writer's Digest Handbook of Magazine Article Writing, edited by Jean M. Fredette (paper) $11.95
- Writing Creative Nonfiction, by Theodore A. Rees Cheney $15.95

Fiction Writing
- The Art & Craft of Novel Writing, by Oakley Hall $17.95
- Best Stories from New Writers, edited by Linda Sanders $16.95
- Characters & Viewpoint, by Orson Scott Card $13.95
- The Complete Guide to Writing Fiction, by Barnaby Conrad $17.95
- Cosmic Critiques: How & Why 10 Science Fiction Stories Work, edited by Asimov & Greenberg (paper) $12.95
- Creating Characters: How to Build Story People, by Dwight V. Swain $16.95
- Creating Short Fiction, by Damon Knight (paper) $9.95
- Dare to Be a Great Writer: 329 Keys to Powerful Fiction, by Leonard Bishop $16.95
- Dialogue, by Lewis Turco $13.95
- Fiction Is Folks: How to Create Unforgettable Characters, by Robert Newton Peck (paper) $8.95
- Handbook of Short Story Writing: Vol. I, by Dickson and Smythe (paper) $9.95
- Handbook of Short Story Writing: Vol. II, edited by Jean M. Fredette $15.95
- How to Write & Sell Your First Novel, by Collier & Leighton (paper) $12.95
- One Great Way to Write Short Stories, by Ben Nyberg $14.95
- Manuscript Submission, by Scott Edelstein $13.95
- Plot, by Ansen Dibell $13.95
- Revision, by Kit Reed $13.95
- Spider Spin Me a Web: Lawrence Block on Writing Fiction, by Lawrence Block $16.95
- Storycrafting, by Paul Darcy Boles (paper) $10.95

Theme & Strategy, by Ronald B. Tobias $13.95
Writing the Novel: From Plot to Print, by Lawrence Block (paper) $10.95

Special Interest Writing Books

Armed & Dangerous: A Writer's Guide to Weapons, by Michael Newton (paper) $14.95
The Children's Picture Book: How to Write It, How to Sell It, by Ellen E.M. Roberts (paper) $18.95
Comedy Writing Secrets, by Melvin Helitzer $18.95
The Complete Book of Scriptwriting, by J. Michael Straczynski (paper) $11.95
Deadly Doses: A Writer's Guide to Poisons, by Serita Deborah Stevens with Anne Klarner (paper) $16.95
Editing Your Newsletter, by Mark Beach (paper) $18.50
Families Writing, by Peter Stillman $15.95
How to Write a Play, by Raymond Hull (paper) $12.95
How to Write Action/Adventure Novels, by Michael Newton $13.95
How to Write & Sell a Column, by Raskin & Males $10.95
How to Write and Sell Your Personal Experiences, by Lois Duncan (paper) $10.95
How to Write Mysteries, by Shannon OCork $13.95
How to Write Romances, by Phyllis Taylor Pianka $13.95
How to Write Science Fiction & Fantasy, by Orson Scott Card $13.95
How to Write Tales of Horror, Fantasy & Science Fiction, edited by J.N. Williamson $15.95
How to Write the Story of Your Life, by Frank P. Thomas (paper) $11.95
How to Write Western Novels, by Matt Braun $13.95
Mystery Writer's Handbook, by The Mystery Writers of America (paper) $11.95
The Poet's Handbook, by Judson Jerome (paper) $10.95
Travel Writer's Handbook, by Louise Zobel (paper) $11.95
TV Scriptwriter's Handbook, by Alfred Brenner (paper) $10.95
The Writer's Complete Crime Reference Book, by Martin Roth $19.95
Writing for Children & Teenagers, 3rd Edition, by Lee Wyndham & Arnold Madison (paper) $12.95
Writing the Modern Mystery, by Barbara Norville $15.95
Writing to Inspire, edited by William Gentz (paper) $14.95

The Writing Business

A Beginner's Guide to Getting Published, edited by Kirk Polking (paper) $11.95
The Complete Guide to Self-Publishing, by Tom & Marilyn Ross (paper) $16.95
How to Sell & Re-Sell Your Writing, by Duane Newcomb $11.95
How to Write with a Collaborator, by Hal Bennett with Michael Larsen $11.95
How You Can Make $25,000 a Year Writing, by Nancy Edmonds Hanson (paper) $12.95
Is There a Speech Inside You?, by Don Aslett (paper) $9.95
Literary Agents: How to Get & Work with the Right One for You, by Michael Larsen $9.95
Professional Etiquette for Writers, by William Brohaugh $9.95
Time Management for Writers, by Ted Schwarz $10.95
The Writer's Friendly Legal Guide, edited by Kirk Polking $16.95
Writer's Guide to Self-Promotion & Publicity, by Elane Feldman $16.95
A Writer's Guide to Contract Negotiations, by Richard Balkin (paper) $11.95
Writing A to Z, edited by Kirk Polking $19.95

To order directly from the publisher, include $3.00 postage and handling for 1 book and $1.00 for each additional book. Allow 30 days for delivery.

Writer's Digest Books
1507 Dana Avenue, Cincinnati, Ohio 45207
Credit card orders call TOLL-FREE
1-800-289-0963
Prices subject to change without notice.

Write to this same address for information on *Writer's Digest* magazine, *Story* magazine, Writer's Digest Book Club, Writer's Digest School, and Writer's Digest Criticism Service.